In the Footsteps of Nonna

In the Footsteps of Nonna

Recipes and Ramblings in Southern Italy and Sicily

By Bill Abruzzo

PELICAN PUBLISHING COMPANY

GRETNA 2016

The word "Pelican" and the depiction of a pelican are trademarks of Pelican Publishing Company, Inc., and are registered in the U.S. Patent and Trademark Office.

Library of Congress Cataloging-in-Publication Data

Abruzzo, Bill, author.
 In the footsteps of Nonna : recipes and ramblings in southern Italy and Sicily / by Bill Abruzzo.
       pages cm
 Includes index.
 ISBN 978-1-4556-2162-0 (pbk. : alk. paper) — ISBN 978-1-4556-2163-7 (e-book) 1. Cooking, Italian. 2. Italy—Description and travel. I. Title.
 TX723.A27 2016
 641.5945--dc23

                              2015035503

Printed in the United States of America
Published by Pelican Publishing Company, Inc.
1000 Burmaster Street, Gretna, Louisiana 70053

Contents

Acknowledgments

To my wife, Jennifer Abruzzo:

"Tesoro, . . .primo, ho provato, . . . per tanti anni, ho perseverato . . . finalmente, ho vinto . . . ma sempre, con mia moglie al fianco!"

Words cannot express the love and gratitude that I give to you. The several years that I spent writing this cookbook were an incredible journey for both of us. You inspired me, encouraged me, and stood by my side the entire time. For this and so much more, I dedicate this cookbook to you. I cannot imagine having a better partner in life to ramble through Italy with, to enjoy good food with, and to love.

To my parents, Charles and Maria Abruzzo; my grandparents Carl and Vera Scannella; and my grandparents William and Josephine Abruzzo:

You are the people who molded me as a child into the person I am today. You instilled in me a passion for Italian food, culture, travel, and, most importantly, family. All of my life, I have aspired to be like you. I could not have had better role models. Now, I am proud to pass along your traditions to the future generations of our family. I am proud to be your son and grandson.

To my brother Joseph Abruzzo:

I may be twenty years your senior, but your intelligence and skills never cease to amaze me. You spent countless hours building my website, recipesandramblings.com, and teaching me all of all the "techy" stuff that I needed to know in order to run it smoothly. For this, I will be forever grateful. We are two brothers born of the same parents who did not grow up together and have never lived in the same state, yet the years and distance between us have never diminished our brotherly love.

Finally, to all my dear friends in Italy:

You welcomed me into your homes and treated me like one of the family. Your hospitality and generosity have made every visit to Italy feel more like coming home than being away on vacation. Thank you for keeping me grounded in my Italian roots. I look forward to many more wonderful times together, in Italy and here in the United States. *Grazie mille!*

Southern Italy

Abruzzo

Lazio

Molise

Adriatic Sea

Apulia

Basilicata

Campania

Tyrrhenian Sea

Calabria

Sicily

Ionian Sea

Introduction

Benvenuto! Welcome to ***In the Footsteps of Nonna: Recipes and Ramblings in Southern Italy and Sicily!*** In this cookbook, part of my culinary travel series *Recipes and Ramblings*, we will explore many wonderful places from the tranquil vineyards of Frascati near Rome to the bustling city of Palermo with its Byzantine and Arab influenced architecture. I will take you to energetic cities, charming seaside villages, and idyllic places in the countryside. Along the way, I will introduce you to the foods and culinary traditions that make each region so unique. By the end of the journey, you will share my passion for all that Italy has to offer: the people, food, culture, and history.

As we ramble from region to region, I will introduce you to a few locals who are just as passionate about Italian food and culture as I am. Here in the US, you will meet my two proud grandmothers, one Sicilian and the other Campanese. Over the years, I have incorporated their distinct regional recipes and culinary techniques into my own personal cooking style. In Italy, there are my dear friends Anna and Salvatore, who live in the heart of Palermo and run a bakery with their children, Gemma and Lorenzo. They have a beautiful seaside villa in Calabria, where I have been fortunate to spend many wonderful summer days. Finally, there are my friends Rita and Salvo, who live in Bagheria, Sicily. Rita is retired, but Salvo still sells fresh vegetables on the street each day. We will meet many other people too. Perhaps we will chat with a woman selling olive oil in a small hilltop town in Apulia or ask a young man at the beach in Basilicata to share some of the sea urchins he just plucked from the sea. By the end of our journey it will be clear that food nourishes not only the body but the soul. It is an expression of our personality, passion, and desire to live life to its fullest.

A Few Words About Me

Before we begin, let me tell you a little more about myself! Surely you want to know what drives my passion. For me, *In the Footsteps of Nonna* is a culinary journey that has been thirty-five years in the making. My love of Italy and Italian food started when I was a child, growing up in an Italian American family in New Jersey. Food was a big part of what defined us. Our Sunday dinners and holiday meals were always an extravaganza. My mother and grandmothers would cook for hours, and then we would all gather at the table and eat for hours. There was a certain order in which the courses of our meal were served, and often we enjoyed a rest, or *spada*, in between.

There were particular foods that we ate on certain holidays. We made pasta with sardines for St. Joseph's Day, roasted lamb for Easter, and salted cod on Christmas Eve. These were the sorts of things that set us apart as Italian Americans. These were the things that drew me into the kitchen at a young age and enticed me to stir a pot of sauce or watch my grandmother fry holiday pastries. Today, I keep these traditions alive and prepare many of the cherished recipes that have been handed down in my family for generations.

While my passion for Italian food is innate, my love of Italy was acquired. It was a gift given to me by my grandparents. I grew up in a cookie cutter suburb. There were no majestic mountains or amber fields of grain in sight, just rows of houses. Oftentimes I escaped by spending time with my Sicilian grandmother, who told me stories about Italy. Her words conjured up images of an exotic place that fascinated me. On my twelfth birthday, she and my grandfather took me there. We meandered our way down the boot from Rome to Sicily. We explored ancient ruins, climbed Mount Etna, and walked through the villages of my ancestors. I returned home with the unquenchable desire to see more. That Christmas, when most kids wanted an Atari computer game, all I wanted was a map of Italy. I told my parents that I needed one to trace my journey. "Someday, I will go back to every single place," I said. I still have that map. It is faded, torn, and held together by tape in many places. Over the years, I have used it to keep track of my ramblings. As you can imagine, it is crisscrossed with ink! Today, there is no corner of Italy that I haven't visited and there is more ink on that map than I could have ever dreamed possible.

Along with my map, whenever I travelled to Italy I brought a journal to document my adventures. Soon, I realized that I was writing mostly about food. It seemed that each time I travelled to a different region, I came across a tasty new dish or a unique style of cooking, and I just had to write it down! I also learned many recipes from my friends who live in Sicily. Anna and Salvatore, in particular, are masterful chefs who love to cook up a seafood feast! I promise to take you to their apartment for a Sunday dinner. And nobody prepares vegetables better than Rita, as Salvo's produce is always the freshest! We will certainly prod her for a recipe. After I returned from each trip, I would recreate the wonderful new dishes that I enjoyed. And, of course, I would add a few touches of my own. It was only a matter of time before I had a pile of recipes and the beginnings of what would eventually become this cookbook. But how did it all come together? Well, for starters, I could not think of a reason why I should not share my passion for Italy and Italian food with others. Perhaps I might ignite a passion in someone, just as I was impassioned as a child when my grandparents took me to Italy for the first time.

I then spent seven years researching, writing, and testing recipes. Of course, there were many calls to my mother, grandmother, and friends in Italy. It sometimes took four or five attempts before I truly nailed down a recipe and made it my own. During this grand endeavor, I became fascinated by the history of Italian regional cuisine. There were many things that I wanted to understand. How did salted cod from the North Atlantic become so popular in Italy? Why do Sicilians incorporate raisins and pine nuts into so many recipes? Why do the people from Piedmont prefer *risotto* over pasta? Soon, food became the focus and highlight of my trips to Italy. In fact, I once drove many hours to a small town in the central Apennines just to sample the local wild boar sausage. Whether I was attending a food festival, touring an olive oil factory, or simply watching an old woman make tomato paste beside the street, I was captivated. I wanted to see and learn more, and I wanted to pass my knowledge and enthusiasm on to others.

In 2008, *In the Footsteps of Nonna* was more than a vision; it was becoming a reality. That was also the year I married my wife, Jen. We traveled to Italy together and her passion for all things Italian was ignited too. Soon, I had a partner in the kitchen who shared my love of Italian food and helped me recreate the wonderful dishes we experienced while rambling through the Italian countryside. In 2009, Jen and I purchased a small farm in the foothills of the Blue Ridge Mountains of Virginia. Here rows of grapevines grow alongside tranquil country roads, and cows and sheep graze on grassy slopes. It is as close to Tuscany as you can get on the east coast of the United States and a world away from the cookie cutter suburbs of New Jersey where I grew up. Living here was the ultimate inspiration that turned this book into a reality. What setting in the United States could inspire you to cook Italian food more than this? The rolling hills, grapevines, and a garden bursting with fresh vegetables and herbs make my little slice of Tuscany every cook's dream! I promise, at the end of our journey I will take you for a stroll through my vegetable garden and let you peek into my kitchen pantry. These are the places from which every great Italian meal begins.

Setting the Stage for Our Ramblings in Southern Italy and Sicily

Before our journey begins, allow me to set the stage. On the Italian mainland, we will visit the regions of Lazio, Abruzzo, Molise, Campania, Basilicata, Apulia, and Calabria. Then we are off to the mysterious island of Sicily. These are places of varied geography and climate zones that bear the footprints of many civilizations. They have marked the crossroads of the Mediterranean for countless centuries and served as a link between Europe, Africa, and the Middle East. Greeks, Romans, Arabs, Normans, Spaniards, and many others have occupied parts of these regions at one time or another. They cleared the land, cultivated the soil, established thriving colonies, and built iconic monuments that still stand today. Traces of these ancient peoples can still be seen in the local traditions, customs, dialects, and cuisines. What does this mean? Well, in Sicily, Spanish-style turnovers called *'mpanate* are a favorite snack, and in Calabria a flat, round loaf called *pita* is a traditional bread. Although cultural influences help shape a region's cuisine, geography and climate ultimately dictate what foods are available. Beyond that, economics dictates who eats those foods and how they are prepared. The regions we will visit have experienced periods of economic prosperity and instability throughout history. In modern times, oppression and corruption have kept many people impoverished, creating a dichotomy between the opulent cuisine of the rich and the simple cuisine of the poor. That being said, understanding the interplay of all these factors against the backdrop of history is the key to understanding the foods of these fascinating regions that are steeped in beauty, culture, and tradition.

Heading south down the Italian peninsula, we reach Lazio and Abruzzo first. Here, the peaks of the Apennine Mountains rise to heights approaching ten thousand feet. They form a nearly impenetrable boundary between the Mediterranean side of

Italy to the west and the Adriatic side to the east. The verdant pine forests, grassy hillsides, and glaciers are reminiscent of the Swiss Alps. This is where we will find one of Italy's largest nature preserves, the Parco Nazionale d'Abruzzo. Wild boar, game, trout, mushrooms, and other bounties from the mountains are incorporated into the simple cuisine of this region's shepherds. On the high plateau of L'Aquila, cows and wild horses graze on alpine grasses that sway in the mountain breezes. The cool climate here is also perfect for growing lentils and crocuses, which produce the fine saffron that is used to flavor the local dishes. Where the high peaks give way to rolling hills, we will find the fabled provinces of Viterbo, in Lazio, and Teramo, in Abruzzo. Here, cypress trees stand like soldiers alongside quiet roads leading to medieval hilltop towns reminiscent of nearby Tuscany and Umbria. The orchards in these regions overflow with cherries, plums, hazelnuts, chestnuts, and walnuts, making these provinces the fruit and nut basket of Southern Italy.

Sheep are the preferred livestock in Lazio, Abruzzo, and the rest of Southern Italy. In Abruzzo, pasta or potato dumplings are sure to be topped with a thick lamb *ragu*. However, in Lazio, lamb is typically grilled with fresh sage and other herbs gathered alongside the ancient Appian Way. They say that all roads lead to Rome—in Lazio, this is true! Ancient Roman tombs, temples, and palaces dot the landscape. As you approach the eternal city, they stand as sentinels in the countryside pointing the way. The warm, coastal areas of both regions produce a cornucopia of vegetables, including artichokes, zucchini, peppers, and legumes of every kind, including chickpeas and fava. The coastlines of Lazio and Abruzzo are both fringed by long, sandy beaches and are well-equipped for tourism. Roman holidaymakers prefer the nearby beaches of Lazio, but it is the Northern Italians who flock to Abruzzo's sunny shores. Unlike Lazio, which has a broad coastal plain, Abruzzo's olive- and vine-covered hills stretch all the way to the Adriatic Sea, which always produces a bountiful catch for the commercial fisherman of Pescara and Ortona. Here, seafood is sure to be prepared in a grand stew flavored with plenty of saffron from L'Aquila.

South of Rome, the land and climate are less forgiving and sometimes harsh. Here, we find the semi-arid Appennino Meridionale, or Southern Apennine Mountains, which cover most of the regions of Campania, Basilicata, and Molise. Earthquakes are common here, and serious ones strike at least once every twenty years. Nonetheless, the rugged beauty and tranquility of these endless mountains are beyond compare. Remote towns sit perched on hilltops overlooking deep valleys filled with olive groves. In the summer, rivers are sure to run dry, and from the towns above, the dry river beds look like ancient Roman highways built of stone. This region has been nicknamed Mezzogiorno, or "midday," because of the intense heat of the midday summer sun, which inhabitants traditionally avoid by taking a *siesta*, or nap. At the turn of the twentieth century, poor economic conditions forced waves of immigrants to leave these mountains in search of a better life. Today, Mezzogiorno has come to symbolize a place that is economically disadvantaged and plagued by corruption. In many places, it seems that time stands still, but in a good way. In the oldest towns, such as Matera, primitive, cave-like houses built into the side of the mountain are still inhabited. They are a pleasant reminder of much simpler times.

The rustic cuisine of the Southern Apennines is uncomplicated, but the flavors are bold. Dishes are typically made with only a few ingredients, and pasta is a mainstay. Here, eggplants, peppers, artichokes, tomatoes, legumes, and olives grow well in the hot, dry climate, and dishes are typically flavored with plenty of garlic, oregano, basil, and flakes of dried hot chilies. In the rolling, grassy hills, near Campobasso, you are sure to see shepherds tending flocks that are sometimes several hundred head strong! Lamb and pork are more widely consumed than beef in this area, and less desirable cuts of meat, such as tripe and sweetbreads, are never wasted. Wild and cultivated greens—such as broccoli rabe, escarole, spinach, Swiss chard, and kale—are stewed with cannellini beans for a nourishing meal, and day-old bread is used to make bread soup or stuffed into vegetables and meat roulades as a filler. In the heart of Basilicata lies a rugged region called the Piccole Dolomiti Lucane, or the "little Dolomites." The jagged peaks resemble the famous Dolomite Mountains of Northern Italy. In these wild and remote regions, cured hams, dried sausage called *soppressata*, salted cod, preserved anchovies, and aged cheeses such as pecorino and provolone were a mainstay before the advent of refrigeration. Today, even the most rural areas of Basilicata have electricity and enjoy modern conveniences, but cured meats and cheeses are still prepared the traditional way.

By far, the most iconic place in Southern Italy is the Bay of Naples. This area was favored by the ancient Romans, who built elaborate villas along the bay's alluring shores. Unfortunately, today this is one of Italy's most densely populated areas and the beauty of the bay has been compromised by Naples' urban sprawl. Despite the area's reputation for pickpockets and petty thieves, a walk through one of Naples' working class neighborhoods should not be missed. With clotheslines crisscrossed over the streets, sidewalk vendors peddling their goods, and a constant crowd, it is sure to be an atmospheric, albeit chaotic, place. Italy's finest tomatoes are grown in the countryside south of Naples and they have become the backbone of Neapolitan cooking. The tomatoes are used to make sauce for braising meats and spooning over pasta. This area is also famous for its creamy mozzarella, which is made with milk from water buffalo that graze on the coastal plain of Sele. It is perfect for baking in a hearty pasta casserole or spreading atop Naples' signature dish: pizza. Also, south of Naples lies the rocky Sorrentine Peninsula, which juts into a crystalline Mediterranean Sea. Here you will find the fabled Amalfi Coast, which for good reason has become Italy's premier tourist destination. The dramatic scenery and charming fishing villages are beyond compare. Today, Amalfi, Positano, and other towns on the peninsula have been transformed into chic resorts for the Italian elite.

The Italian peninsula eventually splits into two smaller peninsulas, which form the "heel" and "foot" of Italy's boot. Apulia occupies the "heel" and lies between the Adriatic and Ionian Seas. Calabria occupies the "foot" and lies between the Ionian and Tyrrhenian Seas. Most of Northern Apulia is a tableland where the best wheat in Southern Italy is grown. Needless to say, pastas, breads, biscuits, and rustic dishes made with cooked whole grain and *farro* are prominent in the local cuisine. In central Apulia, you will find *trulli*, which are cone-shaped stone houses that resemble beehives. This quirky style of architecture is unique only to the area around Alberobello. With clusters of *trulli* farmsteads set amidst a green sea of olive groves and vineyards, this area has the look and feel of a fairyland. Artichokes, eggplants, zucchini, peppers, legumes, and greens such as chicory and dandelion are cultivated by farmers who have been working their family plots for generations. Along Apulia's Adriatic Coast, whitewashed fishing ports, such as Mola and Monopoli, have the look and feel of nearby Greece. The deep sea fishing fleets bring in an abundance of seafood, which is the mainstay of Apulia's coastal cuisine. Today, the shallow bays and lagoons of Apulia's Ionian coast are also home to a thriving aquaculture industry where oysters, mussels, and clams are farmed commercially.

The Calabrese Peninsula is an extension of the rugged Apennine Mountains, which become even more arid and unforgiving as they march southward. Hearty plants, such as almonds, cactus pears, capers, and figs, thrive in the dry climate, which is also perfect for growing citrus. Along the Tyrrhenian coast, groves of oranges, lemons, and citrons stretch for miles. This part of Calabria is also famous for its lovely beaches. The seaside towns from Praia a Mare to Pizzo are quickly developing into "second home" communities for Neapolitans and city dwellers from Reggio in search of a weekend retreat. As with any beautiful place, overdevelopment is now a concern. Chili peppers thrive in Calabria's unrelenting summer heat. In quaint hilltop villages where the buildings are donned with terracotta-tiled roofs, chilies are hung to dry from the eaves or outside the windows of every home. They are added to many dishes along with garlic, olive oil, and lemon. In the center of the peninsula is the high Sila plateau. Here, the temperatures are cooler than along the coast, and the forested mountain slopes reach down to the shores of several beautiful lakes. Calabria was once home to numerous ancient Greek colonies, and the Scilla promontory, which stands guard over the Strait of Messina, is rumored to be the home of the sea monster Scylla of Homer's *Odyssey*. Today, passenger ferries and cargo ships traverse the swirling waters between Reggio and Messina, but subtle remnants of ancient Greece are still evident in the culture and traditions of the region.

Finally, we come to Italy's largest island, Sicily. Corruption keeps Sicily's economy depressed, but drought, earthquakes, and the sporadic eruptions of Mount Etna also take their toll. The barren hills of the Sicilian interior produce wheat in the spring, but they are parched in the summer. Here, durum wheat is used to make pasta, semolina bread, and couscous, which was brought to the island by the Arabs centuries ago. The old quarter of Palermo is rich with Byzantine and Arab architecture, and the city's chaotic marketplace with its crowded, narrow streets has the look and feel of a Middle Eastern bazaar. In Palermo, dishes of Arab origin are prepared in a sweet and sour sauce and sprinkled with pine nuts, raisins, capers, and olives. Outstanding Greek temples can be found across the island, the best preserved of which are located in the Valley of the Temples near Agrigento. In Trapani, there is a thriving tuna and swordfish industry; however, along the southern coast, anchovies and sardines are the prized catch. Almonds, pistachios, cactus fruit, and citrus grow in the shadow of Mount Etna and eventually make their way into irresistible confections. The volcanic Aeolian Islands, which lie just offshore, are like a string of black pearls in the blue Mediterranean Sea. Once lonely outposts, they are now popular with tourists who travel there to see the active lava flows on Stromboli. Farther afield is the tiny island of Pantelleria, which has the look and feel of North Africa. Here, the arid climate and salty sea breezes create the perfect environment for growing the best capers in the entire Mediterranean.

My Thoughts on Rambling in Southern Italy and Sicily

For me, the start of any great trip to Southern Italy usually begins in Rome, which is the transportation hub through which all international flights arrive and from which emanates a reliable network of regional flights, trains, and autostradas that link the city to Southern Italy's Apennine and coastal regions. The nearby port of Civitavecchia is also a hopping on or off point for those travelling by cruise ship or ferry. Within a few hours' drive of Rome, you can be basking in the sun at a chic seaside resort on the Amalfi Coast or skiing on the slopes of the Gran Sasso in Abruzzo. If you wander farther you can be in the wild heart of mountainous Basilicata or a whitewashed seaside town on Apulia's Gargano coast. For me, the perfect two week vacation in Southern Italy starts with a few days in a bustling, energetic city such as Rome, Naples, or Palermo followed by five days in the countryside and then five days by the sea. When I want to experience *la dolce vita*, I head to the countryside of northern Lazio, which has the feel of Tuscany, or to the chic seaside resorts of the Amalfi Coast. When I prefer simple pleasures, I may choose to get lost in the endless olive groves of Apulia or stroll on a black sand beach in the Aeolian Islands. The possibilities for a unique and diverse travel experience are truly endless!

Whenever I travel, I like to feel the heartbeat of the land. Whether I am in the rugged interior of Sicily or a vibrant Adriatic fishing port, such as Pescara, I want to experience the rhythm of daily life. Travelling should be more than just snapping photos of historic buildings and churches. You must step out of the tour bus! Take a few minutes to chat with the shopkeepers, the locals sitting beside you at the café, and the old women selling fruit at the outdoor market. Walk into a crowded butcher shop or stroll through a fish market to see how the locals do their daily food shopping. Attend a small town festival, head to a winery to see how grapes are pressed into wine, or watch an artist hand paint a ceramic vase in his workshop. And if you do not speak the language, fear not! Sometimes trying to communicate makes your experience all the more fun. It is sure to bring out a smile on everyone's face.

The best way to feel the heartbeat of the land is to stay with locals. I prefer to stay at guest houses and bed and breakfasts rather than large hotels. The owners are sure to be friendly and helpful, and living like a local is always such fun. An even better option is to stay at an *agriturismo*, where you can experience rural life. *Agriturismi* are working farms, usually family run, that also operate as bed and breakfasts. Why not spend a few days on an olive plantation in Apulia or a vineyard in Lazio? The experience is sure to be memorable and rewarding! Oftentimes *agriturismi* are housed in traditional structures, historic farmsteads, or old castles. They are charming and intimate places where the owners take the time to teach you about their trades. As a guest, you may be asked to participate in the harvest, assist with cheese-making, or press olives into oil. Most *agriturismi* also operate a small restaurant or offer home-cooked meals to their guests. They are sure to serve traditional regional dishes made with the freshest ingredients. If you head to a family run *agriturismo* in Campania, no doubt there will be a grandmother in the kitchen rolling fresh pasta dough or pulling curds into fresh mozzarella cheese!

Wherever I chose to stay, I always make sure that kitchen facilities are available so that I can cook. I will either rent an apartment or check with the owners of a bed and breakfast beforehand to see if they will allow me to use their kitchen. For me, there is no greater joy than shopping in the open air markets and then preparing a meal with regional products. To ensure that I am using the highest quality ingredients, I always purchase products certified with a "Protected Designation of Origin" (PDO) label.

By European Union law, only traditional products originating in a particular region are allowed to be marketed as such. This protects against inferior products in the marketplace. PDO laws protect the names of hams, cheese, olives, vegetables, fruits, wines, and much more. For example, a cheese can only be labeled as "Parmigiano-Reggiano" if it is produced in the designated Parma region following the traditional cheese-making methods. Other similar cheeses must be called something else. By using ingredients with a PDO label, you can be certain that any dish you prepare while rambling through Southern Italy and Sicily is truly authentic and delicious.

Another great way to sample the foods of a region is to attend a food festival. Italians love a celebration, and what could be better to celebrate than a bountiful catch or harvest? Nearly every town from Abruzzo to Sicily holds an annual food festival, or *sagra*, to celebrate whatever food or product the town is famous for. Along the coast of Sicily, it may be a sardine festival in a town that has a fishing fleet, whereas in Calabria it may be an onion festival in a town that is famous for growing onions. That being said, there is sure to be a food festival somewhere in Southern Italy or Sicily on any given day. Be sure to search them out—or better yet, plan your next trip so that it coincides with a celebration of your favorite food! It is guaranteed to be a memorable and tasty experience.

Let the Journey Begin!

I hope this brief introduction to Southern Italy and Sicily has enticed you. Now it is time to ignite your passion for the culture and foods of these regions. Welcome to *In the Footsteps of Nonna: Recipes and Ramblings in Southern Italy and Sicily.*

Laundry hanging to dry in Naples

Fishing boats pulled ashore at the end of a sunny day in Sorrento

The fortified town of Lipari in the Aeolian Islands with the dazzling blue Tyrrhenian Sea as a backdrop

The ancient tuna fishing port of Castellammare del Golfo on Sicily's rugged northwestern coast

Apennine pastures and wooded hills along the border of Lazio and Abruzzo

The ancient town of San Giovanni Piro, Campania

The author in the enchanting town of Tropea, Calabria, perched above the sea

I

Antipasti e Spuntini (Appetizers and Savory Snacks)

Fine Food and Misbehaving Children in Marineo

A Rambling in Sicily

Several years ago, I was invited to attend the wedding of Rita and Salvo's daughter, Caterina, in Bagheria, Sicily. I was travelling to Sicily that summer with my close friend Jeff, whom they had never met. I explained that Jeff did not speak Italian and would sightsee on his own for a few days while I celebrated with them, but Rita and Salvo insisted that he attend all the festivities too. As soon as we arrived, the first order of business was a pre-wedding dinner hosted by Salvo at a popular restaurant in the small town of Marineo, which is located in Madonie Mountains high above Bagheria. The dinner was attended by the families of the bride and groom and the wedding party. We were honored to attend. As Jeff will tell you, it was an experience that neither one of us will ever forget!

We drove for nearly an hour on a road that snaked its way deep into the countryside past olive groves and grassy pastures. We ascended higher and higher into the mountains until we reached the restaurant, which sat at the edge of a ridge with glorious views of the agricultural valley below. The sign in front of the restaurant proudly announced "Rocca Bianca." We were amazed by the tranquil setting, which was caressed by a cool breeze even though it was summer and the rest of the island was sweltering. According to Rita and Salvo's other daughter, Paola, this is the best restaurant in Sicily and a favorite day trip for Palermitani who want to escape the city and enjoy authentic Sicilian cuisine. Before we left that morning, Paola explained that Rocca Bianca is a family style restaurant with no menu. Instead, families go there and sit for hours laughing and drinking wine as a parade of food is brought to the table. Jeff and I were very excited and forewent breakfast to save room for a grand feast.

Our group that day was thirty strong with just under a dozen young, unruly children. The restaurant had prepared one long table for our party. As we all sat down there was plenty of confusion. Some people were meeting for the first time, others were greeting each other with hugs and kisses, and the children were playing games and running around the table. Rita pulled me in one direction to meet a cousin and then Salvo pulled me in the other direction to meet someone else. Then, suddenly, everyone settled into a seat. But somehow during all the confusion, I lost track of Jeff! I wound up sitting at one end of the table next to Paola and he was all the way down at the other end. How terrible, I thought. He cannot speak Italian! Who will he talk to? Then I realized something even worse; he was sitting at the children's end of the table right in the middle of a rambunctious group of five to twelve year olds! How did this happen?

Paola and I walked over to speak with Jeff about the unfortunate situation. We all agreed that it would be best for him to remain where he was seated, rather than move people around. We would then visit him between courses. Just as Paola and I returned to our seats, the parade of food began. First came platters of sliced cured ham, dried *salumi*, fresh caciocavallo cheese, olives, *caponata*, and turnovers filled with fresh ricotta. Next was an assortment of cold seafood *antipasti*, which included several seafood salads and sweet and sour tuna smothered in onions. It was already a feast beyond compare and the pasta had not yet arrived. And there were many more courses still to come! I craned my neck to see Jeff at the other end of the table. There he was, sitting amongst a cacophony of screaming children with nobody to talk to. Then, the boy sitting next to Jeff stood up on his chair and threw a piece of bread at another child across the table. That was when Paola and I decided to go keep him company for a while.

We walked over and Paola asked, "Are the children misbehaving?"

Jeff rolled his eyes. "The chubby girl is crying because little Antonio punched her in the face, and there are two children under the table touching my feet. But they are not bothering me," he explained.

We pushed the tablecloth back and looked down to see the giggling offenders, Paola's nephews, Roberto and Silvio, ages six and seven. She immediately shooed them away and apologized.

Jeff then said, "There is no reason to apologize; I have died and gone to heaven! These kids aren't eating a thing! Look, there is a whole tray of octopus, and nobody is eating it but me."

We glanced down at the table. There were platters full of food lined up in front of Jeff. He appeared to be blissfully content despite the chaos going on all around him and underneath the table. The children were apparently more interested in playing than eating, which meant more food for him.

"I guess they don't do happy meals for kids here, or chicken fingers and fries, but I am not complaining," he said. "Now please, go back to the other end of the table. I have lots to eat before the next course arrives!"

The parade of food continued. Next came bowls of homemade pasta with different sauces, trays of baked *cannelloni*, grilled swordfish and tuna, stuffed squid, roasted lamb and pork, eggplant casseroles, and tender artichokes cooked over a flame until slightly charred. We continued to check up on Jeff between courses, and each time he remained blissfully content with platters full of food lined up in front of him and no children challenging him for a morsel. At some point, Roberto and Silvio went back under the table, and a few pieces of bread were thrown in Jeff's direction. But nothing could distract him from this extraordinary feast! He proceeded to eat and savor each bite. Despite all of the commotion, he truly enjoyed the meal. When the dinner finally ended we were all stuffed. Jeff and I agreed that it was the best meal we had ever eaten.

Before we headed back to Bagheria, everyone stood outside the restaurant to chat and enjoy the view. Rita and Salvo told Jeff, "Next time you will have a better seat!" Paola introduced him to the adults that he did not have a chance to meet. One woman even thanked him for watching over her two children. Paola then explained to her that Jeff was not put there to watch the children. The woman was embarrassed for assuming that he was the babysitter and apologized for not checking up on them. She asked Jeff if they were well behaved, but he refrained from mentioning that her son threw the bread and that her daughter punched another little girl in the face.

The bride and groom's families then gathered for a photo, and Jeff and I were included. It was a wonderful day of family, friends, and fine food. And if you ask, Jeff will tell you that he had the best seat in the house, despite the misbehaving children.

The sun-drenched hills of the Val di Salso, Sicily

The town of Rivello, perched atop a mountain in the heart of Basilicata

A street festival in the cheerful town of Lipari, Sicily

A friendly face in Pisticci, Basilicata

Bruschetta (Grilled Country-Style Italian Bread)

ABRUZZO/MOLISE

The word bruschetta *is derived from the Italian word* bruscare, *which means "to grill something over hot coals." In the hills of Abruzzo and Molise,* bruschetta *is made by brushing thick slices of a round loaf of country-style bread with olive oil, grilling them until crisp and golden, and then rubbing them with cloves of fresh garlic. This wonderful, rustic preparation is also a favorite in Lazio, Tuscany, and Umbria. Today,* bruschetta *is a popular menu item at Italian American restaurants, where it is typically served with a topping of fresh chopped tomatoes and herbs. However, in Abruzzo and Molise,* bruschetta *is also topped with sautéed wild mushrooms, mashed beans, roasted peppers, and much, much more! The possibilities for topping* bruschetta *are truly endless, and modern Italian chefs are quite inventive. If you don't have a grill or weather does not permit, simply toast the bread in the oven. When toasted in the oven,* bruschetta *is referred to as* crostini.

1 loaf country-style Italian bread
Olive oil, for brushing
6 cloves garlic

Slice the Italian bread into ½ inch thick slices and lightly brush them on both sides with olive oil.

Grill the sliced bread over a low flame until crisp and golden. Alternatively, preheat an oven to 425 degrees and toast the bread for 5 minutes.

Slice the cloves of garlic in half, rub the cut sides over the hot, crisp bread, and then discard the garlic. Top with your favorite spread or topping. Serve warm. Serves 6 adults.

Bruschetta con Ceci in Mortaio (Bruschetta Topped with Chickpea and Garlic Mash Made in a Mortar)

ABRUZZO/MOLISE

Ceci, *or chickpeas, are an essential ingredient of Southern Italian and Sicilian cooking. A staple in all rural kitchens, they are traditionally dried for storage and then used throughout the year. Once dried, chickpeas must be soaked overnight before they can be used. Then they must be boiled to become tender and delicious. Today, chickpeas are available canned, which eliminates the need for soaking and makes them convenient and easy to use. They are a great item to keep stocked in your pantry. Toss them in soups, stews, risotto, and pasta dishes or mash them up for a great* bruschetta *or crostini topping!*

No kitchen in rural Molise would be complete without a mortaio e pestelo, *or mortar and pestle. They are the perfect implements for mashing and grinding all sorts of things. In Basilicata and Calabria, the mortar and pestle are used to crush dried chilies into flakes that can be sprinkled over soups and pastas. In Sicily, they are used to grind almonds into a paste for confections such as marzipan. In Molise, a simple mash of chickpeas, black peppercorns, and garlic in the* mortaio *is topped with the finest extra virgin olive oil and a pinch or two of sea salt. Spooned on top of* bruschetta *or crostini, it is a simple and tasty* antipasto *that captures the flavor of Molise's pastoral countryside. Serve it with a glass of red Montepulciano d'Abruzzo wine for a truly authentic regional treat.*

2 cans (15 oz. each) chickpeas
½ tsp. black peppercorns
1 clove garlic
1 tsp. Sicilian sea salt
¾ cup extra virgin olive oil, divided

2 tbsp. finely chopped, firmly packed Italian flat leaf parsley
Bruschetta, enough for 4 to 6 adults *(see page 23)*

Drain the chickpeas. Mash the peppercorns in a large mortar. (If you do not have a mortar and pestle, prepare the spread using a food processor.) In the same mortar, mash the garlic along with the sea salt. Stir in ¼ cup of olive oil and then add the chickpeas. Mash the chickpeas into a thick, chunky spread, adding the rest of the olive oil, ¼ cup at a time, as you mash. If you prefer, mash the chickpeas until smooth and creamy.

Season with additional salt, if needed. Top the chickpea spread with a final drizzle of olive oil, and sprinkle with the chopped parsley.

Serve at room temperature with *bruschetta*. Serves 4 to 6 adults.

Bruschetta con Purea di Peperoni e Pomodori Secchi (Bruschetta Topped with Roasted Red Bell Pepper and Sundried Tomato Spread)

CAMPANIA

I once drove south from Naples to the bustling port of Salerno. The autostrada took me out of the city and ran alongside the bay, passing ancient towns such as Torre del Greco and Ercolano, which sit beneath Mount Vesuvius. It is a region shrouded in mystery that is still haunted by the ghosts of Pompeii and Herculaneum. It has been centuries since mighty Vesuvius last roared, but the people living in its shadow keep a watchful eye! With the richest volcanic soil in all of the Mediterranean, it is no wonder that this region is famous for growing a cornucopia of fine vegetables, including tomatoes, peppers, onions, zucchini, broccoli, greens, and legumes of all kinds. On the terraced slopes of Vesuvius, grapes grow plump and flavorful and are pressed into the local wine, la Crema Christi, which means "cream of Christ." In a place where a volcanic eruption could occur at any time, the name given to the local wine certainly says it all!

Here is a recipe from the cornucopia of Vesuvius. Red bell peppers are roasted with sweet onions and garlic and then pureed into a spread made flavorful with the finest sundried tomatoes. The concentrated, tangy flavor of the sundried tomatoes is a true taste of the Bay of Naples, or la Baia di Napoli, as it is called. There, tomatoes are set to dry on the rooftops. They are then stored sott´olio, *or "under olive oil," and used throughout the year in many dishes. They are certainly the star of this wonderful spread that is perfect for smearing atop* bruschetta *or* crostini. *I also served it alongside* polpette, *or meatballs that are pulled piping hot from the frying pan.*

6 large red bell peppers
1 medium Spanish or Vidalia onion
Olive oil, for brushing and drizzling
5 cloves garlic
Salt to taste
¾ cup chopped, firmly packed jarred sundried tomatoes preserved in olive oil

¾ tbsp. red wine vinegar
1 rounded tsp. sweet paprika
Black pepper to taste
¼ cup finely ground dry bread crumbs, if needed
Bruschetta, enough for 4 to 6 adults *(see page 23)*

Preheat the oven to 415 degrees. Quarter the peppers, removing and discarding the seeds. Quarter the onion. Place the peppers and onions in a baking dish that has been brushed with olive oil and toss in the whole garlic cloves. Drizzle lightly with olive oil and season with salt.

Cover the baking dish with aluminum foil and place it in the oven for 45 to 50 minutes or until everything is soft. Transfer the roasted vegetables to a food processor using a slotted spoon to strain off all of the residual cooking liquid. Add the sundried tomatoes, vinegar, paprika, and black pepper and process until smooth and creamy. If necessary, re-season with salt and spices and adjust the acidity level by adding another splash of vinegar. If the spread is too thin, add some bread crumbs.

Serve at room temperature with *bruschetta* or as a condiment for grilled meats. Serves 4 to 6 adults.

Bruschetta con Insalata Tropeana (Bruschetta Topped with Cherry Tomatoes, Mixed Olives, Capers, and Red Onions)

CALABRIA

The Aeolian Islands lie off the coast of Western Calabria. On a clear day, they can be seen from the charming seaside town of Tropea. If you wish, hop on a hydrofoil at Tropea's harbor and head to Stromboli for the day! In Greek mythology, the Aeolian Islands were the home of Aeolus, god of the winds. Once a lonely outpost, today they have been discovered by tourists in search of an authentic Italian vacation spot. If you want to get away from it all, there are six islands to choose from, and each one is more tranquil than the next. On the island of Stromboli, you can rent a villa on a black sand beach and take an excursion to see an active lava flow. Don't worry—it is safe! Villagers have lived on Stromboli since the days of the ancient Greeks and violent eruptions are rare. If you prefer, stay in Tropea at a cliffside hotel overlooking the sea. From there you can watch the smoke rising from Stromboli's crater as the sun sets over the Mediterranean.

Aeolian islanders have harvested the bounties of the sea and tilled the rich volcanic soil for centuries. Sweet cherry tomatoes, briny capers, green olives, oregano, and basil are common ingredients in Aeolian cuisine. They are also popular in the cuisine of coastal Calabria and make their way into many of the dishes served at Tropea's restaurants. In Tropea, they also grow sweet red onions, which are a perfect match for the bright flavors of Aeolian ingredients. Here is my version of a simple chopped salad that captures all of wonderful flavors of the region. Dressed with extra virgin olive oil and lemon, it is the perfect topping for bruschetta *with a Calabrese flair. The bright, bold flavors will transport you to Tropea, the Aeolian Islands, and beyond!*

⅓ cup Sicilian capers preserved in salt
½ medium red onion, diced
3 cloves garlic, finely chopped
1½ tbsp. finely chopped, firmly packed oregano
1½ tbsp. finely chopped, firmly packed basil
1 dry quart cherry tomatoes, halved
½ cup pitted, halved Kalamata olives
½ cup pitted, halved Sicilian green olives
Salt and black pepper to taste
Extra virgin olive oil, for drizzling
Juice of 2 large lemons, divided
Bruschetta, enough for 6 to 8 adults
(see page 23)

Remove the salt from the capers by soaking them in warm water for 10 minutes. Rinse them under cool running water and pat them dry.

Combine the capers, red onion, garlic, oregano, basil, cherry tomatoes, Kalamata olives, and green olives in a mixing bowl and season with salt and black pepper.

Squeeze the juice of one lemon over the mixture, drizzle generously with extra virgin olive oil, and toss well. If you prefer more acidity, add the juice of the second lemon. Serve with *bruschetta*. Serves 6 to 8 adults.

Bruschetta con Rucola, Purea di Fave, e Pecorino (Bruschetta Topped with Field Greens, Fava Bean Spread, and Shaved Pecorino Cheese)

APULIA

It is said that favas are the favorite bean of the Pugliese people. To understand why, head to the town of Giovinazzo in August and attend the annual Sagra delle Fave. It is a festive evening of bonfires and fava beans! The bonfires are lit to celebrate the harvest of Apulia's most beloved legume. There is sure to be music, dancing, and plenty of dishes made with fava beans. Grab a snack at a food stall, take a stroll, and admire the Romanesque cathedral and fine limestone buildings that seem to glow in the firelight.

Food festivals such as this are common in Italy. In fact, it seems that every town has a sagra *to celebrate its gastronomic specialty. Whether it is an onion festival in Calabria or a chestnut festival in Lazio, more likely than not there is a food celebration happening somewhere in Italy on any given day. Most large towns in Italy now have a website that is sure to provide the dates and details of their annual* sagra.

Here is a simple fava bean bruschetta *that you are sure to find at Giovinazzo's Sagra delle Fave. The fava beans are boiled until tender and then mashed into a puree with garlic and olive oil. In Apulia, the puree is traditionally made with dried favas and served with stewed bitter greens, but I like fresh favas and fresh greens best.*

2½ lbs. fava beans in the pods (yields 2 cups beans)

2 cloves garlic

¾ cup extra virgin olive oil, divided, plus additional for drizzling

Sea salt and black pepper to taste

1 bunch arugula or dandelion greens

1 splash red wine vinegar (optional)

Bruschetta, enough for 4 to 6 adults *(see page 23)*

Shaved Pecorino Romano cheese, for topping

3 eggs, hard-boiled and sliced into rounds

Shell 2 cups of fava beans. Fill a 4½ quart pot ⅔ of the way with water and add 2½ teaspoons of salt. Boil the beans for 20 minutes or until tender. Allow the beans to cool, remove the skins, and place them in a food processor along with the garlic. Add ¼ cup of olive oil, season with sea salt and black pepper, and process. Continue processing, adding as much of the remaining ½ cup of oil as needed to achieve a smooth, creamy consistency.

Finely chop the arugula or dandelion greens and toss with a drizzle of olive oil and an optional splash of vinegar. Place some chopped arugula on each slice of bruschetta and sprinkle generously with cheese.

Add a dollop of fava spread and a slice of egg on each piece of *bruschetta*. Drizzle with additional olive oil and sprinkle lightly with salt and black pepper. Serves 6 adults.

Bruschetta con Fegato di Lepre (Bruschetta Topped with Rabbit Liver Pate and Fig Preserves)

LAZIO

If you are making whole rabbit, do not discard the liver and heart. Do as they would in the hills of Northern Lazio near the enchanting medieval town of Vitorchiano—prepare a creamy, luxurious pate! In this part of rural Lazio, which lies nestled between Tuscany to the west and Umbria to the north, nothing goes to waste when an animal is slaughtered. With a little ingenuity, even the least desirable cuts and organs are transformed into something delicious. This pate is one of them. Smeared atop crisp bruschetta *made with country-style Roman bread, it is the perfect* antipasto *or prelude to a rustic dinner of rabbit stew and roasted vegetables. It also makes a delectable* spuntino, *or late-afternoon snack, after a day of rambling around Vitorchiano and other enchanting hillside towns. For a* merenda, *a light lunch that is typically eaten at midday, serve the* bruschetta *with wedges of sharp, nutty Parmigiano-Reggiano cheese and fig preserves. This is the type of* antipasto *or* spuntino *that you are sure see on the menu at family-run* trattorias *in Northern Lazio.*

2 young rabbits (2½ to 3 lbs. each)
4 tbsp. butter, divided
Salt and black pepper to taste
½ small Spanish or Vidalia onion, chopped
1 clove garlic, chopped

2 eggs
1 splash cream or milk, if needed
Bruschetta, enough for 4 to 6 adults *(see page 23)*
Fig preserves

Remove the livers and hearts from the rabbits. Remove the scrap meat (flaps of meat over the rib cage and strip of meat that extends from the top of the neck down the spine). Set the rabbits to the side. Slice the livers, hearts, and scrap meat into strips.

Add two tablespoons of butter to a frying pan over medium-low heat. When the butter has melted, add the livers, hearts, and scrap meat, season with salt and black pepper, sauté the meat until fully cooked, and then transfer it to a food processor.

Add another tablespoon of butter to the frying pan and sauté the onions over low heat until soft. Add the garlic, sauté for another minute, and then transfer the sautéed onions and garlic to the food processor.

Add the last tablespoon of butter to the frying pan and fry the eggs over easy. Transfer them to the food processor.

Process until smooth and creamy, and add additional salt and black pepper to taste. If the pate is too thick, add a splash or two of cream or milk.

Serve room temperature atop *bruschetta* that has been smeared with fig preserves. Serves 4 adults.

Caponata (Sweet and Sour Eggplant with Cherry Tomatoes, Green Olives, Pine Nuts, and Capers)

SICILY

Caponata *is the bold and flavorful signature dish of Palermo. It is an eggplant salad flavored with a tangy Sicilian sweet and sour sauce called* agrodolce. *Of Arab origin, it can be traced back to the time when Palermo was the site of a great mosque and a sultan's palace. Today, remnants of Palermo's Arabic past can be seen in the architecture, dialect, and cuisine. Just take a walk down the narrow, crowded streets of the Vucciria market, which has the feel of a Middle Eastern bazaar, or stroll past the red domes of the church of San Giovanni degli Eremiti, which was once a mosque! Palermo has a feel like no other city in Italy. It is a place where the sights, smells, and tastes are truly exotic and intriguing.*

Although the flavors in caponata *are complex, it is rather simple to prepare. A splash of vinegar and a sprinkle of sugar add a sweet and sour component, capers and olives add saltiness, and tomatoes add plenty of bright tang. It is a delectable combination that elevates the mild flavor of eggplant. Your taste buds will certainly agree! While the traditional* caponata *recipe starts by frying the eggplant in olive oil, I like to roast mine instead. Roasting caramelizes the eggplant, enhances its pleasant flavor, and prevents it from absorbing too much oil. I also cut back on the tomato paste and throw in a handful of sliced cherry tomatoes. The result is a* caponata *that is light and flavorful, not oily and overpowering. I prepare it as an* antipasto *for holiday meals and serve it with wedges of hard-boiled eggs.*

3 lbs. eggplants (preferably large, plump purple variety)	⅔ cup red wine vinegar
Olive oil, for brushing and sautéing	¾ cup water
Salt and black pepper to taste	1½ tbsp. sugar
2 tbsp. pine nuts	2 tbsp. finely chopped, firmly packed oregano
1 large Spanish or Vidalia onion, sliced	2 tbsp. finely chopped, firmly packed basil
2 large stalks celery, sliced on the bias into ¼ inch thick pieces	1 cup pitted, halved Sicilian green olives
4 large cloves garlic, sliced	2 tbsp. capers in brine
4 rounded tbsp. tomato paste	2 cups halved cherry tomatoes

Preheat the oven to 400 degrees. Slice the eggplants into ½ inch thick rounds, brush them with olive oil, and season them with salt and black pepper. Place the slices on baking trays that have been lightly brushed with olive oil. Bake for 12 minutes, flip the slices, and continue baking for another 10 to 15 minutes or until soft and golden on both sides.

Meanwhile, toast the pine nuts in a small frying pan over low heat until golden. When the eggplant is done, remove it from the oven and slice it into bite-sized pieces. Set aside.

Coat the bottom of a 5½ quart frying pan generously with olive oil and set it over medium-low heat. Add the onions, season with salt and black pepper, and sauté until soft. Add the celery and continue sautéing for another 2 minutes or until the celery is tender but still firm. Add the garlic and sauté for another minute.

Push the sautéed items to one side of the frying pan, tilt the frying pan so that the oil pools to the other side, and fry the tomato paste in the oil for 1 minute. Combine the tomato paste with the sautéed items and stir in the vinegar, water, and sugar.

Add the oregano, basil, pine nuts, olives, capers, and cherry tomatoes and re-season with salt and black pepper. Continue sautéing for another 2 minutes or until the cherry tomatoes soften and their skins begin to pucker. Stir in the roasted eggplant and continue sautéing for another 3 minutes or until the eggplant has absorbed the sauce.

If necessary, adjust the seasoning and the ratio of sweet to sour by adding more sugar or vinegar. Serve at room temperature. Serves 6 to 8 adults.

Melanzane Rollitini (Eggplant Roulades Stuffed with Chickpeas, Sundried Tomatoes, Capers, and Fresh Herbs)

APULIA

Fresh vegetables, beans, and olive oil are the foundation of Apulia's simple, rustic cuisine, and the Pugliese people know how to combine them in creative and delicious ways. In central and southern Apulia, the flat countryside is a patchwork of fields and olive groves. Should you ramble through this region, no doubt you will stumble upon a frantoio *or olive oil mill. Today, there are many modern mills to process Apulia's olives into oil. However, at an* antico frantoio, *or ancient olive oil mill, the oil is sure to be made using traditional methods. Before the advent of modern machinery, olives were pressed under the weight of massive stone wheels that were usually turned by a donkey. The stone press method ensures that extra virgin oil from an* antico frantoio *is always the very best!*

In Apulia, the best extra virgin olive oil is always reserved for drizzling over salads, fresh vegetables, pasta, and bread. A true Pugliese would never use it to fry because that would destroy its fine flavor. Here is the perfect antipasto *from the countryside of Apulia that is always best when served with a generous drizzle of fine extra virgin olive oil from an* antico frantoio. *Plump, purple eggplants from the fields of Salentino are sliced, roasted in the oven, and then rolled up with a simple filling of mashed chickpeas, sundried tomatoes, and garlic. It is the perfect summertime* antipasto *from the heart of Apulia. Be sure to serve it at room temperature with crusty bread to mop up the olive oil!*

4 large, plump purple eggplants	½ small red onion, diced
Olive oil, for brushing and drizzling	1 large clove garlic, minced
Salt and black pepper to taste	1½ tbsp. finely chopped, firmly packed basil
Dried oregano to taste	
2 cans (15 oz. each) chickpeas	1 rounded tbsp. capers in brine
¾ cup chopped, firmly packed jarred sundried tomatoes preserved in olive oil	1 tbsp. red wine vinegar
	Extra virgin olive oil for drizzling

Preheat the oven to 400 degrees. Slice the eggplants lengthwise into slices that are just under ½ inch thick, brush them with olive oil, and season them with salt, black pepper, and dried oregano. Place the slices on baking trays that have been lightly brushed with olive oil. Roast for 12 minutes and then flip the slices and continue roasting for another 10 to 15 minutes or until soft and golden on both sides. Allow the slices to cool.

Meanwhile, prepare the filling: Drain and coarsely chop the chickpeas by pulsing them in a food processor. Add the chickpeas to a mixing bowl with the sundried tomatoes, onion, garlic, basil, capers, and vinegar. Drizzle with extra virgin olive oil, season with salt and black pepper, and combine thoroughly to form a thick, chunky spread. If necessary, adjust the acidity by adding a splash of additional vinegar.

Spread some filling on each slice of eggplant and then roll up. Place the eggplant rolls on a serving platter and drizzle with extra virgin olive oil. Serve at room temperature. Serves 6 to 8 adults.

Verdure Sott'acetto (Pickled Mixed Vegetables)

CAMPANIA

Pickled vegetables are popular throughout Italy. Vegetables jarred with vinegar are referred to as sott'acetto *or "under vinegar," whereas vegetables jarred with olive oil are referred to as* sott'olio. *In Naples, they prepare Insalata Rinforzo at Christmas time. It is a hearty mix of cauliflower, carrots, red bell peppers, and mixed olives marinated in a vinaigrette dressing. In the United States, Italian-style jarred vegetables are called* giardiniera, *which means "from the garden." It is a nickname that is distinctively Italian American. So when you are in Naples, if you ask the grocery store clerk for* giardiniera, *his likely response will be, "Che cosa?"*

In Sicily, my dear friend Anna jars pickled baby artichokes and mushrooms the old fashioned way, by sealing the jars and boiling them in an enormous pot of water for fifteen minutes. Her husband, Salvatore, does the same with sundried tomatoes, which he skillfully packs in small jars with a slice of garlic and basil between them. Whenever I return from a visit to Sicily, I always find a few jars of both packed in my bags! No doubt, Anna snuck them in when I wasn't looking. Here is my recipe for mixed pickled vegetables. I prepare it two ways—with a simple vinegar brine or, as in this recipe, by adding sugar to create an agrodolce, *or sweet and sour flavor. I add my own unique blend of spices and sometimes stick a small hot pepper in the jar to add some zing. My friends Anna and Salvatore would certainly approve!*

3 small cloves garlic	Mixed sliced vegetables, enough to
1 fresh bay leaf	fill a 1 quart jar
1 tsp. mustard seeds	1 cup white distilled vinegar (5%
1 tsp. celery seeds	acidity)
1 tsp. black peppercorns	1 cup water
1 tsp. coriander seeds	1 tbsp. kosher salt
1 small Cayenne pepper (optional)	¼ cup dark brown sugar

Use any of the following vegetables: zucchini, onion, red bell pepper, carrots, cauliflower, green tomatoes, and green cherry tomatoes.

Sterilize the jar in the dishwasher using the sanitize cycle. Place the garlic, bay leaf, mustard seeds, celery seeds, peppercorns, coriander seeds, and Cayenne pepper in the jar. Add the vegetables to the jar, packing them in snugly.

In a saucepan, bring the vinegar, water, salt, and brown sugar to a boil and then remove the saucepan from the burner. Pour the hot brine over the vegetables, covering them completely and leaving ½ inch headspace from the top of the jar. Seal the jar and shake it gently so that any trapped air bubbles will rise to the top. Unseal the jar to release any air bubbles, and if necessary, add more brine. Then reseal the jar tightly and process it in a boiling water bath for 13 minutes. Store the jar in a cool, dark place for 3 weeks before eating. Makes 1 quart.

Carpaccio di Tonno con Insalata di Finocchio (Tuna Carpaccio with Fennel Slaw, Grapes, and Pistachios)

SICILY

Ancient tuna fisheries called tonnara *can be found along Sicily's western coast. A traditional* tonnara *is sure to be located on a protected bay, where the fishing boats would be safe from rough seas. Inside the perimeter walls of an ancient* tonnara *you will find vaulted, stone buildings for processing tuna, houses where the fishermen lived, and a central courtyard for storing nets and building boats. Today, most of Sicily's ancient* tonnara *have been abandoned as the tuna industry has moved to modern ports such as Trapani and Mazara del Vallo. A few, however, have been converted to wonderful bed and breakfasts. They are charming places to stay that are full of Sicilian character. My favorite is located in Scopello, on a picturesque cove that is the perfect place for an afternoon swim!*

There are many traditional methods for preparing and preserving tuna in Sicily. In fact, this region produces Italy's finest jarred tuna and dried tuna roe. Whenever I am in Sicily, I buy plenty to take home! Tuna has always been a favorite seafood that Sicilians enjoy eating crudo, *or raw. Today, modern chefs in Palermo and Catania use fresh, locally caught tuna raw in delicious dishes such as this. This recipe was inspired by a wonderful tuna* carpaccio *that I enjoyed while vacationing in Taormina. Here, the distinctively Sicilian combination of fennel and orange compliments the freshness of raw tuna, making this dish a perfect summertime* antipasto. *The added crunch and burst of flavor from the grapes and pistachios add interest and intrigue that is sure to please today's foodies.*

1 large California navel orange
½ cup olive oil
1 tbsp. white vinegar
Salt and black pepper to taste
1 bulb fennel with fronds
1 cup halved small, seedless red grapes

1½ lbs. fresh tuna steak, sliced very thin
1 small handful pistachios, roasted

Finely zest the orange and extract 3 tablespoons of juice. Whisk together the olive oil, orange zest, orange juice, and vinegar and season with salt and black pepper. Set aside.

Shave the fennel as thinly as possible using a mandolin and coarsely chop a small handful of fronds. Place the fennel, fronds, and grapes in a mixing bowl and toss with enough dressing to moisten.

Arrange the sliced tuna on a serving platter and place some fennel slaw on top of each slice. Coarsely chop the pistachios, sprinkle them over top, and then drizzle with the remaining dressing. Serve lightly chilled. Serves 6 adults.

Pomodorini con Alici Crudi (Cherry Tomatoes Wrapped with Marinated Anchovy Fillets)

CALABRIA

In recent years, fresh anchovies have become widely available in the United States, especially in ethnic markets. If fresh anchovies are available to you, be sure to give them a try! They are absolutely delicious and taste nothing like their salty brown cousins that come in the small pull-top tins. Try fresh anchovies dredged in flour and deep fried with a squeeze of lemon. Or better yet, marinate them in lemon juice. It is a quick and easy preparation. The acid in the lemon juice will cook the anchovies, and they will become firm, white, and full of lemony flavor. They are wonderful eaten alone or with other assorted antipasti. *This is a simple dish that I enjoyed in Scilla, which is perched on a cliff above a crescent-shaped beach of golden sand. It was no doubt made with fresh lemons grown on the nearby plains of Santa Eufemia and anchovies plucked straight from the azure sea. The lemony flavor of the anchovies contrasts nicely with the sweetness of the cherry tomatoes. A good drizzle of extra virgin olive oil and a sprinkle of fresh herbs add even more freshness. It is the perfect* antipasto *for al fresco dining in the summer by the sea.*

2 dozen fresh anchovies (3 or 4 inches in length)
Salt to taste
Juice of 6 lemons
3 cloves garlic, chopped
Olive oil, for drizzling

2 dozen cherry tomatoes
Extra virgin olive oil, for drizzling
Black pepper to taste
3 tbsp. finely chopped, firmly packed Italian flat leaf parsley

Dress the anchovies by removing the scales, heads, fins, innards, and backbone. Rinse the fillets under running water and pat them dry.

Place the fillets, skin side down, in a shallow 10 by 13 inch ceramic or glass baking dish. Season them lightly with salt and squeeze over enough lemon juice to completely cover them. Cover the dish with plastic wrap and refrigerate for 24 hours. The lemon juice will cook the fillets, turning them firm and white.

Pat the fillets dry and discard the juice. Place the fillets in a jar with the garlic and then pour over enough olive oil to cover them. The anchovies can be stored in the refrigerator for up to 5 days.

Wrap each cherry tomato with an anchovy fillet and secure it with a toothpick. Arrange them on serving platter, drizzle with extra virgin olive oil, season with salt and black pepper, and sprinkle with parsley. Serve at room temperature or lightly chilled. Serves 4 to 6 adults.

Peperoni Ripieni con Mollica, Pomodori Secchi, e Alici (Hot Cherry Peppers Stuffed with Bread Crumbs, Sundried Tomatoes, and Anchovies)

CALABRIA

Hot peppers are a favorite in Southern Italian cuisine. There are many varieties of hot peppers in Southern Italy, and some are hotter than others. The long, red chilies are the most common, but beware of the smaller ones that are about one inch long. They may look innocent, but they are sure to deliver a punch! In Calabria, Abruzzo, and Basilicata, hot peppers are sautéed with olive oil and eaten alongside roasted and grilled meats, stuffed with bread crumbs and preserved under olive oil, and sewn into long strands that are hung out to dry in the sun. If you really enjoy the heat of hot peppers in your food, then head to Calabria! This region is said to have the spiciest cuisine in all of Italy. And it is quite delicious, too.

Hot cherry peppers grow plentifully in my vegetable garden. Unfortunately, they all ripen at the same time. At some point in late July, I always find myself with a few baskets full of bright red cherry peppers sitting on the kitchen counter. My wife says the same thing every year: "Why did you plant so many?" Plump, round cherry peppers are perfect for stuffing. They can be pickled and then stuffed with cheese and salami or stuffed with bread crumbs and then jarred in olive oil. Either way, they are the perfect finger food! I stuff mine Calabresi style with a flavorful bread crumb mixture. I then roast them in the oven until tender and golden on top. It is a delicious treat from the sun-drenched hills of Calabria.

½ loaf country-style Italian bread
½ cup chopped, firmly packed jarred sundried tomatoes preserved in olive oil
8 fillets Italian jarred anchovies in olive oil
2 cloves garlic
2 tbsp. finely chopped, firmly packed oregano

Black pepper to taste
Olive oil, for moistening (about ¼ cup) and brushing
2 dozen hot cherry peppers
Salt to taste

Grate enough bread in a food processor for 2 cups of firmly pressed crumbs and set them to the side in a bowl.

Next, grind the sundried tomatoes, anchovies, garlic, and oregano in the food processor. Return the bread crumbs to the food processor and season with black pepper. Pulse while adding a steady stream of olive oil until you achieve a moist, fluffy filling.

Preheat the oven to 400 degrees. Remove and discard the tops and seeds from the peppers and stuff them with the filling. Place the peppers on a baking tray that has been brushed with olive oil, and then tent it with aluminum foil. Roast the peppers for 30 minutes. Then remove the foil and bake for another 5 to 10 minutes to crisp the tops. Serve at room temperature. Serves 6 adults.

Mozzarella in Carozza (Pan Fried Mozzarella Pockets)

CAMPANIA

Mozzarella is the signature cheese of Naples. The best mozzarella is said to be produced in the Salerno province, near the town of Battipaglia. Here, ancient cheesemakers have mastered the art of pulling, stretching, and cutting the curds into a semi-soft cheese that is truly divine. The tradition was passed down over the centuries and eventually spread to Lazio, Abruzzo, Molise, Apulia, and Basilicata, which have all incorporated mozzarella into regional cuisines. Today, almost one hundred years after the massive migration of Southern Italians to the United States, mozzarella is the number one ingredient associated with Italian American food. However, high demand from a society obsessed with shortcuts has now caused our supermarket shelves to be stocked with low quality, manufactured mozzarella that comes pre-shredded in a re-sealable bag. What a shame!

In Neapolitan dialect, this simple peasant dish is called "mozzarella in a carriage." It is one of my favorite comfort foods. When I was a child, my mother would make it for lunch on cold, snowy days when my siblings and I were off of school. It was a tasty, satisfying treat that filled our stomachs and warmed us up after a few hours of playing in the snow. The preparation is quick and easy. A mound of shredded mozzarella is enclosed in a pocket of fresh country-style Italian bread that is then soaked in beaten egg and pan fried in butter. The bread, or "carriage," holds the melted cheese, and when sliced the cheese is released with all of the wonderful gooeyness one would expect from mozzarella. Children and adults alike find it irresistible! After all, who doesn't like mozzarella that stretches from the plate to your mouth as you eat?

2 round loaves country-style Italian bread
8 extra-large eggs
1 lb. mozzarella cheese (low moisture), shredded
2 sticks butter
Salt and black pepper to taste

Cut the bread into slices just under ½ inch thick and remove the crust. Use a 5 inch round cookie cutter to press twelve rounds out of the white part of the bread.

Beat the eggs with a splash of water. Place some cheese in the center of a bread round, cover it with another round, and seal it by pressing firmly around the edges. Repeat to make five more cheese pockets.

Melt the butter in a 5½ quart frying pan over medium-low heat. Dip each cheese pocket into the beaten eggs, and allow the egg to thoroughly soak into the bread. Fry the pockets until golden brown on each side and sprinkle with salt and black pepper. Serve hot. Serves 6 adults.

Crocchette di Patate e Zafferano (Pan Fried Saffron Potato Croquettes)

ABRUZZO/MOLISE

If there is any one ingredient of Italian cookery that is most associated with Abruzzo, it has to be zafferano, *or saffron. Saffron is the pistil of the tiny crocus flower. On the high plateau of Navelli, the soil conditions and cool autumn weather are perfect for growing saffron crocuses. Each October, the crocus buds push their way up through the soil to bestow upon the world a most beautiful purple blossom. Once the crocus bud emerges, it must be picked right away, before the blossom opens. It is an arduous and backbreaking task for the harvesters! Once harvested, the red pistils are plucked from the buds and set to dry over hot coals. The crocus buds can only be harvested by hand, which makes saffron very expensive. In fact, it is said to be the most expensive spice in the world by weight. In Rome or Milan, an ounce of Abruzzese saffron is likely to cost over $200! Fortunately, it only takes a pinch to add wonderful flavor and a tantalizing yellow color to any dish. In the small towns of the Navelli Plateau, saffron is added to crisp, savory potato croquettes called* frittatina. *I always add a handful of grated Pecorino Romano cheese to the potato filling for extra depth of flavor. Served piping hot with a glass of red wine, they are the perfect wintertime snack.*

3 lbs. russet potatoes
½ cup milk
3 pinches saffron threads
5 tbsp. melted butter
2¼ cups grated Pecorino Romano cheese, divided
Salt and black pepper to taste

6 extra-large eggs
3 cups finely ground dry bread crumbs
2 tbsp. finely chopped, firmly packed Italian flat leaf parsley
Olive oil, for frying

Peel the potatoes and chop them into 1½ inch chunks. Place the potatoes in a pot, cover them with water, season lightly with salt, and boil for 20 minutes or until tender. Drain the potatoes well, transfer them to a mixing bowl, and allow them to cool completely.

Meanwhile, place the milk and saffron in a small saucepan over low heat and steep the saffron until the milk turns bright yellow. Strain out the saffron threads using a mesh sieve, discard, and allow the milk to cool.

When the potatoes are room temperature, mash them. Then incorporate the milk, melted butter, and 1½ cups cheese and season with salt and black pepper to taste. The mixture should be smooth and firm enough to form croquettes. If the mixture is too dense, add an additional splash or two of milk.

Beat the eggs in a mixing bowl with a splash of water. Combine the bread crumbs, parsley, and remaining ¾ cup of grated cheese in another bowl. Form oval shaped croquettes from the potato mixture, dip the croquettes in the beaten egg, and then dredge them in the bread crumbs. After you have breaded all of the croquettes, let them sit for 10 minutes and then pass them through the egg and bread crumbs a second time.

Add ½ inch of olive oil to a 5½ quart frying pan over medium heat. When the oil has heated, fry the croquettes on each side until golden brown. Place the croquettes on paper towels to absorb the excess oil and sprinkle lightly with salt. Serve hot. Makes 18 to 22 croquettes, depending upon size. Serves 6 to 8 adults.

Arancini di Riso (Saffron Rice Croquettes Filled with Beef Ragu, Peas, and Mozzarella)

SICILY

I love the city of Palermo. The streets are full of hustle and bustle, with cars coming at you from every direction, horns blowing, and people pushing their way down crowded sidewalks. That being said, it is no wonder that Palermo is such a great city for street food. After all, one must certainly work up an appetite navigating through the traffic and crowds! In Palermo, there are friggitorie *or "fry shops" on every corner ready to serve up Sicily's version of fast food: rice croquettes called* arancini, *chickpea fritters called* panelle, *and batter-fried artichokes and vegetables. A line of people at the fry shop window and plenty of more people eating nearby are always the sign of a good* friggitoria. *When you are in Palermo, be sure to grab a snack at one.* Arancini *means "little oranges" in Sicilian dialect. They are tasty croquettes of saffron-tinged rice filled with ground beef* ragu *and peas. When breaded and fried to golden perfection, they resemble little oranges, just as the name implies.* Arancini *are a sure find at every* friggitoria *in Palermo. They are traditionally eaten as a snack, but I also serve them as a warm* antipasto *on special occasions.*

1½ quarts chicken broth	1 heaping tbsp. finely chopped
3 large pinches saffron	prosciutto
Olive oil, for sautéing	2 rounded tbsp. tomato paste
3 cups Arborio rice	½ cup red wine
Salt and black pepper to taste	1 cup tomato puree
1½ cups white wine, divided	1 rounded tsp. dried oregano
6 tbsp. butter	1 rounded tsp. dried basil
1½ cups grated Parmigiano-Reggiano cheese	⅔ cup frozen peas (thawed)
¾ lb. ground sirloin (90% lean)	⅓ lb. mozzarella cheese (low moisture), cubed
½ small Spanish or Vidalia onion, finely chopped	6 extra-large eggs
1 clove garlic, minced	1 lb. finely ground dry bread crumbs
	3 quarts corn oil, for deep frying

Set the broth to simmer in a pot with the saffron for 7 minutes so that the saffron infuses the broth. Remove the threads with a mesh skimmer and discard.

Coat the bottom of a 5½ quart frying pan with olive oil. Add the rice and sauté over medium-low heat for 2 to 3 minutes or until opaque, stirring constantly. Then season the rice with salt and black pepper.

Add ½ cup of white wine to the rice. Stir constantly until the wine is absorbed. Then add the remaining white wine ½ cup at a time. Continue stirring constantly, making sure the wine has been absorbed before more is added.

Add the hot broth to the rice one ladle at a time, stirring constantly and adding the next ladle after the rice has absorbed the broth. This process will tenderize the rice. It will take about 20 to 25 minutes for the rice to become tender. Depending on the rice and desired tenderness, you may or may not use all of the broth.

Whisk in the butter and then the grated cheese. Continue sautéing for another minute or until the rice is thick and creamy. Transfer the rice to a bowl and allow it to cool to room temperature. If possible, allow it to cool further in the refrigerator, covered, for several hours or overnight, as this will make it easier to mold into balls.

Brush the bottom of a frying pan with olive oil, add the ground sirloin, and season it with salt and black pepper. Brown the meat over medium-low heat, breaking it up with the back of a wooden spoon. Drain off any excess grease and set it to the side in a bowl.

Coat the bottom of the frying pan with olive oil and sauté the onion until soft. Add the garlic and prosciutto and continue sautéing for another minute. Push the sautéed items to one side of the frying pan, tilt the frying to the other side to pool the oil, and fry the tomato paste in the oil for 1 minute. Add the red wine, followed by the tomato puree, oregano, and basil and season lightly with salt and black pepper. Simmer on low heat for 5 minutes, stir in the ground beef, and continue sautéing for another 5 minutes. If necessary, add more wine or some water to moisten the mixture. Stir in the peas, remove the frying pan from the burner, and allow the meat mixture to cool completely.

Set a piece of wax paper on your work surface. Take a handful of rice, form it into a ball, and then press it on the wax paper into a round patty that is about 5 inches in diameter and just under ½ inch thick. Place some of the meat mixture and a cube or two of Mozzarella in the center of the patty. Slip your hand under the wax paper, lift the wax paper and patty, and, using the wax paper as an aid, fold in the edges of the patty to completely enclose the filling within the rice. Shape into a ball, set it on a baking tray, and continue making rice balls.

Beat the eggs with a splash of water. Place the bread crumbs in a wide bowl. Dip the rice balls in the beaten egg, dredge them in the bread crumbs, and let them sit for 10 minutes. Then pass them through the egg and bread crumbs a second time.

Heat the corn oil in a deep pot, fry the *arancini* until golden brown, about 3 to 5 minutes, and set them on paper towels to absorb any excess oil. Serve hot. Makes 8 *arancini*, with enough filling left over to make a second batch. Serves 8 adults.

Crocchette di Gamberi (Pan Fried Shrimp Croquettes)

CAMPANIA

In Positano, colorful houses with bougainvillea-covered terraces cascade down a steep slope to the sea. On the pebble beach below, small boats sit in neat rows looking out at the warm azure waters. Once a sleepy fishing village, Positano's seductive climate and dramatic scenery have helped transform it into a chic resort. Today, the Costiera Amalfitana has become the Cote d'Azur of Italy, surpassing Liguria's Riviera Ponente as the preferred destination of jetsetters. Here, rooms at the best hotels will set you back $1,000 per night. But sitting on the balcony of your hotel room and sipping a glass of wine as the sun sets over the Mediterranean is worth every cent. If only I had enough pennies!

Here is a recipe inspired by the Costiera Amalfitana, where there is a fine tradition of croquette making. Croquettes are typical of rustic Italian cooking. They are a way to turn a few meager ingredients or leftovers into another meal or snack. The specialty of Positano is a potato croquette, which is deep fried until golden brown and crisp. It is a popular snack at restaurants and snack bars all along the Costiera Amalfitana. As the cuisine of this region is tied to the sea, fish and shrimp are sometimes cooked in tasty croquettes too! Here is my version, which is made with sweet, succulent shrimp. I chop the shrimp, toss them in a stiff batter, shape the mixture into patties, coat them in bread crumbs, and pan fry them until crisp and delicious. Serve them as an entrée, antipasto, *or afternoon snack with a squeeze of fresh lemon.*

2½ lbs. shrimp	1 tbsp. olive oil, plus additional for frying
1 cup all-purpose, pre-sifted flour	2 tbsp. finely chopped, firmly packed Italian flat leaf parsley
1 tsp. baking powder	5 cups finely ground dry bread crumbs
¾ tsp. garlic powder	
½ tsp. black pepper	
½ tsp. salt	Salt to taste
1 extra-large egg	3 lemons, cut in wedges
½ cup milk	

Peel, devein, and finely chop the shrimp. Combine the flour, baking powder, garlic powder, black pepper, and salt in a mixing bowl.

In a separate bowl, beat together the egg, milk, and olive oil. Add the liquid ingredients to the flour mixture and whisk to form a smooth, thick batter. Then incorporate the shrimp and parsley.

Sprinkle the bottom of a baking tray liberally with bread crumbs and place the rest in a bowl. Drop a scoop (about ⅓ cup) of the shrimp mixture into the bowl, dredge it in the bread crumbs, shape it into a patty, and set it to rest on the baking tray.

When you are done forming patties, place ½ inch of olive oil in a 5½ quart frying pan over medium-high heat. When the oil has heated, fry the patties on each side until golden brown. Place the patties on paper towels to absorb the excess oil and sprinkle lightly with salt. Serve hot, with lemon wedges. Serves 6 adults.

Fiori di Zucchine Ripieni (Batter Fried Zucchini Blossoms Stuffed with Ricotta Cheese, Prosciutto, and Herbs)

LAZIO

The Campo de Fiori is a large square located in the heart of Rome, not far from the Piazza Navona. This is where you will find the Mercato di Campo de Fiori, Rome's most splendid outdoor produce market. The name Campo de Fiori *means "field of flowers," which certainly seems odd as the square is located in the urban core of Rome. Back in the days of Julius Caesar, however, the area was a meadow that stretched to the banks of the Tiber. The* mercato *is a lively place in springtime when young vegetables, fresh greens, aromatic herbs, and bouquets of bright, golden zucchini blossoms fill the stalls. There is always a large variety of produce to choose from, most of which comes in fresh each day from the surrounding countryside. Discerning Romans will go from vendor to vendor searching out the best produce and haggling for a good price. No doubt, they always leave with their shopping sacks full!*

Zucchini blossoms are popular throughout Italy, but they are especially favored by the Romans. They are fried until crisp, stuffed with cheese and ham, tossed with pasta, or cooked in omelets. This recipe was inspired by the stuffed zucchini blossoms I ate at a small family-run restaurant near the Spanish Steps. I'd bet the zucchini blossoms were purchased that morning at the Mercato di Campo de Fiori! It was a simple preparation of batter-dipped flowers filled with creamy ricotta cheese. In my recipe, grated Parmigiano-Reggiano cheese, finely diced prosciutto, and fresh herbs add extra flavor. Serve them with a glass of Frascati wine from the verdant hills outside of Rome for a taste of Lazio in the springtime.

¼ oz. active dry yeast
1¼ cups warm water
1¼ cups all-purpose, pre-sifted flour
¼ tsp. salt
1 extra-large egg yolk plus 1 extra-large whole egg
2 cups ricotta cheese
2 tbsp. grated Parmigiano-Reggiano cheese

2 tbsp. finely diced prosciutto
1 tbsp. finely chopped, firmly packed Italian flat leaf parsley
Salt and black pepper to taste
2 dozen zucchini blossoms
Corn oil, for frying

In a mixing bowl, dissolve the yeast in the water and let it sit for 5 minutes. Add the flour, salt, and the yolk of one egg, whisk to form a frothy batter, and let it rest for 20 minutes.

Meanwhile, prepare the filling: Stir together the ricotta cheese, Parmigiano-Reggiano cheese, prosciutto, parsley, and the remaining whole egg. Season the ricotta mixture with salt and black pepper.

Remove the pistil or stamen from the blossoms. Place the filling in a pastry bag and squeeze some into each flower. Twist the petal tops gently so the filling will not escape.

Add 1 inch of corn oil to the bottom of a large, deep frying pan over medium-high heat. When the oil is hot, push down the batter with a wooden spoon. (As the batter is resting, the yeast will cause it to rise.) Dip the stuffed blossoms in the batter, and fry them in the oil until golden brown. Set the fried zucchini blossoms on paper towels to absorb the excess oil and sprinkle lightly with salt. Serve hot. Serves 6 to 8 adults.

The enchanting side streets of a medieval town in the Chieti Province of Abruzzo

II

Pane, Pizze, Pizze Ripiene, e Frittate
(Breads, Pizzas, Savory Pies, and Egg Dishes)

An Unusual Place for Hot Dogs

A Rambling in Calabria

Scalea is a small beach town that lies on a rugged stretch of Calabria's Tyrrhenian coast far to the south of the famous resorts of Amalfi and Positano. It is off the radar of international tourists, and certainly few Americans ever venture there. My friends from Palermo, Anna and Salvatore, have a summer villa in Scalea. Every August, they leave the hot, crowded city and head to Scalea with their family for vacation. One summer, I was lucky enough to join them. Each day we swam in the sea and then stopped for a snack at one of the food vendors along Scalea's main boulevard. Full of Calabrian charm, this little town was the last place I expected to eat hot dogs. Even more bizarre was the unusual place I found them!

One afternoon, their daughter, Gemma, took me to a *trattoria*, and she ordered a pizza for us to share. When it arrived, the waiter proudly announced, "Here is your pizza with *wurstel*!" He placed the pizza on the table, and much to my surprise it was topped with hot dogs. They were cocktail wieners, to be exact. I found this quite odd. Here I am in Italy, and America's number one fast food is served to me on a pizza! While I enjoy hot dogs at a Yankees game, they are not something I would choose to eat on pizza, especially when I am in Italy. Gemma sensed my bewilderment.

"This is pizza with hot dog," she explained. "You are American. You do like hot dog?"

I cracked an uneasy smile and replied, "Of course." I then sheepishly added, "But Americans would never put hot dogs on their pizza."

Gemma defended her choice of topping. "But you are in Italy, and Italians do put hot dog on pizza!" she exclaimed.

She then grabbed the menu and pointed it out. "You see, pizza with *wurstel* is written here. That is hot dog," she proudly stated.

Gemma then stuck the menu close to my face. I looked at it carefully and then with a smirk, I prodded her one last time. "Maybe this is a tourist menu, and they put hot dogs on the pizza for Americans like me!"

Gemma became frustrated and replied, "American tourists do not come to Scalea! This is where Italians go. And I did not ask the restaurant to put hot dogs on the menu because you were coming!"

I then grabbed one of the cocktail wieners with a fork, popped it in my mouth, and smiled. Gemma ended our heated conversation by cracking a smile back and then we each grabbed a slice of the pizza. The crust was thin and crisp and the cocktail wieners were scattered atop of a layer of wonderful, fresh mozzarella cheese. I explained to Gemma how Americans wrap the little hot dogs in dough and serve them with a fancy toothpick at cocktail parties. She was quite amused by the name "pigs in a blanket." We finished the pizza and headed back to the beach. It was truly an unusual place for hot dogs, and I'll never forget it.

Village market on the island of Lipari, Sicily

A window in the colorful town of Procida, Campania

The town of Orsomarso, Calabria, cascades down a mountainous slope

A view of the Trapani coast and Monte Cofano from Erice, Sicily

Olive groves and wheat fields in Southern Lazio

A day at the beach in Tropea, Calabria

Biscotti di Semola (Braided, Ring-Shaped Semolina Biscuits with Sesame Seeds)

SICILY

My friends Salvatore and Anna own a paneficio, *or bread bakery, in Palermo. Their son, Lorenzo, heads to the bakery early each morning to make the breads and biscuits. Locals go to the* paneficio *every day to buy a fresh loaf. It is a place where neighbors bump into each other and spend a few minutes chatting. In the morning, there is always a line at the counter and plenty of people gossiping by the door. I once suggested to Lorenzo that he set up a coffee bar. "Absolutely not!" he said. "I want the customers in and out of the door quickly. If everyone is standing around drinking coffee, how can I sell my bread?" Here is my take on a crispy Sicilian biscuit. It is the sort of treat that Lorenzo sells by the bagful at Salvatore and Anna's* paneficio *in the bustling heart of Palermo! I use semolina flour, which imparts a nutty flavor and turns the biscuits a pleasant shade of yellow. Coated with plenty of sesame seeds, they are a delicious savory snack. Or serve them with a glass of red Nero d'Avola wine from Sicily or alongside a bowl of hot soup in wintertime.*

2¼ cups all-purpose, pre-sifted flour	½ cup olive oil
1½ cups semolina flour	1 tsp. salt
4 tsp. baking powder	3 extra-large egg whites
1¼ cups plus 2 tablespoons water, divided	3 cups raw hulled sesame seeds

Whisk together the two flours and baking powder in a large mixing bowl and make a well in the middle. In a separate bowl, whisk together the water, olive oil, and salt. Pour the liquid ingredients into the well and beat with a fork, pulling in flour from the sides until the dough pulls together.

Turn the dough onto a lightly floured work surface and knead for 2 minutes or until glossy. Divide the dough into 2 balls, cover each with plastic wrap, and allow them to rest for 1 hour.

Break off walnut-sized pieces of dough and roll them into thin, 4 inch long cords. Twist 2 cords together and then shape into a fancy braided ring and pinch together the ends. Continue until all dough has been used.

Preheat the oven to 350 degrees. Whisk together the egg whites and 2 tablespoons of water. Place the sesame seeds in a shallow bowl. Dip the biscuits into the egg wash, dredge them in sesame seeds, and place them on an ungreased, non-stick baking tray. Bake for 50 to 55 minutes or until the sesame seeds are golden brown. Serve at room temperature. Makes 1½ dozen biscuits.

Taralli (Ring-Shaped Fennel Seed Biscuits)

ABRUZZO/MOLISE

Savory biscuits called taralli *are a popular snack in Abruzzo, Molise, Apulia, and Campania. They are typically eaten with* antipasto *or as a* spuntino, *which is a snack between meals.* Taralli *are now popular in the United States, especially in areas where there is a large Italian American community. When I was a child, my father would pick up a box of fresh baked* taralli *from the Italian market on his way home from work. He would set the box on the kitchen counter, and my brother and I would sneak a handful before dinner. Inevitably we were caught, and our mother would yell, "Stop or you will spoil your appetite!" Dinner always ended with my brother being scolded for not eating all the food on his plate. However, thirty minutes later he was back to sneaking* taralli *from the box!*

It seems that each town in Southern Italy has its own way of making taralli. *In Campania and Apulia, they are sure to be made with a yeast dough, which makes them light and airy, whereas in some parts of Molise no yeast is added, and they are always firm and crisp. Regardless of the dough, one step is essential when making* taralli—*they must be boiled first before being baked in the oven. This gives them their signature shiny crust. Here is a recipe typical of Molise, which is known for its fine rustic breads. My recipe does not call for yeast, an omission that makes the dough easy to assemble and the* taralli *crisp. Aromatic fennel seeds, flecks of black pepper, and a hint of garlic make them extra special. For the perfect* spuntino, *serve them with aged provolone cheese and a glass of red Montepulciano wine from Abruzzo.*

3¾ cups all-purpose, pre-sifted flour	2 cloves garlic, minced
4 tsp. baking powder	1 rounded tsp. salt
1 cup water	1 tsp. black pepper, freshly cracked
¾ cup olive oil	2 tsp. fennel seeds

Whisk together the flour and baking powder in a large mixing bowl and make a well in the middle. In a separate bowl, whisk together the water, olive oil, garlic, salt, black pepper, and fennel seeds. Pour the liquid ingredients into the well and beat with a fork, pulling in flour from the sides until the dough pulls together.

Turn the dough onto a lightly floured work surface and knead it for 2 minutes or until glossy. Divide the dough into 2 balls, cover each with plastic wrap, and allow them to rest for 45 minutes.

Break off walnut-sized pieces of dough and roll them into 4 inch cords. Shape the cords into rings and pinch together the ends.

Fill a 12 quart pot ⅔ of the way with water and bring it to a boil over medium-low heat. Drop a few *taralli* at a time into the boiling water. They will sink to the bottom and then quickly rise to the surface. Let them boil at the surface for 30 seconds and then remove them with a skimmer or slotted spoon. Set the *taralli* on wax paper to dry for 5 minutes and then transfer them to an ungreased, non-stick baking tray.

Preheat the oven to 350 degrees. Bake for 30 minutes, flip the *taralli*, and then continue baking for another 15 to 20 minutes or until golden brown. Serve room temperature. Makes 2½ dozen *taralli*.

Foccacia (Country-Style Bread with Fresh Herbs and Pecorino Cheese)

APULIA

Whenever I am in Apulia, I search out a panetteria *that has fresh baked* focaccia. *A* panetteria *is a bakery that specializes in both breads and pastries. It is typically much larger than a* paneficio, *which sells only breads, or a* pasticceria, *which sells only pastries. Focaccia bread is the specialty of Bari. If you ask a Baresi grandmother, she will tell you that a traditional* focaccia *must be soft and spongy in the middle, crisp and golden on the bottom and top, and moistened by a drizzle of the freshest Pugliese olive oil. Here is my version! It is something we make quite often at our farm with fresh-picked herbs from our garden. I like to serve it with* antipasto *or alongside my main course in place of regular bread. Sometimes I make two loafs and wrap one up in plastic wrap to freeze. Then, whenever I want, I just pop it in a 400 degree oven for 10 minutes to warm and crisp it up.*

For the dough:
2 cups warm water
1 packet active dry yeast
1½ tsp. sugar
5 cups all-purpose, pre-sifted flour
2 tsp. salt
3 tbsp. olive oil, plus additional for brushing

For the topping:
Coarse salt and black pepper to taste
4 cloves garlic, finely chopped
1 tbsp. finely chopped, firmly packed rosemary
1½ tbsp. finely chopped, firmly packed Italian flat leaf parsley
1 cup shaved or shredded Pecorino Romano cheese
Extra virgin olive oil, for drizzling

Combine the water, yeast, and sugar in a small bowl and let it sit for 10 minutes or until frothy. Place the flour and salt in the bowl of a standing mixer. Add the yeast mixture and 3 tbsp. olive oil to the mixing bowl and beat on low speed using the paddle attachment until a soft, sticky dough forms. Switch to a dough hook and knead on medium-high speed for 4 minutes or until the dough is smooth. If the dough is too sticky, work in a tablespoon or two of additional flour.

Transfer the dough to a large bowl that has been brushed with olive oil, and then brush the top of the dough with olive oil. Cover the dough loosely with plastic wrap and let it rest in a warm place for 1½ hours or until it has doubled in size.

Brush an 11 by 17 inch pizza tray with olive oil. Turn the dough onto the tray and spread it out evenly. Press your fingertips deep into the dough to make indentations all over the surface and then season with coarse salt and black pepper. Sprinkle the garlic, rosemary, parsley, and cheese and drizzle generously with extra virgin olive oil. Let the *focaccia* rest for another hour or until it has doubled in size.

Preheat the oven to 475 degrees. Make more indentations with your fingers and bake for 20 to 25 minutes or until golden brown on the bottom. Serves 6 adults.

Pandolce di Pasqua (Braided Easter Sweet Bread with Colored Eggs)

CAMPANIA

In most regions of Italy, fancy breads are made to celebrate Easter. The breads are sometimes braided or shaped into rings and studded with hard-boiled eggs. In Sicily, they make small Easter breads called pupi cu l'uova *that are shaped like dolls and have an egg in the center. In Campania, the Easter breads are sure to be flavored with lemon, and sometimes bits of candied citron or a sprinkle of raisins are added too. It is said that the bread symbolizes abundance and the eggs symbolize the rebirth of Christ. Step into a traditional Neapolitan bakery during Easter week and you will see skillfully braided, ring-shaped Easter breads proudly set out for display. Be sure to take one home!*

Here is my mother's recipe for Easter sweetbread. It is typical of the region of Campania. She has been making it for as long as I can remember; she always baked it the night before Easter so that it was soft and delicious the next morning. When I was a child, I woke up every Easter morning to find her sweetbread proudly set on display next to the Easter baskets. Neatly braided with dyed eggs tucked into each twist and a sprinkle of colorful nonpareils on top, it was always the show piece of the breakfast table. A touch of lemon and orange zest add bright flavor to this pleasantly sweet and tasty bread. A slice of pandolce di Pasqua *is the perfect snack to enjoy on Easter morning with your espresso.*

½ oz. active dry yeast	1½ cups sugar
2 cups warm water, divided	1 tsp. salt
8½ cups all-purpose, pre-sifted flour, divided	4 large eggs, divided
1 small lemon	5 uncooked, dyed eggs (multi-colored)
1 small orange	Colored nonpareils, for decorating
1 cup vegetable shortening	

Dissolve the yeast in ½ cup of warm water and let it stand for 7 minutes. In a large mixing bowl, combine 1½ cups of flour with 1½ cups of warm water. Add the yeast mixture and beat until smooth. Cover the bowl loosely with plastic wrap and let it sit in a warm place for 1½ hours.

Meanwhile, zest the lemon and orange and extract 2 tsp. of juice from each. Cream the shortening with the sugar, salt, zest, and juice. Beat 3 eggs into the creamed ingredients and then beat in the yeast mixture to form a smooth batter. Add the remaining flour, 1 cup at a time, until the dough pulls together.

Turn the dough onto a lightly floured work surface and knead it until smooth and shiny. Shape the dough into a ball and place it in a large bowl that has been sprayed with non-stick cooking spray. Spray the top of the dough lightly with cooking spray to prevent it from forming a skin. Cover the bowl with a dish towel and let it sit in a warm place for 2 hours or until doubled in size.

Punch down the dough, divide it into 2 equal balls, and let them sit, covered, for 20 minutes. Roll each ball of dough into a cord 2½ inches in diameter and about 2½ feet long. On a lightly greased, round baking tray, loosely braid the cords into a ring. Be sure there are 5 twists in the braid to hold the dyed eggs.

Place a dyed egg inside each twist. Cover the bread with a dish towel and let it stand for about 1½ hours or until doubled in size.

Preheat the oven to 350 degrees. Bake the bread for about 40 minutes. Beat the remaining egg with a splash of water and brush the bread with the egg wash. Quickly sprinkle with nonpareils and continue baking for another 15 to 20 minutes or until golden brown. Serves 6 to 8 adults.

'Mbriulate (Spiral Semolina Bread with Sausage, Cheese, Sundried Tomatoes, and Black Olives)

SICILY

At one time, Sicily was the breadbasket of the Roman Empire. Vast areas of the Sicilian interior were cleared of forests by the Romans and given over to the cultivation of wheat, which is still grown there today. No wonder Sicily has such a fine tradition of pastamaking and breadmaking! Farina di semola, *or semolina flour, is made from a hard variety of wheat called durum. It is said that the Romans brought durum wheat to Italy from other parts of the Mediterranean Basin. Unlike soft wheat that is milled into your typical white flour, durum wheat produces flour that is coarse and pale yellow. In Sicily,* farina di semola *is used to make bread, pasta, and couscous. In Agrigento, crumbled pork sausage, cheese, briny olives, and sundried tomatoes are rolled into a semolina dough that is baked into a large, round loaf called* 'mbriulate, *the preparation of which is truly unique. First, the filling is encased in a long cord of dough. Then the cord is twisted into a spiral. When baked, it looks like a giant snail shell! The semolina gives the bread a unique yellow color, which is certainly symbolic of the sun-drenched hills of Agrigento. However, the filling is what sets this bread apart. The bold, vibrant flavors are distinctively Sicilian and match well with the nutty flavor of the semolina.*

For the dough:
½ oz. active dry yeast
1½ cups warm water
2¼ cups all-purpose, pre-sifted flour
1¼ cups Semolina flour
1 tbsp. olive oil
1 tsp. salt

For the filling:
1 lb. Italian pork sausage
Olive oil, for sautéing
1 red bell pepper, seeded and chopped
½ medium Spanish or Vidalia onion, chopped

Salt and black pepper to taste
4 cloves garlic, finely chopped
¾ cup pitted, halved, black Cerignola olives
½ cup chopped and firmly packed jarred sundried tomatoes preserved in olive oil
1 tbsp. finely chopped and firmly packed oregano
1 tbsp. finely chopped and firmly packed basil
¾ lb. mozzarella or caciocavallo cheese, cubed

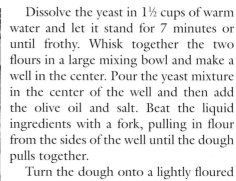

Dissolve the yeast in 1½ cups of warm water and let it stand for 7 minutes or until frothy. Whisk together the two flours in a large mixing bowl and make a well in the center. Pour the yeast mixture in the center of the well and then add the olive oil and salt. Beat the liquid ingredients with a fork, pulling in flour from the sides of the well until the dough pulls together.

Turn the dough onto a lightly floured work surface and knead it until smooth.

Shape the dough into a ball and place it in a lightly greased bowl. Cover the bowl with a dish towel and set it in a warm place for 2 hours or until the dough has doubled in size.

Meanwhile, prepare the filling: Remove the sausage from the casing. Brush the bottom of a frying pan with olive oil and set it over medium-low heat. Brown the sausage, breaking it up with the back of a wooden spoon. When the sausage is fully cooked, drain off any excess grease and transfer the sausage to a mixing bowl.

Return the frying pan to the heat and recoat the bottom with olive oil. Add the bell pepper and onion, season with salt and black pepper, and sauté until soft. Add the garlic and continue sautéing for another minute. Transfer the sautéed items to the mixing bowl with the sausage and stir in the olives, sundried tomatoes, oregano, and basil.

When the dough has doubled, punch it down and turn it onto a lightly floured work surface. Roll the dough into a long, narrow rectangle about ¼ inch thick. Spread the filling evenly over the dough, maintaining a 1 inch border from all four edges. Sprinkle the cheese on top of the filling. Roll the dough like a jelly roll and seal the edges. Transfer the roll to a lightly greased baking sheet, twist it into a spiral that resembles a snail shell, and fold the outer edge underneath the spiral. Allow the bread to rest for 40 minutes.

Preheat the oven to 375 degrees. Bake for 50 minutes or until golden brown on top and bottom. Serve warm or room temperature. Serves 4 to 6 adults.

Pasta per la Pizza Napoletana (Basic Neapolitan Pizza Dough)

CAMPANIA

A friend of mine who does not speak Italian was vacationing in Italy. He sat down for lunch at a restaurant and ordered a pepperoni pizza. His pizza arrived topped with green bell peppers, and an argument ensued with the waiter. "This is not what I ordered. I wanted pepperoni on my pizza!" he exclaimed. The waiter responded, "But sir, that is what I brought you!" My friend went on to describe the spicy sausage that he knows as pepperoni. The waiter realized the dilemma. "I am sorry sir, but pepperoni *means "pepper" in Italian, which is what you ordered." My friend then asked, "How can that be?" The waiter then explained, "Unfortunately, what you want is called* salame picante *in Italian!" That being said, my friend apologized and proceeded to eat his pizza with peppers!*

Proud Neapolitans will tell you that pizza was invented in their city. Although the legitimacy of this claim is debatable, one thing is certain: Neapolitans have perfected the art of pizzamaking. No other region of Italy produces pizza that compares! Today, pizza has been hijacked by the rest of Italy: it is a popular snack from the mountains of Piedmont to the shores of Sicily. Its popularity has also spread across the globe. You are sure to find pizza in modern cities such as Tokyo and Dubai. In the United States, pizza is so common that it has become uniquely "American," especially when topped with—you guessed it—pepperoni! Here is a classic Neapolitan pizza dough. Be sure to roll or stretch it thin. Although this requires some elbow grease, you will be rewarded in the end with the crispiest crust ever!

1¼ cups warm water
1 packet active dry yeast
1 tsp. sugar
3½ cups all-purpose, pre-sifted flour

1¾ tsp. salt
1 tbsp. olive oil, plus additional for brushing

Combine the water, yeast, and sugar in a small bowl and let it sit for 10 minutes or until frothy. Place the flour and salt in the bowl of a standing mixer. Add the yeast mixture and olive oil to the mixing bowl and beat with the paddle attachment on low speed until the dough pulls together. Switch to a dough hook and knead on medium-high speed for 3 minutes or until the dough forms a smooth ball. If the dough is too sticky, work in a tablespoon or two of additional flour. Turn the dough onto a lightly floured work surface, knead it a few times with your hands, and then shape it into a ball.

Place the dough in a large bowl that has been brushed lightly with olive oil, and then brush the top of the dough lightly. Cover the dough loosely with plastic wrap and let

it stand in a warm place for 1½ hours or until it has doubled in size. Punch down the dough, knead it for 1 minute, shape it into a ball, lightly brush the top with olive oil, and let it sit for another hour, or until it has it doubled in size. Makes enough dough for 1 large pizza.

Pasta Frolla (Savory Pie Crust—Done 2 Ways)

APULIA

Savory deep dish pies are popular in all regions of Italy. They are eaten throughout the year, but most especially at Easter. The short crust pastry used for making both savory and sweet pies is called pasta frolla. *There are many different recipes for* pasta frolla, *some of which call for sugar to add sweetness and others that call for white wine and olive oil to add a layer of savory flavor. In Southern Italy, a closed pie with a savory filling is called either* pizza *or* calzone, *depending upon the region. Here are my two favorite savory pie crusts. The first recipe is typical of Campania and Basilicata and is flavored with extra virgin olive oil and black pepper. The second recipe is from Apulia and is made with dry white wine, which adds nice flavor and texture to the dough. Both are easy to work with and bake up crisp, top and bottom, every time. Try them with different recipes and decide which you like better!*

Basic Savory Crust:
4 cups all-purpose, pre-sifted flour
1 tsp. baking powder
¾ tsp. black pepper
1½ tsp. salt
⅓ cup water
⅓ cup milk
4 extra-large eggs
½ cup olive oil

Whisk together the flour and baking powder in a large mixing bowl, season with the black pepper, and make a well in the middle. In another bowl, dissolve the salt in the water and then whisk in the milk, eggs, and olive oil. Pour the liquid ingredients into the well and beat with a fork, pulling in flour from the sides until the dough pulls together.

Turn the dough onto a lightly floured work surface and knead until smooth. Wrap the dough in plastic wrap and let it rest for 1 hour. Lightly grease the baking surface when using this dough.

Rustic Crust Made with White Wine:
1¼ cups corn oil
1 cup dry white wine
3 tsp. salt
½ cup water
6¼ cups all-purpose, pre-sifted flour
1 tsp. black pepper

Combine the corn oil, wine, salt, and water in a small saucepan and set it over medium-low heat. Meanwhile, place the flour in a large mixing bowl, season with the black pepper, and make a well in the middle. When the liquid ingredients are almost to a boil, remove the saucepan from the burner and whisk briskly. Pour the wet ingredients into the well and beat with a fork, pulling in flour from the sides until the dough pulls together.

Turn the dough onto a lightly floured work surface and knead until smooth. Roll out the dough right away, while it is still warm. You do not need to grease the baking surface when using this dough.

Pizza Margherita con Rucola e Prosciutto (Margherita Pizza Topped with Prosciutto, Fresh Arugula, and Shaved Parmigiano Reggiano Cheese)

CAMPANIA

You are certain to find a pizzeria on every corner in the cities and towns of Southern Italy. Walk into any pizzeria and there is sure to be a pizzaiolo or pizza maker, stretching and twirling dough. The best pizza is always made in a forno al legno, or wood burning pizza oven. The natural wood fire adds great flavor to the pizza and heats the oven to an incredibly high temperature that cooks it in just a few minutes. That being said, a pizza made in a forno al legno is always crisp and delicious! It is the only way to prepare Naples' most-acclaimed dish, Margherita pizza. This, of course, begs the question: Who is Margherita?

According to legend, Queen Margherita visited Naples in 1889 and was served pizza topped with three ingredients: tomatoes, mozzarella, and basil. She enjoyed the pizza, and so it was named "Margherita" in her honor. Thereafter, red, white, and green became colors associated with Italian nationalism, and today they stand as the colors of the vibrant Italian flag! Here is a recipe that takes this simple classic pizza one step further by topping it after baking with thinly sliced prosciutto, a handful of fresh arugula, and flecks of shaved Parmigiano-Reggiano cheese. The prosciutto adds a depth of rich pork flavor and the crisp, peppery arugula adds unexpected texture. Queen Margherita would have certainly approved! Make one large pie or small, individual pizzette.

1 batch pizza dough *(see page 56)*
3 cups Salsa Marinara *(see page 121)*
1 lb. fresh mozzarella cheese, sliced into strips
1 dozen basil leaves
1 large bunch arugula, coarsely chopped

Extra virgin olive oil, for drizzling
Shaved Parmigiano-Reggiano cheese, for topping
½ lb. prosciutto, thinly sliced

Prepare the dough as instructed on page 56. Roll out the dough on a floured surface and place it on a lightly greased 11½ by 17 inch baking tray. If you prefer, roll out small, individual *pizzette.*

Preheat the oven to 475 degrees. Spread the Salsa Marinara over the dough and then arrange the mozzarella and whole basil leaves on top. Bake the pizza for 15 minutes or until the underside of the crust is golden brown.

Toss the arugula with a few drizzles of extra virgin olive oil. As soon as the pizza comes out of the oven, sprinkle with the arugula and Parmigiano-Reggiano cheese and then arrange the prosciutto on top. Makes one large pizza or four small *pizzette.* Serve hot. Serves 4 to 6 adults.

Pizza alla Tropea (Pizza Topped with Cherry Tomatoes, Red Onions, Black Olives, and Marinated Anchovies)

CALABRIA

Tropea sits on a cliff overlooking a golden beach and a rocky islet called Isola Bella. It is located on the Costa Violetta, which is said to have the best beaches in all of Southern Italy. Tropea is the quintessential beach town and the perfect spot for a brief respite when you are travelling between Naples and Palermo. One summer I spent a few days in Tropea with friends, and we immediately slipped into a wonderful routine: espresso in the morning, beach during the day, afternoon snack, and dinner in the evening. Each afternoon, I would snorkel around the rocky islet of Isola Bella. The water was crystal clear, and there were plenty of fish and other creatures to admire. Sometimes I would even be surrounded by schools of tiny, silver anchovies that seemed to glisten in the rays of sunshine. When I emerged from the sea an hour later, I would head into town for a slice of pizza that could only be described as a true taste of coastal Calabria. Topped with fresh anchovies, black olives, cherry tomatoes, and red onions, it was hearty and delicious. Here is the recipe. If marinated white anchovies are not available, use jarred Italian anchovies packed in olive oil.

1 batch pizza dough *(see page 56)*
1½ dry quarts cherry tomatoes, sliced in half
5 cloves garlic, sliced
2 medium red onions, chopped
2 tbsp. finely chopped, firmly packed basil
2 tbsp. finely chopped, firmly packed oregano

Olive oil, for drizzling
Salt and black pepper to taste
Crushed red pepper flakes to taste
8 oz. marinated white anchovy fillets
1½ cups pitted, halved black Cerignola olives

Prepare the dough as instructed on page 56 and set it aside. Place the cherry tomatoes, garlic, onions, basil, and oregano in a mixing bowl. Drizzle with olive oil, season with salt, black pepper, and red pepper flakes, and toss well.

Preheat the oven to 475 degrees. Roll out the pizza dough on a floured surface and place it on a lightly greased 11½ by 17 inch baking tray. Spread the cherry tomato mixture evenly over the dough and then arrange the anchovy fillets and olives on top. Bake for 15 minutes or until the underside of the crust is golden brown. Serve hot. Makes one large pizza or four small *pizzette*. Serves 4 to 6 adults.

Pizza alla Lipari (Pizza Topped with Tuna, Sautéed Sweet Onions, and Capers)

SICILY

In calm seas, the island of Lipari is a one hour ferry ride from Sicily. When the seas are rough, the bumpy journey takes twice as long. My friends and I travelled to Lipari on a day when the waters were agitated by the anger of Aeolus, the ancient Greek god of the winds. An avid seaman, I was unshaken by the turbulent seas. My friends, unfortunately, were not. When we disembarked, they were quite thankful to be on solid ground. As we walked into town, my first order of business was to find a snack! After a two hour journey, I was hungry. Still blue in the face, my friends questioned, "How can you even think about eating now?" Nonetheless, I stopped at a snack bar and grabbed a slice of thick-crusted pizza topped with sautéed sweet onions, plump capers, and delicate flakes of tuna. It was a tasty treat! The next day, I returned for another slice. My friends, then rosy cheeked, tried a slice and loved it too. I have returned to Sicily many times since then but have not gone back to Lipari, although I did once contemplate hopping on a ferry just to get a slice of that pizza! Here is my recreation of this wonderful local dish.

1 batch pizza dough *(see page 56)*	Salt to taste
½ cup capers preserved in salt	5 cloves garlic, sliced
32 oz. Italian jarred tuna in olive oil	8 fillets Italian jarred anchovies in
Olive oil, for sautéing	olive oil, chopped
3 extra-large Spanish onions, sliced	1 tbsp. dried oregano
into strips	Black pepper to taste

Prepare the dough as instructed on page 56 and set it aside. Rub the salt off of the capers, soak them in a bowl of warm water for 10 minutes, rinse them under running water, and then pat them dry. Remove the tuna from the jar, flake it with a fork, and set it aside.

Coat the bottom of a frying pan with olive oil and set it over medium heat. Add the onions, season very lightly with salt, and sauté until the onions are soft. Stir in the garlic and sauté for another minute. Stir in the anchovies and capers, sauté for another 30 seconds, and remove the frying pan from the heat.

Preheat the oven to 475 degrees. Roll out the pizza dough on a floured surface and place it on a lightly greased 11½ by 17 inch baking tray. If you prefer, roll out small, individual *pizzette*. Spread the tuna evenly over the dough and season with oregano and black pepper. Spread the sautéed onion mixture over top. Bake for 15 minutes or until the underside of the crust is golden brown. Makes one large pizza or four small *pizzette*. Serve hot. Serves 4 to 6 adults.

Pizza Rustica (Easter Pie Filled with Layers of Ricotta Cheese, Soppressata, Salami, and Hard-Boiled Eggs)

APULIA

As a child I loved Easter, but not for the Easter egg hunt. My eager anticipation was always for the food! For Easter breakfast, my mother prepared fancy Easter breads and sweet ricotta pies. There were also trays of Neapolitan cookies, each covered with icing and topped with sprinkles, and a savory pie from Apulia called pizza rustica, *which was prepared by my aunt, Vivian Jacobellis. With such delicacies set out on the table, I could never wait to eat! While my siblings were searching the house for plastic eggs and munching on yellow marshmallow chicks, I was happily sitting at the kitchen table eating a slice of savory, delicious* pizza rustica. *It was always the first thing I went for. With layers of sliced hard-boiled egg, salami,* soppressata, *and fresh ricotta cheese baked in a savory crust, it was the ultimate Easter treat.*

Savory Easter pies are a tradition throughout Italy. In Campania and Basilicata, a similar Easter pie is called pizza chini. *It is typically filled with crumbled hard-boiled eggs, diced salami, and ricotta cheese, and it is sometimes made with a sweet crust. In Northern Italy, they serve a savory Easter pie called* torta pasqualina, *which is filled with sautéed greens and sometimes artichokes. It is certain to be made with a light, flaky crust. My aunt's recipe for* pizza rustica *came from her mother-in-law, who hailed from a small town just outside the bustling city of Bari in Apulia. Made with a* pasta frolla *that is typical of the region, it is an authentic Pugliese recipe that is sure to please. Make it part of your Easter tradition or serve at your next brunch or luncheon instead of sandwiches or quiche.*

1 batch Rustic Crust Made with White Wine dough *(see page 57)*
3 extra-large eggs
2 tbsp. grated Pecorino Romano cheese
½ lb. shredded mozzarella cheese (low moisture)

2 cups ricotta cheese
9 extra-large hard-boiled eggs, sliced
½ lb. *soppressata*, thinly sliced
½ lb. Genoa salami, thinly sliced

Prepare the dough as instructed on page 57 and set it aside. Beat 3 eggs with the grated Pecorino Romano cheese. In a separate bowl, combine the mozzarella with the ricotta.

Divide the dough into 2 balls. Roll out the balls on a lightly floured work surface into two 14 inch circles that are ¼ inch thick. Place one sheet of dough on a baking tray, preferably a round one. Spread half of the cheese mixture on the bottom, staying 1½ inches in from the edge of the dough. Next, add a layer of hard-boiled egg and drizzle half of the beaten egg over top so that it drips into all the nooks and crannies. Add a layer of *soppressata*, then a layer of salami. Continue by layering the remaining cheese mixture, hard-boiled eggs, beaten egg, *soppressata*, and salami.

Preheat the oven to 375 degrees. Cover the filling with the second sheet of dough and crimp the edges. Poke holes in the top with a knife so the steam will escape. Bake for 1 hour and 15 minutes or until golden brown. Serve at room temperature. Serves 6 to 8 adults.

Torta Romana (Country-Style Pie Filled with Sautéed Escarole, Pine Nuts, and Raisins)

LAZIO

The verdant Alban Hills lie just twenty miles south of Rome. The hills are actually a dormant volcanic region with two large lakes that formed thousands of years ago in the ancient calderas. The Alban Hills were a favorite summer retreat for wealthy ancient Romans who built villas and country estates along the shores of the lakes. Today, the Alban Hills are still favored by the Roman upper class and are known as the Castelli Romani, or land of Roman castles. The rich volcanic soil of this region also makes it the cornucopia of modern Rome. Here, the soil and climate are perfect for growing all sorts of vegetables and greens. Should you decide to ramble through this fabled region, be sure to visit the towns along the shores of Lake Albano. There, you will find many fine restaurants where you can sample true Roman cuisine made with the freshest vegetables that Rome has to offer!

Sautéed escarole with pine nuts and raisins is a traditional dish that I ate while travelling through this fabled hinterland of Rome. Topped with shaved Pecorino Romano cheese, the combination of sweet and salty flavors reminded me of Sicilian cookery and was truly delicious. When I returned home, I was inspired to recreate the dish, and in doing so I also improved upon an old recipe in my collection for escarole pie. Here it is! I am sure any Roman chef or home cook would approve. If escarole is not available, substitute spinach or Swiss chard, or use a combination of different greens. For a truly authentic taste of the Alban Hills, serve it with a glass of white Frascati wine from the Castelli Romani region.

1 batch Basic Savory Crust dough or Rustic Crust Made with White Wine dough *(see page 57)*
1½ tbsp. pine nuts
3 large heads escarole (about 2½ to 2¾ lbs.)
Olive oil, for sautéing and drizzling
½ medium Spanish or Vidalia onion, diced

4 cloves garlic, chopped
½ cup water
Salt and black pepper to taste
3 heaping tbsp. grated Pecorino Romano cheese
⅓ cup firmly packed raisins
1 egg

Prepare the dough as instructed on page 57 and set it aside. Toast the pine nuts in a small frying pan over low heat until golden brown and set aside. Remove and discard the core of the escarole, chop the leaves, and set aside.

Coat the bottom of a large, deep frying pan with olive oil and sauté the onion and garlic over medium-low heat until soft. Add the escarole and the water, which will allow the greens to steam. Season with salt and black pepper and continue sautéing for another 10 minutes or until the escarole is wilted and tender. If the frying pan becomes too dry, add more water. When the escarole is done, transfer it to a colander and drain off any excess liquid by pressing it lightly. Then transfer the escarole to a mixing bowl and stir in the grated cheese, raisins, pine nuts, and a drizzle of olive oil.

Divide the dough into 2 balls. Roll out the balls on a lightly floured work surface into two 14 inch circles that are ¼ inch thick. Place one sheet of dough on a baking tray, preferably a round one, and spread the filling evenly on top, staying 1½ inches in from the edges.

Preheat the oven to 375 degrees. Cover the filling with the second sheet of dough and crimp the edges. Poke holes in the top with a knife so the steam will escape. Bake for 30 minutes. Beat the egg with a splash of water and brush the top of the pie lightly with the egg wash. Continue baking for another 20 to 25 minutes or until golden brown. Serve at room temperature. Serves 4 to 6 adults.

'Mpanate con Salsiccia e Bietola (Sicilian Turnovers Filled with Pork Sausage, Swiss Chard, Leeks, and Green Olives)

SICILY

What culinary tradition does Sicily share with Spain? Empanadas! Although the Sicilian version is spelled and pronounced differently, its origin dates back to the time when Spaniards ruled Sicily. Like the Arabs before them, the Spanish brought culinary traditions and new ingredients to the island. In fact, the Spanish introduced all of Europe to many new foods from the Americas, such as tomatoes, peppers, corn, and cocoa. Empanadas were no doubt introduced to Sicily by Spanish merchants and transplanted Spanish nobility who were sent there to govern the island. Whatever the historical case may be, Sicilian 'mpanate are always a tasty treat! They can be filled with just about anything. In Siracusa, a traditional filling is swordfish, capers, and olives. In Palermo, you might find them stuffed with cauliflower, pine nuts, and raisins. There is even an old recipe from Ragusa in which they are stuffed with ground lamb and chocolate! I have devised my own tasty filling that I am sure you will enjoy. With flavorful pork sausage, sautéed Swiss chard, and briny green Sicilian olives, it is a treat you might just find at a snack bar or pizzeria in Sicily. Be sure to make some for your next picnic!

1 batch Basic Savory Crust dough *(see page 57)*
1 lb. Italian pork sausage
Olive oil, for sautéing
½ medium Spanish or Vidalia onion, diced
2 large leeks, trimmed and diced
Salt and black pepper to taste
3 cloves garlic, minced

2½ lbs. Swiss chard, chopped
½ cup water
¾ cup pitted, quartered Sicilian green olives
⅔ lb. mozzarella or caciocavallo cheese, cubed (optional)
Grated Pecorino Romano cheese, for topping
1 egg

Prepare the dough as instructed on page 57 and set it aside. Remove the sausage from the casing. Brush the bottom of a frying pan with olive oil and set the sausage over medium-low heat. Brown the sausage, breaking it up with the back of a wooden spoon. When the sausage is fully cooked, drain off any excess grease and set the sausage to the side.

Coat the bottom of a deep frying pan with olive oil and set it over low heat. Add the onions and leeks, season with salt and black pepper, and sauté for 10 minutes or until caramelized. Add the garlic, sauté for another minute, and then add the Swiss chard and water, which will allow the greens to steam. Raise the heat to medium low and continue sautéing for 10 minutes or until the Swiss chard is wilted and tender, adding more water if necessary. Stir in the sausage and olives, adjust the seasoning if necessary, and continue sautéing until any excess liquid has cooked off.

Preheat the oven to 375 degrees. Roll the dough out on a lightly floured work surface to ¼ inch thickness. Using a cookie cutter or other tool, cut circles from the dough that are 5 inches in diameter. Place some of the filling and a few cubes of cheese in the middle of each circle, sprinkle with grated cheese, and then fold one end over and crimp the edges. Set the *'mpanate* on a lightly greased baking sheet and bake for 20 minutes. Beat the egg with a splash of water and brush the tops lightly with the egg wash. Continue baking for another 20 to 25 minutes or until golden brown. Serve warm or at room temperature. Makes 8 to 10 *'mpanate*.

Calzone Baresi (Country-Style Pie Filled with Sautéed Sweet Onions and Green Olives)

APULIA

The people of Bari are said to be amazing cooks. This is a truth I can attest to, as my uncle Gaetano Jacobellis was of Baresi descent. He introduced our family to many fine traditional recipes from Apulia—including this one, which is so good that I hijacked it for my cookbook! By description it sounds odd, and to some people the idea of a pie filled with onions may seem off-putting. But I assure you this unusual, quirky pie is delicious. It is a specialty of the countryside west of Bari, where whitewashed towns dot the agricultural plains. There they grow all sorts of fine vegetables, including sweet onions, and the olive groves produce plump green olives. We serve Calzone Baresi as an antipasto on Christmas, as is traditional in Bari and other towns in Apulia. My uncle always makes the calzone in a large, round pizza tin. It is large enough to feed a Christmas crowd twenty strong! The peppery crust and briny green olives contrast nicely with the sweet sautéed onions. Be sure to serve it with a dry white Frascati wine from Lazio. Make a Calzone Baresi for your next dinner party and you will be the talk of the town for serving a truly unique and tasty dish!

1 batch Rustic Crust Made with White Wine dough *(see page 57)*
    Olive oil, for sautéing
    Salt and black pepper to taste
    5 lbs. Spanish or Vidalia onions, sliced into strips

3 cloves garlic, minced
1½ cups pitted, halved green Sicilian or Spanish Manzanilla olives

Prepare the pie dough as instructed on page 57 and set aside. Coat the bottom of a deep frying pan with olive oil and set it over low heat. Add the onions, season with salt and black pepper, and sauté until soft and translucent. Stir the onions frequently so they cook evenly. When the onions are done, add the garlic and olives and continue sautéing for another minute. Remove the frying pan from the heat and allow the mixture to cool.

Preheat the oven to 375 degrees. Divide the dough into 2 balls. Roll out each ball of dough on a lightly floured work surface into two circles that are ¼ inch thick and 16 inches in diameter. Place one sheet of dough on a round, 14 inch, ungreased baking pan that is ½ inch deep. Spread the filling evenly on top using a slotted spoon to drain off any excess cooking liquid. Cover the filling with the second piece of dough and crimp the edges. Poke holes in the top with a knife so the steam will escape. Bake for 60 to 70 minutes or until golden brown. Serves 10 to 12 adults.

Fiori di Zucchine in Fritella (Zucchini Blossom Omelet)

LAZIO

The town of Sperlonga sits on a rocky promontory above the sparkling Tyrrhenian Sea. It is one of Lazio's most beautiful coastal towns. But be forewarned, it gets quite crowded in summertime, when the Romani flee the heat of Rome for the mild breezes of the coast. North of Sperlonga, fertile agricultural lands lie just beyond the sandy beaches where Romani bronze all summer long. Here, fields of lofty zucchini plants with large green leaves and bright-orange blossoms sway in the sea breezes. Romani like to cook the blossoms in a fritella, *or omelet. Here is my version. The method is easy and the presentation beautiful! Simply arrange the blossoms in a circular pattern on the bottom of a sizzling frying pan and pour a thin layer of beaten egg over top. When you flip the omelet, the pointed blossoms look like a brilliant Mediterranean sun. Flavored with grated Pecorino Romano cheese and fresh herbs, it is a dish typical of Lazio's rustic cuisine.*

3 extra-large eggs
1 tbsp. finely chopped, firmly packed Italian flat leaf parsley
12 large zucchini blossoms
Olive oil, for sautéing
Salt and black pepper to taste
1 heaping tbsp. grated Pecorino Romano cheese

Beat the eggs. Add the parsley to the beaten eggs and set aside. Remove the stamens and pistils from each zucchini blossom and gently tear the blossoms so that they open in one piece that lays flat.

Brush the bottom of a 13 inch frying pan lightly with olive oil and set it over medium-low heat. Arrange the blossoms bright-orange side down in a circular, sunburst pattern on the bottom of the frying pan. Season the blossoms with salt and black pepper and press gently with a spatula until they soften. Sprinkle with grated cheese and gently pour the beaten eggs over top. Allow the eggs to set, and then flip the omelet and let the other side cook until firm. Serve warm. Serves 2 adults.

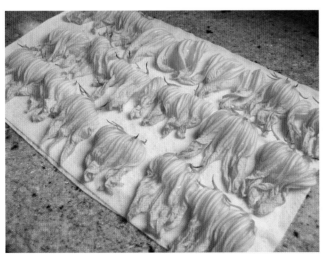
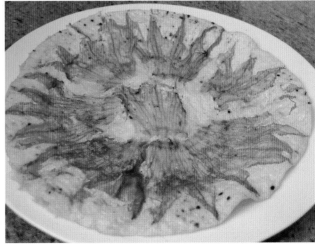

Ciambotta in Frittata (Frittata with Sautéed Vegetables, Sausage, and Mozzarella)

BASILICATA

Frittata is a traditional Italian omelet. Unlike French or American omelets, a frittata *is started on the stove top and then finished in the oven without being flipped, folded, or removed from the pan. When one thinks of an omelet, cheese usually comes to mind; and in Southern Italy, any decent* frittata *is sure to be made with plenty of mozzarella cheese. There are several types of mozzarella. The highly prized* mozzarella buffala *is made with milk from water buffalo. It is considered to have the best taste and creamiest texture. It is typically eaten by itself or with fresh tomatoes. Mozzarella made with cow's milk is called* fior di latte. *It is less expensive and commonly used for cooking. When fresh,* fior di latte *has a high moisture content and is creamy. When it is commercially produced, the moisture content is much lower, which makes the cheese firm and perfect for shredding. A low-moisture* fior di latte *is always best for a* frittata!*

In Southern Italy, ciambotta *refers more to a style of cooking than a particular recipe. In Basilicata, food was sometimes scarce and peasants made due with the ingredients on hand. Oftentimes, a little of this and a little of that would be thrown together in a frying pan to make a* ciambotta, *or mixed fry, that could feed the whole family. Leftover* ciambotta *never went to waste. With a few eggs and some mozzarella cheese, it would be turned into a delicious, satisfying* frittata *for the next day's meal. This hearty* frittata *truly captures the flavors of Basilicata. Vegetables typical of Southern Italy are sautéed with pork sausage and a sprinkle of crushed red chili flakes and then baked with plenty of mozzarella. If you prefer, add or substitute whatever else you have on hand. As this is* ciambotta, *there is no precise recipe that must be followed, and you can make this dish all your own!*

¾ lb. Italian sausage
Olive oil, for sautéing
1 small red bell pepper, seeded and chopped
½ Spanish or Vidalia onion, chopped
4 cloves garlic, finely chopped
2 small Italian eggplants, chopped
2 small zucchini, chopped
3 medium tomatoes, chopped
2 tbsp. finely chopped, firmly packed basil

2 tbsp. finely chopped, firmly packed oregano
1 cup white wine
Crushed red pepper flakes to taste
Salt and black pepper to taste
10-12 extra-large eggs
1½ cups grated Parmigiano-Reggiano cheese, divided
3 tbsp. butter
¾ lb. mozzarella cheese, shredded

Preheat the oven to 400 degrees. Roast the sausage for 25 minutes or until fully cooked and then slice it into rounds.

Coat the bottom of a frying pan with olive oil, set it over medium-low heat, and sauté the pepper and onion until soft. Add the garlic and continue sautéing for another minute.

Add the eggplants, zucchini, tomatoes, basil, oregano, wine, red pepper flakes, and salt and pepper. Continue sautéing for another 10 minutes or until the vegetables are tender. If necessary, add more wine.

Preheat the oven to 375 degrees. Beat the eggs with a splash of water and ½ cup of grated cheese. Place the butter in a deep, 13 inch, oven-proof frying pan and melt it over low heat. When the butter has melted, swirl it around to coat the sides of the frying pan and then add the eggs. When the egg begins to set along the edges, sprinkle over the sautéed vegetables and sausage. Check the underside of the frittata by lifting it with a spatula. When the bottom is firm, remove it from the burner and sprinkle with the mozzarella and remaining Parmigiano-Reggiano cheese. Bake for 20 minutes or until the egg has fully set and the top is crisp and golden. Serve hot. Serves 4 to 6 adults.

Zucchine e Pomodorini con Uova Stracciata (Sautéed Zucchini and Cherry Tomatoes with Egg Strands and Pecorino Romano Cheese)

LAZIO

Pecorino Romano is a hard sheep's milk cheese from Lazio. Today, it is popular throughout Italy, and for good reason. Its sharp, nutty flavor makes it absolutely perfect for topping pasta and flavoring all sorts of dishes. Here is one of my signature recipes, which calls for plenty of grated Pecorino Romano cheese. It is a rustic preparation for sautéed vegetables and torn eggs. It was inspired by the popular torn egg soup of Rome, called Stracciatella alla Romana. In this simple recipe, zucchini and cherry tomatoes are sautéed in olive oil until tender and then egg whites are added to the frying pan at the very last minute. As the egg whites cook, they tear into shreds, or stracciata, *that then become interlaced between the sautéed vegetables and holds them together. The dish is then finished with a generous sprinkle of grated Pecorino Romano cheese. And the more cheese the better! Serve it as a unique alternative to a traditional* frittata, *or layered between two slices of crusty Italian bread for the ultimate sandwich.*

Olive oil, for sautéing
½ small Spanish or Vidalia onion, diced
3 medium zucchini (about 8 inches long), chopped
Salt and black pepper to taste
Crushed red pepper flakes to taste
¾ dry quart cherry tomatoes, sliced in half
4 cloves garlic, finely chopped

2 tbsp. finely chopped, firmly packed basil
2 tbsp. finely chopped, firmly packed oregano
Whites of 8 extra-large eggs
Grated Pecorino Romano cheese, for topping

Coat the bottom of a deep frying pan with olive oil and set it over medium-low heat. Add the onion and zucchini, season with salt, black pepper, and red pepper flakes, and sauté until the vegetables are tender. Add the cherry tomatoes, garlic, basil, and oregano. Continue sautéing for another 2 minutes or until the cherry tomatoes begin to pucker. Raise the heat to medium high and push the sautéed items towards the sides of the frying pan. Pour the egg whites into the middle. As the egg white cooks, scrape it with a spatula and tear it into strands. Stir everything together so that the egg strands are interlaced with the sautéed vegetables. Transfer to a serving platter and top with plenty of grated cheese. Serve hot. Serves 4 adults.

III

Zuppe (Soups)

Making Tomato Paste on the Sidewalk in Bagheria

A Rambling in Sicily

Sicilians love their *stratto*, or tomato paste. The concentrated, pungent tomato flavor is used as a base for all types of sauces and soups. Rita and Salvo's neighbor, Angela, performs the time-honored ritual of making *stratto* each summer. At seventy-five years old, Angela is feisty and full of character. She is short and rotund with milk-white hair and a sun-baked face. Now a widow, she is always clad in a black dress, even on the hottest days. When the August sun is bright and warm overhead, Angela sets up a table on the sidewalk, lays a long, wide board on top, and spreads tomato puree over the board. She sits nearby in a chair and scrapes the tomato puree every few minutes until it has thickened into a paste. It takes an entire day!

Meanwhile, the street is buzzing with activity. There are people hurriedly walking by and a constant parade of cars whizzing down the street. As the day goes on, the sweet aroma of the *stratto* attracts flies and soon there is a whole swarm circling over the table. Armed with a folded section of newspaper, Angela swooshes them away whenever they get too close. For Angela, making *stratto* on the sidewalk is also a time to socialize. There are always neighbors stopping by to chat and sometimes other women set up tables beside her and make *stratto* too!

I asked Rita and Salvo's daughter, Paola, "Is your neighbor not concerned that the exhaust from the cars and dust from the street will get into the *stratto*?"

She replied, "No. Here, they don't care about such things. She would rather make her own, even if she must do it alongside a dusty road. This is just the way it is."

She then explained that making *stratto* is still a tradition in Bagheria and other Sicilian towns, even though tomato paste is now available at the supermarket. Many older women have been making it for decades just as their mothers and grandmothers did before them, and they are not ready to give up the tradition. How wonderful, I thought.

Paola then added, "Besides, sitting out on the sidewalk is how the women in this town catch up on the gossip! I do not like to walk by the women when they are making *stratto*, because I know once I leave they will talk about me!"

I then asked Paola, "Your mother and Angela are good friends; does she give *stratto* to your mother?"

Paola laughed and said, "Oh yes, but my mother tries not to take it, and if Angela insists, she takes only a little bit and never uses it."

I asked Paola why. She explained, "Because my mother is just like you! She sees the dust, the exhaust from the cars, and the flies, and she does not want to eat it!"

Paola went on to explain that her mother now buys *stratto* from the supermarket because today commercial brands are of high quality. In fact, Rita uses a brand that comes in a convenient squeeze tube. Many years ago, they too made *stratto*; however, Rita never made it in on the sidewalk in Bagheria. She always insisted that Salvo take her into the countryside where the air was fresh and clean. Surely, this was fodder for gossip in Bagheria when the other women were making their *stratto* in the street!

The fine sandy beach of Tropea, Calabria

Chilies are a favorite spice in Basilicata

Typical Neapolitan street scene

A traffic jam near Salaparuta, Sicily

Houses perched near the sea in Cefalu, Sicily

Buying produce the old-fashioned way in Bagheria, Sicily

Zuppa di Scarola con Fagioli (Escarole and Cannellini Beans in Tomato Broth)

CAMPANIA

Most Americans use escarole for salad without giving any thought to cooking it. How unfortunate! Truth be told, escarole is much better cooked than raw. The stems of the escarole leaves can be fibrous, making it inferior for salads as compared to other greens. Moreover, stewing or sautéing the escarole removes any bitterness, making it mild and delicious. The people of Campania have known this for centuries, and their wonderful and tasty tradition of cooking escarole is still popular today, even in the United States. Head into an Italian American restaurant in the northeast, and sautéed escarole with beans and garlic may just be on the menu.

Now that I have extolled the virtues of cooked escarole, here is a recipe! It is a simple, hearty soup from the town of Teggiano in southern Campania. This is where my maternal grandmother's family was from. Teggiano is a medieval citadel, perched high atop a mountain with a commanding view over the Diano Valley. The tightly packed, ancient buildings with terracotta rooftops look down upon a patchwork of neatly tended fields where wonderful greens such as escarole, spinach, kale, and Swiss chard are grown. Tasty soups and stews made with greens and legumes from the valley have been prepared by the Teggianese people for centuries. Here is one such dish that has been handed down in my family for generations. It is nourishing and delicious. Be sure to serve it with a slice of crusty Italian bread!

Olive oil, for sautéing
½ Spanish or Vidalia onion, diced
3 oz. thinly sliced prosciutto
4 cloves garlic, minced
Crushed red pepper to taste
Salt and black pepper to taste
1 can (28 oz.) whole, peeled San Marzano tomatoes, diced (juice reserved)
3 cans (15 oz. each) Cannellini beans, drained

1 tbsp. dried oregano
2 rounded tsp. paprika
2 pieces Parmigiano-Reggiano cheese rinds (3 by 3 inches each)
2 large heads escarole (about 2 to 2¼ lbs.), chopped
Grated Parmigiano-Reggiano cheese, for topping

Coat the bottom of a large soup pot with olive oil, set it over medium-low heat, and sauté the onion until soft. Mince the prosciutto and add it to the pot. Add the garlic, season with crushed red pepper, salt, and black pepper, and sauté for one more minute. Add the diced tomatoes and all of the juice from the can. Using the can from the tomatoes, add 3 cans of water. Add the beans, oregano, paprika, and cheese rinds and simmer over low heat for 40 minutes, stirring occasionally.

Remove and discard the cheese rinds. Taste for seasoning and add salt, if necessary. Add the chopped escarole to the pot and continue simmering for another 20 minutes or until the escarole is wilted and tender. Adjust the seasoning as needed. Serve hot, topped with grated cheese. Serves 6 adults.

Minestra di Carciofi e Patate (Artichoke and Potato Soup with Garlic and Herbs)

LAZIO

When one thinks of Lazio, Roman cuisine certainly comes to mind. In the countryside north of Rome, however, many local dishes have a seemingly Tuscan flare. Here, the vine covered hills and fields of wheat and sunflowers are like a scene from Under the Tuscan Sun. *This is a simple Tuscan-style soup that I enjoyed in Capodimonte on the shores of Lake Bolsena. This charming hill town has wonderful views over Lazio's tranquil countryside and the glistening lake. The next time you travel to Southern Italy, make Capodimonte your home base and you will have easy access to the charming hill towns of Tuscany just a short drive to the north, or the hustle and bustle of glorious Rome, just an hour or so to the south!*

In this recipe, fresh, diced artichoke hearts and potatoes are cooked in a light chicken broth flavored with onion, garlic, and fresh herbs. The soup is then thickened with a sprinkle of finely ground bread crumbs—a tasty trick of the rustic Italian kitchen. The result is a soup that is thick, creamy, and bursting with the flavors of northern Lazio. Be sure to top it with a fine aged Pecorino Romano cheese local to the region and a drizzle of extra virgin olive oil. For a rustic lunch, serve it with crusty Italian bread and a glass of dry white Frascati wine from Lazio.

Olive oil, for sautéing
½ large Spanish or Vidalia onion, diced
4 cloves garlic, minced
1½ quarts chicken broth
1 quart water
2 pieces Parmigiano-Reggiano cheese rinds (3 by 3 inches each)
2 tbsp. finely chopped, firmly packed Italian flat leaf parsley
2 tbsp. finely chopped, firmly packed oregano

1 fresh bay leaf
2 large russet potatoes, peeled and chopped
8 large globe artichokes (with at least 3-inch stems)
Salt and black pepper to taste
¼ cup finely ground dry bread crumbs
Grated Parmigiano-Reggiano cheese, for topping

Coat the bottom of a soup pot with olive oil, set it over medium-low heat, and sauté the onion until soft. Add the garlic, continue sautéing for another minute, and then add the broth, water, cheese rinds, parsley, oregano, and bay leaf. Turn down the heat to low and bring the soup up to a simmer.

Add the potatoes to the pot. Use a paring knife to remove the leaves from the artichokes, and then remove the inner chokes. This will leave just the heart and stem. Use a potato peeler to remove the stringy outer fibers of the stems, chop the artichokes into pieces similar in size to the potatoes, and add them to the pot. Season with salt and black pepper and simmer for 40 minutes or until the artichokes and potatoes are tender.

Remove and discard the bay leaf and cheese rinds. Stir ¼ cup of bread crumbs into the soup to thicken the broth. Continue simmering for 5 minutes. If you prefer a thicker soup, add more bread crumbs ¼ cup at a time, as needed. Adjust the seasoning if necessary. Serve hot, topped with a drizzle of extra virgin olive oil and grated cheese. Serves 4 to 6 adults.

Minestra di Cucuzza (Rustic Sicilian Squash and Egg Soup)

SICILY

Anything Sicilian is sure to be larger than life! That being said, it's no wonder that Sicily's native squash, called cucuzza *can grow to be five feet long. That's the same height as my Sicilian grandmother—who, though not tall, was big in a different way. In Sicily, the vines of the* cucuzza *plant climb up trellises in backyard gardens. Once when I was visiting my friend Salvatore in Palermo, he gave me some* cucuzza *seeds. He cautioned, "The vines grow very big. Plant these seeds in a place where there is plenty of room and the vines can grow tall so that the squash hang without hitting the ground." He offered sage advice. One year, the* cucuzza *vines took over my entire vegetable garden and grew up the side of our house, onto the roof, and into the vents of the attic fan on the second floor. This amused my neighbor, who started calling me "Jack and the Beanstalk." He exclaimed, "One day you will climb up that vine and we will never see you again!"*

Cucuzza squash are difficult to find in the United States. You must search them out in Italian markets or grow them yourself. If they are available at the market, be sure to take a few home. Otherwise, you can order the seeds online and test your green thumb. Just be sure you have enough space and a sturdy trellis for the vines to climb on! Cucuzza is similar to zucchini in flavor and texture. It is perfect for stewing with tomatoes, tossing into soups, or sautéing with eggs. Here is my family's recipe for a rustic cucuzza and torn egg soup that is cooked in a light tomato broth. Topped with a sprinkle of grated pecorino cheese, it is absolutely delicious! Although this recipe calls for cucuzza, you can use zucchini instead as it is more readily available at the supermarket. Whichever squash you use, the soup is sure to be tasty. It is homestyle Sicilian cooking at its best!

Olive oil, for sautéing
½ large Spanish or Vidalia onion, diced
4 cloves garlic, finely chopped
1 can (28 oz.) crushed San Marzano tomatoes
3 tbsp. finely chopped, firmly packed Italian flat leaf parsley
2 tbsp. finely chopped, firmly packed basil

8 cups chopped, firmly packed *cucuzza* squash or zucchini (*If you are using* cucuzza, *peel with a potato peeler and scoop out the seeds first.*)
Salt and black pepper to taste
5 extra-large eggs
3 tbsp. grated Pecorino Romano cheese, plus additional for topping

Coat the bottom of a soup pot with olive oil, set it over medium-low heat, and sauté the onion until soft. Add the garlic and continue sautéing for another minute. Turn the heat down to low and add the crushed tomatoes, parsley, basil, and *cucuzza*. Using the can from the tomatoes, add enough water to completely cover the *cucuzza* and season with salt and black pepper. Let the soup simmer for 25 to 30 minutes or until the squash is tender.

In a separate bowl, beat together the eggs and grated cheese. Bring the soup up to a medium boil and add the beaten egg, a little at a time, while stirring briskly. Continue stirring until the beaten egg has cooked and thickened the soup. Turn the heat back down to low and simmer for another minute. Adjust the seasoning if necessary. Serve hot, topped with grated cheese. Serves 4 to 6 adults.

Minestra di Verdure Pugliese (Vegetable Soup Served with Bruschetta and Fresh Pesto)

APULIA

Apulia is often called il Giardino, or the garden of Southern Italy. The soil, flat terrain, and climate of central and southern Apulia are perfect for growing all sorts of wonderful vegetables. In this region, ancient whitewashed towns such as Locorotondo, Cisternino, and Ostuni are set amidst a patchwork of agricultural fields and olive groves. Seen from above, they look like pearls floating atop a vibrant green sea. No wonder vegetable soups are so popular here in springtime! They are sure to include plenty of fresh vegetables such as zucchini, artichokes, peppers, broccoli, and cauliflower. Assorted legumes such as fava, borlotti, garbanzo, and cannellini beans are sure to be thrown into the mix too, as well as chopped fresh greens.

There is no better topping for a springtime vegetable soup than a dollop of fresh, aromatic pesto. It is said that pesto originated in Liguria, but truth be told it is also popular in Southern Italy and Sicily. In Apulia and Campania, it is made with walnuts or pine nuts. But in Sicily, it is typically made with almonds. Here is my recipe for the most delicious vegetable soup ever. For a nice presentation, I plate the soup in a wide bowl and serve it with a slice of grilled bruschetta *and pesto. We swirl the pesto into the soup or smear it on the bruschetta and dunk! It truly captures the flavor and soul of springtime in the verdant countryside near Locorotondo. Give it a try with pesto made fresh from your garden!*

3 ribs celery
1 medium Spanish or Vidalia onion
4 cloves garlic
3 carrots, washed but unpeeled
Olive oil, for sautéing
Salt and black pepper to taste
3½ quarts water
2 pieces Parmigiano-Reggiano cheese rinds (3 inches by 3 inches)
2 bay leaves
2 russet potatoes, peeled and diced
1½ cups canned chickpeas, drained
16 baby artichokes (about 2½ inches long)

2 cups chopped, firmly packed Swiss chard or dandelion greens
1½ cups chopped Italian flat beans
1½ cups chopped zucchini
1½ cups chopped broccoli florets
3 tbsp. finely chopped, firmly packed Italian flat leaf parsley
Grated Pecorino Romano cheese, for topping
Bruschetta, to accompany
Pesto sauce, to accompany

Pulverize the celery, onion, garlic, and carrots in a food processor. Coat the bottom of a large soup pot with olive oil, add the ground aromatics, season with salt and black pepper, and set the pot over medium-low heat. Sauté the ground aromatics (stirring constantly and scraping the bottom of the pot) for 10 to 15 minutes or until it has reduced to a thick, soft paste. Add the water, cheese rinds, and bay leaves and season with salt and black pepper. Bring the soup to a simmer, add the potatoes and chickpeas, and then reduce the heat to low and continue simmering.

Prepare the artichokes: Remove the outer leaves of each artichoke until you reach the soft, pale inner cone. Cut off the top ⅓ of the cone, peel the stem, and cut the artichoke in half. Add the artichokes to the pot right away before they become discolored. Add the greens, Italian flat beans, zucchini, broccoli, and parsley. Simmer for another 20 minutes or until everything is tender. Remove and discard the cheese rinds and bay leaves and adjust the seasoning if necessary. Ladle the soup into serving bowls. Serve hot, topped with grated cheese and accompanied by *bruschetta* topped with pesto. Serves 4 to 6 adults.

Verdure in Brodo alla Siciliana con Cuscusu (Sicilian Vegetable Soup with Couscous)

SICILY

In Palermo, there are small restaurants that serve only couscous. Oftentimes they have no menu, just a choice between two or three stews that are served alongside a heaping plate of tasty, steamed couscous. Anna and Salvatore's son, Lorenzo, took me to such a place. It was a small storefront tucked away in a residential neighborhood. It had no name, just a faded sign stating "Cuscusu." There was graffiti scribbled on the outside wall, but Lorenzo reassured, "This is just the way that it is in Palermo." We ordered our meal, and the owner kept plenty of wine flowing as we waited. I asked Lorenzo, "Is it customary to get drunk before eating couscous?" He laughed and said, "Don't worry, it is worth waiting for." And it was! We were presented with a heaping platter of fluffy couscous and a terrine of savory vegetable soup. We enjoyed every last bite. Now, I cannot wait to go back! Here is my recreation of the delicious cuscusu *that I enjoyed at my favorite hole-in-the-wall in Palermo. It is a medley of fresh Sicilian vegetables simmered in a flavorful saffron broth and then spooned over couscous that has been steamed with almonds and raisins. Serve it with a white Corvo wine from Sicily for a true treat from Palermo.*

8 cups couscous, steamed *(see page 116)*
¾ cup slivered almonds
½ cup raisins
3 carrots, washed but unpeeled
1 large Spanish or Vidalia onion
4 cloves garlic
Olive oil, for sautéing
1 can (6 oz.) tomato paste
2 quarts vegetable or light chicken broth
2 large pinches saffron
2 fresh bay leaves
1 quart water
2 large russet potatoes, peeled and chopped into 1½ inch chunks
2 cups canned chickpeas, drained

14 baby artichokes (about 2½ inches long)
2 medium zucchini (8 inches long), chopped into large chunks
½ head cauliflower, coarsely chopped into florets
2 small red bell peppers, seeded and chopped into large chunks
3 ribs celery, chopped into large chunks
3 tbsp. finely chopped, firmly packed Italian flat leaf parsley
3 tbsp. finely chopped, firmly packed oregano
Crushed red pepper flakes to taste
Salt and black pepper to taste

Prepare the couscous following the recipe on page 116. Toast the almonds in the oven at 375 degrees for 5 minutes or until golden. Stir the almonds and raisins into the couscous before you set it to steam.

Meanwhile, prepare the vegetable soup: Grind the carrots, onion, and garlic in a food processor. Coat the bottom of a soup pot with olive oil, add the ground aromatics, season with salt and black pepper, and set the pot over low heat. Sauté the ground aromatics (stirring constantly and scraping the bottom of the pot) for 10 to 15 minutes or until it has reduced to a thick, soft paste. Push the paste to one side, add a splash of olive oil to the bottom of the pot, and fry the tomato paste for 2 minutes. Then add the broth, saffron, bay leaves, and water and bring the soup to a simmer. Add the potatoes and chickpeas to the pot and continue simmering over low heat.

Prepare the baby artichokes: Remove the outer leaves of each artichoke until you reach the soft, pale inner cone. Cut off the top ⅓ of the cone, peel the stem, and cut the artichoke in half. Add the artichokes to the pot right away before they become discolored. Add the zucchini, cauliflower, bell pepper, celery, parsley, oregano, red pepper flakes, salt, and black pepper. Continue simmering over low heat for another 10 minutes or until everything is tender. Place a heaping mound of couscous on individual serving plates and spoon the soup over the couscous so that it absorbs all of the delicious the broth. Serve hot. Serves 4 to 6 adults.

Tubettini con Fagioli (Tubettini and Cannellini Beans in Tomato Broth)

BASILICATA

Ask any Italian to name their favorite comfort food, and I'll bet they'll say pasta fagioli. Pasta and beans are staples in nearly all regions of Italy, and they come together in this traditional soup that has nourished Italians for centuries. In Southern Italy, it is made with cannellini beans or chickpeas, but in Northern Italy, they prefer borlotti beans. Beyond regional differences, each family has its own way of turning these two ingredients into something special. Any type of pasta or bean can be used. Just be sure to top off the finished product with plenty of grated pecorino cheese. Here is the recipe that has been handed down in my family. When I asked my Campanese grandmother for it, she said, "What recipe?" Like most Italian nonnas, she cooks by intuition. Her final word of advice after telling me the ingredients was simply, "Just put enough of everything and sprinkle plenty of grated pecorino cheese on top!" After a few tries, I nailed it down. It is Southern Italian comfort food at its best!

Olive oil, for sautéing
½ medium Spanish or Vidalia onion, diced
2 ribs celery, diced
2 carrots, peeled and diced
Crushed red pepper flakes to taste
Salt and black pepper to taste
3 oz. paper-thin prosciutto
4 cloves garlic, finely chopped
1 can (28 oz.) whole, peeled San Marzano tomatoes, diced (juice reserved)

3 cans (15 oz. each) cannellini beans, drained
2 pieces Parmigiano-Reggiano cheese rinds (3 inches by 3 inches)
2 bay leaves
2 tbsp. finely chopped, firmly packed oregano
3 tbsp. finely chopped, firmly packed Italian flat leaf parsley
½ lb. tubettini pasta
Grated Pecorino Romano cheese, for topping

Coat the bottom of a soup pot with olive oil and set it over medium-low heat. Add the onion, celery, carrots, red pepper flakes, salt, and black pepper and sauté until the vegetables are soft. Mince the prosciutto and add it to the pot. Add the garlic and continue sautéing for another minute. Add the tomatoes and their juice, cannellini beans, cheese rinds, bay leaves, oregano, and parsley. Using the can from the tomatoes, add 2 cans of water. Simmer over low heat for 40 minutes, stirring frequently. Remove the cheese rinds and bay leaves, taste for seasoning, and adjust the salt if necessary.

Meanwhile, fill a 6 quart pot ⅔ of the way with water and add 1 tablespoon of salt. Boil the pasta until *al dente*. When the pasta is done, use a skimmer or slotted spoon to transfer it to the soup pot. Then add enough ladles of the pasta cooking water to create a broth. Adjust the seasoning if necessary. Serve hot, topped with grated cheese. Serves 4 to 6 adults.

Orecchiette con Piselli e Prosciutto (Orecchiette with Peas and Prosciutto in Tomato Broth)

APULIA

No trip to Apulia would be complete without a visit to Ostuni. It is a true architectural gem, built in a style and tradition that is unique to central Apulia. This ancient, whitewashed town sits atop a hill surrounded by ramparts. The cubist houses rise above the defensive walls, and from a distance it seems as if the houses are stacked one on top of the other like building blocks. In Ostuni's old quarter, you will find a maze of narrow streets, winding alleys, and stairways that link the different levels of the town. It is a step back in time to the days when cities were built to maximize protection from pirates and marauders. With its dazzling white buildings, this fascinating citadel could easily be mistaken for a town in Greece or Andalusia, Spain. How intriguing!

Ostuni is known for its rustic cooking. Here, clutches of women sit in the alleyways outside of their homes making a traditional pasta called orecchiette, *which means "little ears." As one might expect, this pasta is flat with an indentation in the middle, just like an ear! The shape is formed by pressing the thumb into a small disc of dough to create a dimple to hold the sauce.* Orecchiette *are the perfect pasta to toss with sautéed chopped greens and bits of crumbled sausage. They are also great tossed into a soup! I add them to a simple tomato broth with peas and prosciutto. It is a hearty and tasty dish that is typical of Apulia's rustic cuisine. Topped with plenty of grated Pecorino Romano cheese and served with a slice of crusty bread and a glass of red Primitivo di Puglia wine, it is a true taste of Ostuni!*

Olive oil, for sautéing
1 small Spanish or Vidalia onion, diced
Crushed red pepper to taste
Salt and black pepper to taste
4 cloves garlic, finely chopped
3 oz. slab prosciutto, diced
1 can (28 oz.) whole, peeled San Marzano tomatoes, diced (juice reserved)
2 pieces Parmigiano-Reggiano cheese rinds (3 inches by 3 inches)
2 small bay leaves
2 tbsp. finely chopped, firmly packed oregano
2 tbsp. finely chopped, firmly packed Italian flat leaf parsley
1 lb. frozen peas
½ lb. *orecchiette* pasta
Grated Pecorino Romano cheese, for topping

Coat the bottom of a soup pot with olive oil and set it over medium-low heat. Add the onion, season with red pepper flakes, salt, and black pepper, and sauté until the onion is soft. Add the garlic and prosciutto and continue sautéing for another minute. Add the tomatoes and their juice, cheese rinds, bay leaves, oregano, and parsley. Using the can from the tomatoes, add 2 cans of water. Simmer over low heat for 40 minutes. Remove the cheese rinds and bay leaves, add the peas, and adjust the salt, if necessary.

Meanwhile, fill a 6 quart pot ⅔ of the way with water and add 1 tablespoon of salt. Boil the pasta until *al dente.* When the pasta is done, use a skimmer or slotted spoon to transfer it to the soup pot. Then add enough ladles of the pasta cooking water to create a broth for the soup. Adjust the seasoning if necessary. Serve hot, topped with grated cheese. Serves 4 to 6 adults.

Gnudi di Spinaci e Ricotta in Brodo (Spinach and Ricotta Dumplings in Chicken Broth)

LAZIO

On my first trip to Rome in 1978, my Sicilian grandmother handed me three coins and said, "Here, throw them over your shoulder." She then turned me around so that my back faced the fountain we had been looking at. "Why am I doing this?" I asked. "Because if you do, someday you will fall in love and return to Rome!" At twelve years old, I was not interested in falling in love, so I hesitated. "Go ahead!" my grandmother prodded. I then tossed them over my head and quickly turned around to see if they landed in the fountain. All three did, and so began my love affair with Italy! I returned to Rome several times since then, and I eventually fell in love and got married, but only after a long stint of bachelorhood. Perhaps there is some truth to the legend of the Trevi fountain. Head to Rome and find out for yourself!

This is my recreation of a simple, elegant soup I ate at a trattoria not far from the Trevi Fountain during a return trip to Rome. It is typical of the refined cuisine you are likely to encounter in Rome, Florence, Bologna, or any other grand Italian city. The soft and flavorful dumplings are made with ricotta and spinach. They are called gnudi, which means "nude" in Italian. The dumplings are made from what is essentially a ravioli filling, but they are boiled without being wrapped in pasta. Hence the name! The gnudi float like pillows amongst the thin egg noodles in a light, tasty chicken broth. It is an elegant first course from the heart of the eternal city. Be sure to serve it at your next fancy dinner party!

Olive oil, for sautéing	3 tbsp. finely chopped Italian flat leaf
2 carrots, peeled and diced	parsley
2 ribs celery, diced	2 bay leaves
½ medium Spanish or Vidalia onion,	Black pepper to taste
diced	Salt to taste
3 cloves garlic, finely chopped	1 batch *gnudi* (see page 148)
3 oz. slab prosciutto, diced	6 oz. *spaghetti* or *tagliatelle*
3 quarts chicken broth	

Coat the bottom of a soup pot with olive oil and sauté the carrots, celery, and onion over medium-low heat until soft. Add the garlic and prosciutto, continue sautéing for another minute, and then add the broth, parsley, and bay leaves. Season with black pepper and simmer over low heat for 30 minutes. Adjust the salt if necessary. Remove the soup from the heat.

Meanwhile, prepare the *gnudi* dough following the recipe for Gnudi di Spinaci e Ricotta in Forno on page 148. When the dough is ready, return the soup to the heat and bring it up to a simmer. Break the pasta into 1 inch pieces, add to the soup, and stir to prevent the pasta from sticking together. When the pasta is almost *al dente* (about 7 to 10 minutes), use two spoons to scoop and shape round dumplings from the dough and drop them into the soup. The dumplings will sink to the bottom and then rise to the top. Continue simmering for another 45 seconds after the *gnudi* have risen (or a little longer if the pasta is not yet tender). Serve hot topped with grated cheese. Serves 6 adults.

Lenticchie con Cavolo Nero e Verdure (Lentil Soup with Kale and Diced Vegetables)

ABRUZZO/MOLISE

Lentils have been cultivated in the mountainous Apennine regions of central and southern Italy since the days of ancient Rome. In fact, near the small hilltop town of Santo Stefano di Sessanio, which lies deep in the heart of the mountainous Abruzzo region, the climate and soil are just right for growing tender, flavorful lentils that are touted as the best in Italy. Over the past few decades, Santo Stefano has earned a reputation for producing gourmet lentils that are beyond compare. If you can find them, they are sure to be expensive—but certainly worth the extra penny. They are perfect cooked in a rustic winter soup or boiled until tender and then tossed in a cold summer salad. Be sure to search them out at your local Italian or gourmet market.

During the first week of September, Santo Stefano di Sessanio holds its annual Sagra delle Lenticchie, or lentil festival. It is a lively event with music, dancing, and wonderful regional foods from all over Abruzzo. No doubt, the festival will feature many tasty dishes made with the local lentils: lentils with potatoes, pasta with lentils, grilled sausage with lentils, and hearty lentil soup served with squares of deep fried bread. Here is my recipe for a delicious Abruzzese lentil soup with kale and prosciutto. If you don't have lentils from Santo Stefano di Sessanio, do not despair. Any variety of brown lentils will suffice. For the perfect lunch on a cold winter day, serve it with a piece of crusty Italian bread and a glass of Montepulciano d'Abruzzo.

Olive oil, for sautéing	3 quarts water
½ large Spanish or Vidalia onion, diced	4 tbsp. finely chopped, firmly packed Italian flat leaf parsley
2 carrots, peeled and diced	2 fresh bay leaves
2 ribs of celery, diced	1 rounded tsp. paprika
1 small red bell pepper, seeded and diced	1 lb. brown lentils
Crushed red pepper flakes to taste	2 cups crushed San Marzano tomatoes
Salt and black pepper to taste	3 cups chopped, firmly packed Tuscan kale
3 oz. paper-thin prosciutto	
4 cloves garlic, finely chopped	

Coat the bottom of a soup pot with olive oil and set it over medium-low heat. Add the onion, carrots, celery, and bell pepper. Season with red pepper flakes, salt, and black pepper and sauté until tender. Mince the prosciutto and add it to the pot. Add the garlic and sauté for another minute. Add the water, parsley, bay leaves, paprika, lentils, and crushed tomatoes. Season lightly with salt and simmer over low heat for 45 minutes, stirring frequently.

Meanwhile, remove and discard the entire stalk from each leaf of kale and chop it. Add the chopped kale to the pot and continue simmering for another 15 minutes or until the kale has wilted, the lentils are tender, and the soup is thick and creamy. Remove the bay leaves and adjust the seasoning if necessary. If the soup is too thick for your liking, add additional water. Serve hot. Serves 6 adults.

Minestra Maritata (Baby Meatballs, Pasta, and Swiss Chard in Broth)

ABRUZZO/MOLISE

Most people in the United States are familiar with Italian wedding soup. The natural question is: Is it really served at weddings? I have been to many Italian weddings in the United States and several in Italy, but soup was not served at any of them. So what is fact and what is fiction? Here is the answer! It seems that the name "Italian Wedding Soup" is actually a misnomer. In Italy, any soup containing meat and greens is commonly called minestra maritata *or "married soup." This is because meat and greens are a delicious combination and "marry" well. It is a common preparation throughout Southern Italy. When Southern Italian immigrants brought this concept to the United States, the name was somehow mistranslated as "wedding soup" even though there is no tradition of serving such a dish at weddings in Italy.*

In the small towns and villages of the Apennines, hearty rustic soups are made with baby meatballs, chopped greens, and small pasta. These are popular from Abruzzo to Basilicata. The meat typically used is beef, pork, or a combination of both. As for the greens, that certainly depends upon what grows best in the particular region. In Abruzzo, the soup is sure to be made with Swiss chard or Tuscan kale, whereas in Campania escarole is more likely and in Apulia chicory or dandelions are featured. Here is my version. I use Swiss chard plucked fresh from my vegetable garden, but you can substitute whatever green you like best. My recipe calls for a combination of ground beef and pork. However, if you prefer a healthy alternative, use lean ground turkey instead.

Olive oil, for sautéing
3 carrots, peeled and chopped
3 ribs celery, chopped
½ large Spanish or Vidalia onion, chopped
4 cloves garlic, finely chopped
Salt and black pepper to taste
2 quarts chicken broth
1½ quarts plus ⅓ cup water, divided
1½ cups whole, peeled San Marzano tomatoes, chopped
2 pieces Parmigiano-Reggiano cheese rinds (3 inches by 3 inches)
2 bay leaves
5 tbsp. finely chopped, firmly packed Italian flat leaf parsley, divided
1½ tsp. paprika
½ lb. ground beef (15% fat content)
½ lb. ground pork
1 extra-large egg
¾ cup bread crumbs
½ cup grated Parmigiano-Reggiano cheese
1½ lbs. Swiss chard or Tuscan kale
½ lb. orzo, tubettini, or other small pasta
Grated Parmigiano-Reggiano cheese, for topping

Coat the bottom of a soup pot with olive oil. Add the carrots, celery, onion, and garlic, season with salt and black pepper, and sauté over medium-low heat until tender. Add the broth, 1½ quarts water, tomatoes, cheese rinds, bay leaves, 3 tbsp. parsley, and paprika and bring the soup up to a simmer.

In a mixing bowl, combine the beef, pork, egg, bread crumbs, grated cheese, 2 tbsp. parsley, and ⅓ cup of water. Season the mixture with salt and black pepper. Roll out teaspoon-sized meatballs and add them to the soup.

Remove and discard the entire stalk from each leaf of Swiss chard or Tuscan kale, chop the leaves into small shreds, and add them to the soup. Continue simmering for another 45 minutes and then remove the cheese rinds and bay leaves. Adjust the seasoning if necessary.

Boil the pasta in a separate pot until *al dente* and then add it to the soup before serving. Serve hot, topped with grated cheese. Serves 6 to 8 adults.

Panecotto Rustico (Rustic Bread Soup with Poached Eggs, Prosciutto, and Peas)

CAMPANIA

What do you do with day-old bread? Most people discard it without giving thought to how it could still be used. If there is one thing in an Italian kitchen that never goes to waste, it's bread. In fact, peasants have devised inventive ways of using bread that has passed its prime. It is tossed into soup, stuffed into vegetables, and ground into fine crumbs that are used as a crispy coating for fried cutlets or stirred into soups as a thickener. In Sicily, bread crumbs are even toasted in a frying pan and sprinkled over pasta for a crunchy topping. So before you toss that last piece of hard bread into the trash bin, consider all of the tasty treats you can make with it!

This is my version of my Campanese grandmother's recipe for soup with day-old bread and poached eggs. It is a tasty recipe from the Diano Valley of southern Campania. No doubt it was born of peasant ingenuity. When times were difficult, Campanese peasants made due with whatever ingredients were on hand. My great-grandmother often took a few eggs and some stale bread and transformed it into a delicious meal for the entire family called panecotto, *which means "cooked bread." It is quick and easy to prepare. If you prefer, use fresh bread that is still soft and spongy in the middle. Just be sure to top the soup with plenty of grated Pecorino Romano cheese, and when you break open the poached eggs, swirl the yolk around in the broth so that it becomes thick and tasty. Serve it for dinner, lunch, or even a hearty breakfast.*

1 loaf country-style Italian bread, cubed
Olive oil, for sautéing
3 cloves garlic, finely chopped
3 oz. slab prosciutto, diced
1½ cups frozen peas, thawed
3 tbsp. finely chopped, firmly packed Italian flat leaf parsley
Black pepper to taste
3 quarts chicken broth
8 extra-large eggs
Salt to taste
Grated Pecorino Romano cheese, for topping

Fill four extra-large soup bowls halfway with the cubed bread and set aside. Coat the bottom of a frying pan generously with olive oil, set it over medium-low heat, add the garlic and prosciutto, and sauté for one minute. Stir in the peas and parsley, sauté for another minute, and remove the pan from the heat. Spoon the sautéed items over the bread in each bowl and then drizzle the olive oil from the frying pan over top. Season with black pepper and set the bowls to the side.

Place the chicken broth in a wide pot or deep 5½ quart frying pan, season with salt if necessary, and set it to simmer over low heat. Poach the eggs in the chicken broth, without cooking the yolks. Place 2 poached eggs on top of the bread in each bowl, ladle plenty of broth over top, and sprinkle with grated cheese. When you eat the soup, break open the yolks and mix everything together. Serve hot. Serves 4 adults.

Aquacotta alla Tuscia (Roman Bread Soup with Sausage, Spinach, Sundried Tomatoes, and Cubes of Mozzarella Cheese)

LAZIO

Bread-based soups are just as popular in rural Lazio as they are in Campania, and each region has its own special way of preparing them. Aquacotta *means "cooked water," which is a sure sign that this, too, is a dish of humble origins. This ancient recipe is the traditional soup of cowboys and shepherds from the coastal plains and hills of Northern Lazio. It was traditionally prepared outdoors in an earthenware pot placed over a fire. The ingredients were simple and always included hard bread and aged cheese— ingredients that could last for many days without refrigeration while the cowboys and shepherds moved their herds. A hearty bowl of* aquacotta *was also sure to include wild greens and herbs gathered in the fields. Every so often, a piece of salted cod, a few eggs, or nourishing bits of meat would be thrown in as well. Just about anything can be added to* aquacotta, *including sautéed vegetables, mushrooms, crushed tomatoes, and cubes of mozzarella that melt and become gooey! The traditional cooking style has survived for many centuries—albeit, today it is most likely to be prepared on the stove top and modern cooks may be more inclined to use chicken or vegetable broth instead of water! Here is my rendition. Don't be afraid to experiment, as this is a peasant-style dish that you can make all your own.*

1 loaf country-style Italian bread, cubed
½ lb. mozzarella cheese (low moisture), diced
1 lb. Italian pork sausage
Olive oil, for sautéing
4 quarts chicken broth
3 cloves garlic, sliced

12 ounces spinach, chopped
1 tsp. paprika
Crushed red pepper flakes to taste
Salt and black pepper to taste
½ cup chopped, firmly packed jarred sundried tomatoes preserved in olive oil
Grated Pecorino Romano cheese, for topping

Fill four extra-large soup bowls halfway with the cubed bread and place a few cubes of mozzarella in each bowl. Remove the sausage from the casing. Brush the bottom of a frying pan with olive oil and set it over medium-low heat. Brown the sausage, breaking it up with the back of a wooden spoon. When the sausage is fully cooked, drain off any excess grease and set the sausage to the side.

Place the broth in a pot, season with salt if necessary, and bring it up to a simmer. Coat the bottom of a frying pan with olive oil and sauté the garlic over medium-low heat until soft. Add the spinach and about ¾ cup of broth, which will allow the greens to steam. Season with paprika, red pepper flakes, salt, and black pepper and continue sautéing until the spinach has wilted.

Stir the sausage and sundried tomatoes into the frying pan and then remove the frying pan from the heat. Spoon the sautéed items over the bread in each bowl, then ladle plenty of the hot broth over top. The broth will melt the mozzarella. Serve hot, topped with grated cheese. Serves 4 to 6 adults.

A quiet back street in Termoli, Molise

IV

Insalate (Salads)

Good Wine and Soppressata on Cleaning Day in Frascati

A Rambling in Lazio

One morning, my wife and I went for a ride in the countryside near Frascati, an area famous for producing one of Italy's finest white wines. We drove through an idyllic landscape of olive groves, vine-covered hills, and storybook villages. We came across a small winery housed in an ancient stone building with a wide arched doorway. Terracotta pots overflowing with red geraniums stood beside the entrance. The wood plank double doors were propped open, as if to say, "Please, come in!" And that is what we did! We sat down at a table but did not see anyone. It was a charming little place. There were large wine barrels stacked against the wall and a counter upon which bottles of wine were proudly displayed. The rustic stone walls and wood beam ceiling made this the perfect setting for a sip of fine Roman wine.

Two men entered the winery from a back room. One man went behind the counter and prepared some food. The other walked over to us, smiled, and asked, "How can we help you?"

"We would like to try some of your wines," I replied.

The kind man nodded and said, "Ok. I will bring you each a glass."

He then walked over to the counter and returned to our table with a bottle of white wine and two glasses. He poured us each a full glass and said, "When you finish this, I will let you try another."

My wife and I sat back, relaxed, and enjoyed the tasty wine. We had the quiet little winery all to ourselves. How lucky! A short time later, we asked the man if we could try another wine.

"Certainly," he said with a smile.

"Would you also like to try some of our homemade *soppressata*?"

We agreed, and this time both men came over to the table where we were sitting. One brought a bottle of red wine and poured us each a full glass. The other man brought us a plate of sliced *soppressata* and plenty of fresh crusty bread. The men sat at a nearby table and we chatted. They were brothers from Apulia. There was no work in their town, so they moved to Rome and then found jobs at the winery. We told them we were from Virginia and lived in the countryside where there are many vineyards and small wineries just like theirs. Soon, we were deep into conversation, and they poured us a third glass of wine and one for themselves. What gracious hosts!

When it came time for us to leave, we thanked our new friends, and I asked for the bill. The two brothers looked at each other and laughed.

"There is no bill," one exclaimed.

"But we had many glasses of wine and you brought us *soppressata* and bread. Surely we must pay you something," I replied.

The other brother chimed in. "Sir, there is a sign on the door that says the winery is closed for cleaning today. We are just the cleaning staff. The cash register is locked so we cannot charge you," he explained.

My wife and I were somewhat embarrassed. We apologized for not seeing the sign and thanked the brothers for their hospitality. Certainly they were aware of our misperception the whole time but were still kind and gracious. We told them how much we enjoyed chatting, and I apologized for taking them away from their work.

"That is not a problem. We do not feel like working today," one said.

"When you leave, we will go home too!" the other added.

We all got up, they turned off the lights, and we all walked out of the wide arched door. One brother removed the doorstops, closed the double doors, and locked up. We bid the brothers farewell, and I complemented them again on their delicious *soppressata* and tasty wines. What a wonderful afternoon for everyone. What could be better than good wine and *soppressata* on cleaning day?

Cactus pears in Basilicata

The medieval town of Agira, Sicily

The azure waters of Apulia's Ionian coastline

The tranquil countryside of Molise

Buying fresh produce from the neighborhood market on Lipari Island, Sicily

Garlic for sale in Bagheria, Sicily

Colorful fishing boats under a bright Mediterranean sun

Salmoriglio (Olive Oil and Lemon Dressing with Garlic and Fresh Herbs)

CALABRIA

Gerace is an ancient town that sits on a mountain with a commanding view over endless citrus and olive groves. In Gerace's historic center you will find an old castle and a grand Norman cathedral. With cobblestone streets and plenty of well-preserved medieval buildings, Gerace is one of Calabria's most atmospheric towns. Be sure to visit the castle, where you can enjoy the view over the terracotta rooftops!

I once knew an old man who grew up in Gerace and then immigrated to the United States. He was very proud of his charming town and the wonderful citrus that grows there. He had a small lemon tree in his yard with bright yellow lemons that were as large as softballs. "This tree was grown from seeds that I brought here from my town in Calabria," he proudly said. He plucked a lemon from the tree and handed it to me. "These lemons are so delicious, you can slice them into wedges and eat them like fruit!" he exclaimed. I replied with just one word, "Bellisimo!" That evening, I prepared a traditional lemon dressing from Calabria called salmoriglio. *It is a versatile condiment that bursts with bright Mediterranean flavors and is perfect for drizzling over salads, roasted vegetables, seafood, pork, and chicken. My old friend from Gerace would certainly have approved of the tasty way that I used his fine lemon. Give this dressing a try and you won't be sorry!*

⅓-½ cup fresh lemon juice
1 clove garlic, minced
1 tbsp. finely chopped and firmly packed basil
1 tbsp. finely chopped and firmly packed oregano

¾ tsp. salt
Black pepper to taste
1 cup extra virgin olive oil

Extract ⅓ cup of lemon juice and place it in a mixing bowl. Add the garlic, basil, oregano, and salt and season with black pepper. Whisk the olive oil in a slow, steady stream. Adjust the level of acidity to your liking by adding more lemon juice. Adjust the seasoning if necessary.

Insalata di Arancia e Finocchio (Orange and Fennel Salad with Olives and Toasted Almonds)

SICILY

My Sicilian grandmother's family came from the Val di Salso in central Sicily. Here, olive and citrus groves fill a tranquil valley surrounded by treeless, sun-baked mountains that are shades of yellow and ochre in the summertime. At one end of the valley, the majestic cone of Mt. Etna dominates the horizon, and at the other end the ancient town of Agira clings to a conical mountain as its narrow streets wind their way to the very top. In the middle of the valley is Lago Pozzillo, a shimmering man-made lake that did not exist at the time when my grandmother's family lived in the valley. The lake was constructed in 1959, during a period of economic growth in Southern Italy. Aside from the construction of Lago Pozzillo, very little has changed in the valley and it remains a truly authentic agricultural region. From Agira, there is a wonderful view over the lake with Mount Etna in the distance.

Several years ago, I drove through the Val di Salso on a warm summer day. Along the way, I admired orange trees bursting with fruit, savored the aroma of wild fennel, and purchased olive oil and fresh almonds from a roadside stand near the lake. The flavors and smells took me back to my grandmother's kitchen! This salad captures the flavors of the Val di Salso. It is simple, rustic cuisine from the heart of Sicily. The refreshing combination of fennel and orange makes it the perfect ending to a summertime meal! Any type of briny olive can used, including the Sicilian and Gaeta varieties, but I like Greek Kalamata olives best. Just please don't tell my grandmother! Toasting the almonds makes them flavorful and crunchy!

⅓ cup sliced almonds	¾ cup extra virgin olive oil
1 large bulb fennel	Salt and black pepper to taste
3 large California navel oranges	⅔ cup pitted, halved Kalamata olives

Preheat the oven to 375 degrees. Toast the almonds for 3 minutes or until golden. Mince 2 tablespoons of fennel fronds and finely zest 2 of the oranges. Whisk the olive oil with the chopped fronds and zest and season with salt and black pepper.

Remove and discard the core from the fennel and slice the bulb into very thin strips. Place the sliced fennel and olives in a mixing bowl, toss it with half of the dressing, and transfer it to a serving platter.

Peel the oranges and slice them into rounds. Place the orange rounds on top of the salad, drizzle the remaining dressing over top, and sprinkle with the almonds. Serves 4 to 6 adults.

Insalata di Pomodoro e Basilico (Tomato and Basil Salad with Lemon Dressing)

CALABRIA

No vegetable garden in Southern Italy would be complete without a few tomato vines! Many varieties of tomatoes grow in Southern Italy. There are large, round tomatoes that are perfect for salads, sweet cherry tomatoes that are the pride of Calabria and Sicily, and oval-shaped plum tomatoes from the San Marzano region near Naples that are perfect for making sauce. I grow all three varieties in my vegetable garden in Virginia. I use them to make sauces, roast them in the oven, and set them out to dry under the hot summer sun. However, I always enjoy them best served fresh in a salad with lemon dressing! It is a simple and delicious recipe that I learned from my father many years ago.

When I was a child, there were always tomato vines clinging to stakes in my father's vegetable garden. He prepared this tomato salad for dinner every day when the garden was full of ripe tomatoes. At the end of the meal, the salad bowl was always empty, except for the remaining dressing. After combining with the juice of sweet tomatoes, it was even more delicious and absolutely perfect for sopping up with a piece of crusty bread. My father always wiped the bowl clean! Give this salad a try the next time plump ripe tomatoes are available in the market or ready to be picked from your vegetable garden. Be sure to have a loaf of fresh-baked Italian bread on hand!

4 large beefsteak tomatoes, sliced into wedges
½ red onion, thinly sliced
3 cloves garlic, thinly sliced
8 large basil leaves, chopped

1 cup olives (any variety)
⅔ to ¾ cups extra virgin olive oil, for dressing
Juice of 3 lemons, divided
Salt and black pepper to taste

Place the tomatoes, onions, garlic, basil, and olives in a salad bowl. Drizzle with extra virgin olive oil, squeeze over the juice of 1 lemon, season with salt and black pepper, and toss. Adjust the level of acidity to your liking by squeezing over as much juice from the remaining lemons as you desire. Serves 4 to 6 adults.

Cetriolo in Agrodolce (Sweet and Sour Cucumber Salad with Onions and Capers)

SICILY

In the summer, the Scirocco winds blow into Sicily from North Africa, bringing hot, dry air and sabia, *or sand, that is picked up from the Sahara Desert. On days when the Scirocco winds blow, the sky is sure to be tinged yellow from the dust, which sometimes settles to the ground and leaves a gritty film on cars and anything else left outside. Sunrises and sunsets always take on a mysterious orange glow when there is* sabia *in the air. It is a reminder that the shores of North Africa are not far from Southern Italy. On a warm evening when the Scirocco winds are blowing, nothing is better for dinner than a light, refreshing salad. With a glass of chilled white wine from Casteldaccia and a vibrant orange sunset, it will be a memorable evening in exotic Sicily.*

Here is the perfect summer salad. Do you know the old adage "cool as a cucumber"? People living in the Mediterranean Basin figured this out a long time ago. They have incorporated mild cucumbers into refreshing dishes that are perfect to eat on hot summer days when the Scirocco winds are blowing. In Spain, cucumbers are combined with tomatoes in a cold gazpacho soup; and in the Greece, they are served in a salad with tomatoes and feta cheese. Here is a recipe for Sicilian-style cucumbers! They are thinly sliced and then tossed with garlic, onions, and briny capers in a tangy sweet and sour dressing. The intriguing combination of sweet, sour, and salty flavors adds life to the mild cucumbers, making them perfect summertime fare.

2 large English cucumbers, thinly sliced

½ large Spanish or Vidalia onion, thinly sliced

3 cloves garlic, thinly sliced

3 tbsp. finely chopped, firmly packed Italian flat leaf parsley

1½ tbsp. sugar

3 tbsp. hot water

½ cup red wine vinegar

¾ cup olive oil

⅓ cup capers in brine

Salt and black pepper to taste

Combine the cucumbers, onion, garlic, and parsley in a mixing bowl and set aside. In a separate bowl, dissolve the sugar in the hot water and allow it to cool. Then whisk in the vinegar and olive oil.

Pour the marinade over the salad, add the capers, season with salt and black pepper, and toss well. Let the salad marinate in the refrigerator for at least 4 hours. Use a slotted spoon to transfer the salad to a serving platter and drizzle some of the excess marinade over top. Serves 4 to 6 adults.

Insalata di Peperoni Arrostiti con Provolone e Olive Nere (Roasted Red Bell Pepper Salad with Provolone Cheese and Black Olives)

BASILICATA

The next time you travel to Italy, stay at an agriturismo. *These are family-run, working farms that also operate as bed and breakfasts. Why not spend a few days at an olive plantation in Apulia or a vineyard in Lazio? The experience is sure to be memorable! Many* agriturismi *are housed in traditional structures, historic farmsteads, converted monasteries, or even old castles. They are intimate places where you can interact with the owners and lend a hand. As a guest, you may be asked to participate in the harvest, assist with wine-making, or press olives into oil. Most* agriturismi *also operate a restaurant or offer home-cooked meals to their guests. They are great places to sample regional Italian cuisine.*

You will find bell peppers in most vegetable gardens of southern and central Italy. From Abruzzo to Calabria, bell peppers are fire-roasted on a grill and then stored in jars sott'olio, *or under olive oil. They are sweet and mild in flavor and pair well with cured meats, cheeses, and olives. In Basilicata, they are also included as a traditional* antipasto *before Sunday dinner. Tossed with briny black olives and a robust local cheese, they are the perfect prelude to a hearty rustic meal. Stay at an* agriturismo *in the hills near the ancient town of Matera and you might be asked to pick a few peppers and help roast them over the coals of an outdoor fire! Later, this wonderful salad could be part of your meal, paired with a hearty Aglianico wine from the region.*

9 large red bell peppers
Olive oil, for brushing
2 cloves garlic, finely chopped
1 tbsp. finely chopped, firmly packed basil
1 tbsp. finely chopped, firmly packed Italian flat leaf parsley
Salt and black pepper to taste

Extra virgin olive oil, for dressing
Red wine vinegar, for dressing (optional)
⅓ lb. aged, sharp Provolone cheese, cubed
1 cup black Cerignola olives

Preheat the oven to 425 degrees. Place the peppers on a baking tray that has been lightly brushed with olive oil and roast for 45 to 50 minutes or until the flesh is soft and the skins are puckered and charred. Turn the peppers every 15 to 20 minutes so that they roast evenly.

Place the peppers in a bowl and cover them with aluminum foil. When the peppers have cooled, remove the skins, slice them in half, remove the cores, scrape away the seeds, and slice them into strips. Place the peppers, garlic, basil, and parsley in a mixing bowl, season with salt and black pepper, drizzle with extra virgin olive oil and vinegar, and toss well. Add the provolone cheese and olives, gently toss again, and transfer the salad to a serving dish. Serves 4 to 6 adults.

Insalata di Carciofi e Fave (Mixed Field Greens with Roasted Artichokes and Fava Beans)

APULIA

I love the tradition of Sunday dinner in Southern Italy. After a long work week, extended families gather to eat, drink, and relax. The typical Sunday meal begins with antipasto, *which is then followed by a pasta course, the main meal, and salad. Unlike Americans who eat salad as a first course, Italians prefer to eat their salad at the end of the meal. As my Sicilian grandfather once explained, "The Italians believe that fresh greens and vegetables help you to digest the meal." This is important, as sweet, rich desserts, espresso, and fresh fruits are still to come! While this may seem like a lot of eating, one thing must be said: Sunday dinner in Italy is never rushed! It is eaten at a leisurely pace and a* spada, *or rest, is usually taken between courses. These meals can last all day as family members enjoy wonderful food and engage in conversation and merriment.*

Here is a light, flavorful salad from the agricultural areas of the Murge in central Apulia, where Italy's best artichokes are commercially cultivated and fava beans are grown in almost every garden plot. In Apulia, fresh-picked artichokes are often sliced very thin and tossed into a salad raw or eaten with a drizzle of extra virgin olive oil. I roast the artichokes until tender and crisp, allow them to cool, and then toss them in the salad. Roasting the artichokes helps to develop the flavor. With peppery arugula and a light dressing, this salad is the perfect ending to a Sunday dinner and will prepare you for the sweets that are still to come!

Juice of 2 lemons
18 baby artichokes (2½ inches long)
Olive oil, for drizzling
Salt and black pepper to taste
1½ lbs. fava beans in the pod (yields 1 cup beans)
1 small head Romaine lettuce, chopped

1 bunch arugula, chopped
2 endives, chopped
1 cup black Cerignola olives
Salmoriglio dressing *(see page 95)*
Shaved Pecorino Romano cheese, for topping

Squeeze the lemon juice into a large bowl of cold water, enough to cover the artichoke hearts entirely. Remove the outer leaves of the artichokes until you reach the soft, pale inner cone. Remove the top ⅓ of the cone and peel the stems. Cut the artichokes in half and drop them into the acidulated water to prevent browning while the remaining artichokes are being prepared.

When the artichokes are ready to roast, drain them in a colander and pat them dry. Preheat the oven to 415 degrees. Place the artichokes in a large mixing bowl, drizzle with olive oil, season with salt and black pepper, and toss well. Spread the artichokes evenly on a baking tray, cover it with aluminum foil, and roast for 15 minutes. Remove the aluminum foil and continue roasting for another 10 to 12 minutes or until crispy on top.

Meanwhile, shell 1 cup of fava beans. Fill a 4½ quart saucepan ⅔ of the way with water and add 2½ teaspoons of salt. Add the shelled beans and set them to boil for 15 minutes or until tender but still firm. Allow the beans to cool and then remove the skins. Place the lettuce, arugula, and endives in a large salad bowl. Add the roasted artichokes, fava beans, and olives and toss with the dressing. Transfer the salad to a serving platter and top with flakes of shaved Pecorino Romano cheese. Serves 4 to 6 adults.

Insalata di Farro con Asparagi e Funghi (Farro Salad with Asparagus, Cremini Mushrooms, and Sundried Tomatoes)

LAZIO

Farro is an ancient grain from the Apennine Mountains of central and southern Italy. It has nourished the Mediterranean and Middle Eastern cultures since the days when Julius Caesar ruled Rome. It is similar to durum wheat, but it is not as good for milling into flour. Therefore, it is rarely used for making pasta and bread. Instead, the whole grains are typically boiled or sautéed in broth until plump and tender. Once an underrated and overlooked ingredient of rustic Italian cooking, today farro is gaining popularity as a healthy and unique alternative to pasta and rice. Inventive Italian chefs have discovered that its fine nutty taste and firm texture make it a great addition to soups, stews, and salads. But this is old news to the peasants of Lazio who have been cooking it this way for centuries! Farro is now widely available at high-end supermarkets and health food stores in the United States. This hearty and delicious farro salad comes from the heart of Apennines, where wild mushrooms and tender asparagus are always local favorites. Substitute whatever vegetables you like!

8 oz. farro

1 small bunch asparagus (pencil thin), chopped into 1 inch pieces

Olive oil, for sautéing and dressing

10 oz. cremini mushrooms, sliced

Salt to taste

½ cup sliced, firmly packed jarred sundried tomatoes preserved in olive oil

½ small Vidalia or Spanish onion, diced

2 cloves garlic, finely chopped

2 tbsp. finely chopped, firmly packed Italian flat leaf parsley

Red wine vinegar, for dressing

Black pepper to taste

Add ¾ teaspoon of salt to 2¼ cups of water and bring to a boil over medium heat. Stir in the farro, reduce the heat to low, cover the saucepan, and simmer for 30 minutes. Remove the saucepan from the heat and let it sit for 10 minutes, covered, so that the grains absorb any remaining cooking liquid. Fluff the grains with a fork and allow them to cool to room temperature.

Blanch the chopped asparagus in water for 30 seconds or until tender but still firm. Coat the bottom of a frying pan with olive oil and place it over medium-low heat. Add the mushrooms, season with salt, and sauté until tender. Drain off any excess cooking liquid from the mushrooms and allow them to cool.

Combine the farro, asparagus, mushrooms, sundried tomatoes, onion, garlic, and parsley in a salad bowl. Drizzle with olive oil, splash over enough vinegar to suit your taste, season with salt and black pepper, and toss well. Serves 4 to 6 adults.

Insalata di Rapi e Boconcini (Blanched Broccoli Rabe with Mozzarella Balls and Sundried Tomatoes)

BASILICATA

Southern Italy conjures visions of sun-drenched towns perched above crescent-shaped beaches. Here, coastal towns are sure to have a palm-fringed beach promenade and plenty of umbrellas and lounge chairs arranged in rows on the sand. This region is indeed blessed with the perfect summer climate, not only for sunbathing, but also for sun-drying tomatoes! In August, plump tomatoes grown in garden plots along the Tyrrhenian coasts of Basilicata and Campania are set to bask in the hot Mediterranean sun for at least two days. The warmth of the sun removes all of the moisture from the tomatoes, and they become shriveled, firm, and full of concentrated flavor. But don't tell this to the ladies sunbathing on the beaches of Basilicata's Ionian coast!

In Basilicata, sundried tomatoes are stored in glass jars sott'olio, *or under olive oil, with basil and garlic. The olive oil preserves the tomatoes, giving them a long shelf life. The tomatoes are eaten as an* antipasto *alongside cheeses and cured meats. They are also tossed with pasta, which is then drizzled with the aromatic and flavorful olive oil from the jar. For a burst of bold, vibrant flavor, I add a handful of chopped sundried tomatoes to sautéed vegetables such as broccoli and string beans. In this salad, tangy sundried tomatoes add contrast to the bitter broccoli rabe and creamy mozzarella cheese. A few grinds of spicy black peppercorns make this salad even more interesting! It is a delicious treat you are sure to find in sunny Basilicata.*

1 large bunch broccoli rabe (about 1½ to 1¾ lbs.)
Olive oil, for sautéing and dressing
5 cloves garlic, sliced
Salt and black pepper to taste
½ cup water
¾ cup pitted, halved black Cerignola olives

½ cup sliced, firmly packed jarred sundried tomatoes preserved in olive oil
1 rounded tbsp. capers in brine
1 lb. *bocconcini* (fresh mozzarella balls preserved in water)

Discard any fibrous stems from the broccoli rabe and coarsely chop. Coat the bottom of a large 5½ quart frying pan generously with olive oil and set it over medium-low heat. Add the garlic, let it sizzle in the oil for 30 seconds, and then add the broccoli rabe and season with salt and black pepper. Add the water to create steam. Do this carefully, perhaps covering the pan for a moment, as it will splatter.

Toss the broccoli rabe every two minutes and continue sautéing for 7 minutes or until wilted and tender. Drain off any residual cooking liquid, transfer the broccoli rabe to a salad bowl, and allow it to cool.

Add the olives, sundried tomatoes, capers, and *bocconcini* to the salad bowl, drizzle with olive oil, and toss everything together. Serves 4 adults.

Insalata di Funghi Misti (Marinated Mixed Mushroom Salad with Arugula and Shaved Parmigiano Reggiano Cheese)

ABRUZZO/MOLISE

For a truly Southern Italian experience, go foraging for mushrooms in the hills near the medieval town of Pacentro in the Apennine Mountains of Abruzzo. The people of Abruzzo love mushrooms, and in Pacentro collecting them is serious business. Everyone has their secret spot, and when the time is just right they head into the woods to gather their stash before anyone else finds them. Many varieties of mushroom grow in the Apennine regions of Abruzzo, Lazio, and Campania. Some varieties, such as porcini, are delicious and full of earthy flavor. Others are not so edible! So when you go foraging, take an experienced mushroom forager with you.

The specialty of Pacentro is a wild mushroom salad topped with shaved pecorino cheese. Here is my version, which is best made with wild mushrooms foraged from the woods. There are plenty of interesting mushrooms growing in the woods alongside my farm, but I dare not cook them. If foraging is out of the question for you also, do not despair! There are varieties of cultivated mushrooms available in most supermarkets that will do just fine. Use a combination of cremini, porcini, oyster, and shitake. Skip the white button mushrooms, as they have little flavor and will add no character to the salad. I sauté the mushrooms and toss them with a flavorful dressing made with good-quality red wine vinegar. Allowing the mushrooms to marinate in the refrigerator overnight helps to develop the flavors and makes them even more delicious!

Olive oil, for sautéing	1 tbsp. finely chopped, firmly packed Italian flat leaf parsley
2½ lbs. assorted mushrooms (cremini, porcini, oyster, and shitake), sliced	Extra virgin olive oil, for dressing
3 cloves garlic, finely chopped	Red wine vinegar, for dressing
1 tbsp. finely chopped, firmly packed thyme	1 large bunch arugula
Salt and black pepper to taste	2 large endives
½ small Spanish or Vidalia onion, diced	Shaved Parmigiano-Reggiano cheese, for topping

Coat the bottom of a deep frying pan with olive oil, set it over medium-low heat, and add the mushrooms, garlic, and thyme. Season with salt and black pepper and sauté until the mushrooms are tender. Cook off any excess liquid to intensify the mushroom flavor. (A small amount of excess liquid is fine, as it will combine with the dressing and add a great earthy flavor.) Transfer the mushrooms to a mixing bowl, and allow them to cool.

Add the onion and parsley to the mixing bowl. Drizzle generously with extra virgin olive oil and enough vinegar to suit your taste. Adjust the seasoning, toss well, and allow the mushrooms to marinate for at least 6 hours or overnight.

Arrange the arugula and endives on a serving platter. Place the mushrooms on top of the greens and drizzle with some of the remaining dressing. Sprinkle shaved Parmigiano-Reggiano cheese over top. Serves 4 to 6 adults.

Panzanella alla Romana (Rustic Bread Salad with Tomatoes, Green Olives, and Capers)

LAZIO

Panzanella alla Romana is a traditional bread salad from the countryside of Lazio. It is made by squeezing the juice of ripe tomatoes over thick slices of grilled country-style bread and then topping the bread with diced tomatoes, fresh Roman mint, and plenty of olive oil. It is similar to bruschetta *but must be eaten with a fork, as the soaked bread would certainly fall apart if you were to pick it up with your hands! In my version, the bread is brushed with olive oil, cut into cubes, and toasted in the oven until golden. I then toss the bread with a tasty vinaigrette dressing made with the juice of overripe tomatoes, vinegar, and olive oil. Diced tomatoes, olives, capers, fresh herbs, and garlic are the final touches. The flavors are vibrant and delicious!*

When you make panzanella alla Romana, be sure to have a large salad bowl on hand. If you do not use a large bowl, the salad will be difficult to toss and the bread will not absorb the dressing evenly. If you are lacking, then head to Rome's Mercato della Porta Portese. This is the city's famous open air street market in the Trastevere district. Here, you can purchase traditional Roman housewares and handicrafts, including ceramics, copperware, wooden utensils, and, yes, even a large salad bowl to make panzanella alla Romana! Whenever I am in Rome, I always spend a few hours at the mercato *walking from stall to stall in search of treasures. Be sure to check it out, and pick up the largest salad bowl that you can find! It will come in handy when you prepare this delicious, rustic salad from the heart of Lazio.*

½ loaf country-style Italian bread, cubed

Olive oil, for drizzling

6 large, ripe beefsteak tomatoes

⅓ cup capers in brine

¾ cup pitted, halved green Ascolane or Cerignola olives

½ small Spanish or Vidalia onion, sliced into strips

4 cloves garlic, chopped

2 tbsp. chopped, firmly packed basil

2 tbsp. chopped, firmly packed oregano

Extra virgin olive oil, for dressing

Red wine vinegar, for dressing

Salt and black pepper to taste

Preheat the oven to 400 degrees. Lay the cubed bread on a baking sheet, drizzle the pieces with olive oil, and toast in the oven for 7 to 10 minutes or until golden brown. Set aside and allow to cool.

Cut 4 of the tomatoes into wedges and place them in a large salad bowl with the capers, olives, onions, garlic, basil, and oregano. Slice the remaining 2 tomatoes in half, squeeze the juice of the tomatoes into the salad bowl, and then discard the tomato halves. Dress the salad by drizzling extra virgin olive oil and splashing enough vinegar to suit your taste. Season with salt and black pepper and toss well. Add the cubed bread and toss again so that the bread absorbs the dressing. Serves 6 to 8 adults.

Insalata di Lenticchie (Lentil Salad with Cherry Tomatoes and Red Bell Peppers)

ABRUZZO/MOLISE

With cobblestone streets, pots bursting with geraniums, and a backdrop of jagged peaks, the small town of Santo Stefano has been dubbed one of Italy's most beautiful villages. Today, many Romans head to Santo Stefano for a weekend country retreat. The town's medieval buildings now house bed and breakfasts, art galleries, boutiques, and restaurants that cater to the discerning Romani. The people of Santo Stefano are not only proud of their charming town but also their lentils, which are a Roman favorite. In Santo Stefano, the soil and climate are perfect for growing tender lentils that are full of earthy flavor. They are popular throughout Italy, and there is stiff competition between the village's lentils and the famous Umbrian lentils from Castelluccio. Each town naturally argues that their lentils are best; truth be told, they are both delicious!

Most people think of lentils as a wintertime food. After all, what could be better on a cold, snowy day than a hot bowl of lentil soup? And what Italian doesn't eat roasted sausage with lentils on New Year's Day? This refreshing and light recipe proves that lentils are great all year round, even in summertime! It is a flavorful dish you are likely to be served at a family-style restaurant in Santo Stefano. The lentils are boiled until tender, allowed to cool, and then tossed in a vinaigrette dressing with sweet cherry tomatoes and plenty of crisp, diced red bell pepper, celery, and onions. It is the perfect salad to enjoy on a glorious summer day in the mountains of Abruzzo.

1 lb. dried brown lentils
1 dry pint cherry tomatoes, sliced in half
1 small red bell pepper, seeded and diced
½ Spanish or Vidalia onion, diced
2 ribs celery, diced

3 cloves garlic, finely chopped
3 tbsp. finely chopped, firmly packed Italian flat leaf parsley
Salt and black pepper to taste
Extra virgin olive oil, for dressing
Red wine vinegar, for dressing

Fill a 6 quart pot ⅔ of the way with water and add 1 tablespoon of salt. Add the lentils and simmer until tender but still firm. Depending upon the size of the lentils, this may take anywhere from 15 to 30 minutes. When the lentils are done, drain them well, place them in a salad bowl, and allow them to cool.

When the lentils have cooled, add the cherry tomatoes, bell pepper, onion, celery, garlic, and parsley to the salad bowl and season with salt and black pepper. Drizzle with extra virgin olive oil, splash over enough vinegar to suit your taste, and toss well. Serves 6 to 8 adults.

Insalata di Patate (Roasted Potato Salad with Cherry Tomatoes, Green Olives, and Capers)

CALABRIA

I am always looking for ways to re-use leftovers. Every so often, my doctored-up or re-purposed leftovers are better than the original dish, and I wind up with a tasty new recipe. This is one of them. It started with leftover roasted potatoes. I added a little of this and a little of that, and before you knew it I had an amazing roasted potato salad. It was not long before I perfected the recipe. Now, I will never boil potatoes for a salad again! Roasting them brings out their wonderful, earthy flavor and keeps them firm and delicious. It is a great technique to use when making an Italian-style potato salad. In Calabria, boiled potatoes are sliced, allowed to cool, and then drizzled with olive oil and lemon. It is a simple dish that I transform into something extra special by roasting the potatoes and adding plump, flavorful green olives and sweet cherry tomatoes. I prefer to use the Calabresi variety of olives because they are briny and bold. However, if you prefer a mild olive, try Castelvetrano olives from Sicily or Cerignola olives from Apulia. Refreshing and light, this is a true summertime recipe for potatoes!

Olive oil, for roasting
3½ lbs. russet potatoes
Salt and black pepper to taste
Paprika to taste
¾ cup pitted and halved green Calabresi or Castelvetrano olives
1 dry pint cherry tomatoes, sliced in half
1 large rib celery, chopped
½ small Spanish or Vidalia onion, chopped
4 cloves garlic, finely chopped
2 tbsp. finely chopped, firmly packed Italian flat leaf parsley
2 tbsp. finely chopped, firmly packed oregano or basil
⅓ cup capers in brine
Extra virgin olive oil, for dressing
Juice of 3 lemons, divided

Preheat the oven to 425 degrees. Brush the bottom of a 9 by 13 inch baking dish with olive oil. Peel the potatoes, cut them in half lengthwise, and cut them into 1 inch chunks. Pat the potatoes dry with a dish towel, place them in a mixing bowl, drizzle with olive oil, season with salt, black pepper, and paprika, and toss well. Place the potatoes in the baking dish and roast for 15 minutes. Stir the potatoes and loosen any that are sticking to the bottom. Continue roasting for another 35 to 40 minutes or until crisp and golden brown. Remove the potatoes from the oven and allow them to cool to room temperature.

Place the olives, cherry tomatoes, celery, onion, garlic, parsley, oregano or basil, and capers in a mixing bowl. When the potatoes have cooled, add them to the mixing bowl. Drizzle with plenty of extra virgin olive oil, squeeze over the juice of 1½ lemons, season with salt and black pepper, and toss well. Adjust the level of acidity to your liking by squeezing over as much juice from the remaining lemons as you desire. Serves 4 to 6 adults.

Insalata di Catalogne con Pomodorini e Ceci (Blanched Dandelion Greens Tossed with Cherry Tomatoes, Chickpeas, and Crumbled Provolone)

APULIA

In central Apulia, you will find one of Italy's most unique architectural styles in buildings called trulli. *These houses look like beehives! They are made from stacked stones that are arranged in a conical shape. In the old neighborhoods of Alberobello, cobblestone streets wind between endless clusters of* trulli, *and in the countryside small* trulli *farmsteads dot the landscape. It is a fairytale setting! For an unforgettable visit to the region, stay at an* agriturismo *housed in a traditional* trullo. *With thick stone walls and a high domed ceiling, a traditional* trullo *is sure to be cool during the heat of Apulia's summer and warm in the winter.*

The perfect summertime lunch while visiting this charming region is a salad made with local dandelions. Wild greens have long been a staple of Apulia's countryside. They have been foraged from the fields and olive groves for centuries. Today, dandelions and chicory are commercially cultivated in Apulia for distribution throughout Italy. In Alberobello, these greens are added to soups, stewed with fava beans, baked in casseroles, and tossed with pasta. Here is a rustic salad made with boiled dandelions that is typical of the region. Boiling the dandelions helps to remove some of the bitterness and ensures that they are tender. The bold flavor of the dandelions contrasts nicely with the sharp cheese, sweet tomatoes, and mild chickpeas. It is a wonderful, healthy treat from the enchanting countryside of Alberobello!

1½ lbs. dandelion greens, coarsely chopped

1 dry pint cherry tomatoes, sliced in half

1 can (15 oz.) chickpeas, drained

4 cloves garlic, chopped

⅓ lb. aged, sharp provolone cheese, cubed

Extra virgin olive oil, for dressing

Red wine vinegar, for dressing

Salt and black pepper to taste

Fill a 6 quart pot ⅔ of the way with water and add 1 tablespoon of salt. Boil the dandelion greens in the water for 5 minutes or until tender, drain them well, and allow them to cool. Add the greens to a salad bowl with the cherry tomatoes, chickpeas, garlic, and cheese, drizzle with olive oil, and splash over enough vinegar to suit your taste. Season with salt and black pepper and toss well. Serves 4 adults.

Insalata di Tonno e Fagioli (Tuna and Cannellini Bean Salad)

CALABRIA

Often when I travel to Italy, I try dishes made with unusual combinations of ingredients. Sometimes they are surprisingly good and I add them to my repertoire. This is one such dish. I tried it while staying at Anna and Salvatore's villa in Calabria. One afternoon, their daughter, Gemma, asked "Shall I prepare tuna salad for lunch?" I replied, "Certo!" I was expecting Gemma to make us sandwiches, but instead she prepared a salad made with tuna and beans. Accustomed to tuna with mayonnaise, I was surprised and skeptical about the combination. "I have never eaten tuna with beans before!" I exclaimed. "That's because you Americans eat everything with mayonnaise or ketchup!" she retorted. "This is the way we prepare tuna salad in Calabria." I took a bite and then complimented Gemma on her unusual—but very tasty—salad. The firm, flaky tuna paired nicely with the creamy cannellini beans. These were two ingredients I never would have thought to combine. The vinaigrette dressing and crunchy texture of the diced vegetables make this salad light and delicious. Now, thanks to Gemma, when I want tuna I no longer reach for the jar of mayonnaise. Add this version of tuna salad to your repertoire of healthy dishes.

16 oz. Italian jarred tuna packed in olive oil

½ large red bell pepper, seeded and diced

½ small Spanish or Vidalia onion, diced

1 rib celery, diced

¾ cup pitted, halved black Cerignola olives

3 cloves garlic, finely chopped

2 tbsp. finely chopped, firmly packed Italian flat leaf parsley

1 can (15 oz.) Cannellini beans, drained

Olive oil, for dressing

Red wine vinegar, for dressing

Salt and black pepper to taste

Place the tuna in a mixing bowl and flake it into chunks with a fork. Add the bell pepper, onion, celery, olives, garlic, parsley, and beans. Drizzle with plenty of olive oil and splash over enough vinegar to suit your taste. Season with salt and black pepper and toss gently. Serves 4 adults.

Yachts moored in the harbor, Porto di Maratea, Basilicata

V

Pasta, Gnocchi, e Cuscusu (Pasta, Dumplings, and Couscous)

Sardines and a Swim in the Sea at Messina

A Rambling in Sicily

When I was twelve years old, my grandparents took me to Italy. We travelled from Rome to Palermo by bus, stopping in Messina for two days to break up our journey. We stayed at a hotel near a harbor and small beach with a wonderful view of the sea from our balcony. We spent our first day in Messina visiting the city's many beautiful churches; as we went from one church to the next, I asked my grandmother, "When can we go to the beach?" Each time she replied, "Maybe later." The day quickly passed, and soon there was no time left for a swim. I was quite disappointed.

The next morning, my grandmother woke me with a boisterous roar. "Put on your bathing suit. I will take you for a swim!" I walked out on the balcony squinting in the bright sunlight. It was warm and the sea was calm—a perfect day for a swim. I put on my bathing suit and we walked across the street, towels in hand, to the harbor. We saw a fisherman unloading his catch. His nets were piled on the sidewalk, and there were wooden boxes filled with fish. There were plenty of sardines in one box and many different kinds of fish in another. We stopped to look and chatted with the fisherman.

"What beautiful fish," my grandmother commented. "We are staying at the hotel, but if I had a kitchen, I would make my grandson pasta with sardines and wild fennel." she added.

The fisherman smiled and pointed to a small restaurant across the street. "That is where I am bringing the fish. If you would like, I will tell the owner that you are coming and she will prepare pasta with sardines tonight."

My grandmother accepted his kind offer and thanked the fisherman. When we reached the small, sandy beach at the end of the harbor, we laid our towels near the edge of the water. My grandmother made herself comfortable on the shore as I quickly jumped in the water

"Do you think there are fish swimming beneath my feet?" I asked her.

She laughed and replied, "No, the fisherman caught all the fish."

I then asked, "Grandma, you cannot swim. What if I drown?"

She smiled and offered me reassurance. "Don't worry, I will call the fisherman and he will scoop you up in his net like a sardine!"

We continued to joke and laugh all morning long as I swam back and forth in front of her. It was a most unexpected and pleasant start to the day!

Later that evening, we went to the restaurant across from the harbor. It was a small, unadorned place. We sat ourselves at an outside table so that we could look at the boats. The matron came over with a small dish of toasted bread crumbs and a bottle of water. "We have been waiting for you!" she cheerfully exclaimed. "We will bring you pasta with sardines and wild fennel and more fish for dinner." I was excited; I had been waiting all day to eat the sardines that the fisherman caught!

Soon, a heaping platter of tubular spaghetti was placed on the table. It was tossed with sardines and a pungent sauce of wild fennel, pine nuts, and raisins. We sprinkled it with toasted bread crumbs, and I ate until my stomach could hold no more. After that came a platter of mixed fried fish. Each time I took a fish from the platter, I asked my grandmother, "Do you remember seeing this one in the box?" She smiled each time and responded, "Of course!" It seemed as if we were eating for hours. After dinner, we went for a stroll—but much to my grandparents' surprise, I was too full for *gelato*!

Before we left the next morning, I took a photograph from our balcony of the little harbor and the beach where my grandmother took me to swim. Although my visit to Messina was short, I did get to see every church in the city. Now, thirty years later, I do not remember all the beautiful churches that my grandmother dragged me to. Instead, my memories are mostly of sardines and a swim in the sea.

A window in a mountain village high in the Apennines of Abruzzo

Rambling around in Canicatti, Sicily

Each region has its own special pasta

A tranquil cover in the Gargano region of Apulia

Aged cheeses on display at an artisanal cheese shop

A tranquil scene in the countryside of Molise

Grapes in Alberobello, Apulia

Pasta Fresca alla Abruzzese (Fresh Semolina Pasta)

ABRUZZO/MOLISE

In Southern Italy, pasta is typically made with course, yellow semolina flour and water. The dough is pushed through extruders to form countless shapes—from long, thin spaghetti to thick, tubular rigatoni and curly corkscrews called cavatappi. *Pasta made with semolina is typically dried, which means a longer cooking time. However, when prepared al dente ("firm to the tooth") it is sure to be delicious and full of nutty semolina flavor. In Abruzzo, semolina pasta is often made with eggs and eaten fresh. The classic pasta shape of the region is* pasta alla chitarra, *which is made with a curious guitar-like device. The dough is rolled into a sheet and spread over a* chitarra, *a wooden frame fitted with rows of thin metal strings spaced barely a millimeter apart. The dough is then rolled with a rolling pin, and the metal strings cut it into long strands of thin pasta that resemble* linguine. *Cutting pasta with a* chitarra *takes some skill. However, an Abruzzese nonna who has been doing it for many years can easily roll and cut a few pounds of pasta in under an hour. Here is my recipe for an Abruzzo-style semolina pasta dough. If you do not have a* chitarra *or an Abruzzese nonna to help you, do not despair! Simply roll your dough into sheets with a pasta-maker and then cut it into linguine using the narrowest setting.*

2 cups semolina flour	4 extra-large eggs
1 cup all-purpose, pre-sifted flour	2 tsp. olive oil
½ tsp. salt	

Place the semolina flour, all-purpose flour, and salt in a food processor and pulse it a few times. Beat the eggs with the olive oil and add them slowly to the food processor while pulsing. Pulse until the egg is thoroughly incorporated and the dough clumps. If the dough is too dry, add a splash of water and pulse again. If it is too wet, add a sprinkle of flour.

Turn the dough onto a floured work surface and knead it for 5 minutes. Shape the dough into a ball, wrap it in plastic wrap, and let it rest for 45 minutes. Follow the instructions on your pasta maker to roll the dough into sheets of medium thickness (#5 on a standard pasta maker). If you are using an authentic *chitarra*, press the sheets through the *chitarra* strings. Otherwise, use the narrowest cut on your pasta maker to make linguine. Fill a 12 quart pot ¾ of the way with water and add 3 tablespoons of salt. Boil the pasta for 3 to 5 minutes. Dress with your favorite sauce. Serves 4 adults.

Cuscusu (Sicilian Couscous)

SICILY

Along Sicily's western coast, there is a cherished tradition of couscous that dates back to the eleventh century when Arabs from North Africa occupied the island. Generations of families in this region have passed on the practice of 'ncocciata, or swirling semolina with water in a wide-rimmed bowl until the grains clump into small clusters of couscous. The couscous is then set to dry before it is steamed in a double boiler, called a cuscuseria. *Although the process of making couscous is time consuming, the method is quite simple. In lazy coastal towns caressed by warm Mediterranean breezes, old women retreat to the shaded alleys during the hottest part of the day to swirl semolina into couscous and pass away the time. It is always a social affair—catching up on the gossip is just as important as making couscous for the evening meal!*

Instant couscous is available today in most supermarkets, and some of the brands are quite good. They are a quick alternative when you are crunched for time. However, if you set yourself upon the task of 'ncocciata, you will be rewarded with a dish that is truly beyond compare! If you do not have a cuscusaria, *you can improvise by placing the couscous in a colander, suspending it in a large pot that is half full with boiling water, and covering it with foil. Just be sure that the bottom of the colander sits at least 2 inches above the water. Serve the couscous as they do in Sicily, alongside a thick and flavorful vegetable or fish stew. I also like to toss it with garlic-infused olive oil, toasted almonds, and raisins. It makes the perfect side dish for roasted and grilled lamb, pork, and chicken.*

1 lb. semolina flour
Water, as needed
Olive oil, for drizzling
Salt to taste
2 cloves garlic, minced (optional)
2 tbsp. minced, firmly packed Italian flat leaf parsley (optional)

Place two tablespoons of semolina on a wide plate towards the side of the plate. Drop a tablespoon of water in the center of the plate. Use your fingers to push the semolina over the water, rubbing it gently in a swirling motion. The grains of semolina will form small clumps of couscous. Continue rubbing until all of the semolina and water have been incorporated and the clumps are of a small uniform size. Empty the plate onto a linen tablecloth and repeat the process. Allow the couscous to sit for at least an hour or until dry.

When the couscous has dried, transfer it to a large mixing bowl. Drizzle lightly with olive oil and season with salt. Incorporate the olive oil and salt into the couscous by gently rubbing and fluffing it with your hands. If you prefer seasoned couscous, work in some garlic and parsley also. Set the couscous in a *cuscuseria* or large double boiler and steam it for 2 hours or until tender, stirring and fluffing with a wide fork every 15 minutes. Serves 4 to 6 adults.

Cavatelli (Ricotta Dumplings)

CAMPANIA

I once asked my Campanese grandmother, "What is your favorite type of pasta?" She smiled and said, "My mother always made cavatelli. *That is what I like best!" She then posed the same question to me, and I responded, "Cavatelli—because that is what my mother always made, too!" Food is perhaps the most important way that Italians pass along traditions. As you travel from one region to the next in Southern Italy, you are sure to see countless varieties of pasta. Preparing pasta is perhaps the first skill taught by a proud Italian nonna to her grandchildren. No doubt she will teach them how to make the traditional pasta that has been prepared in their town for centuries! Cavatelli are a traditional, homestyle pasta in Campania, Molise, and Basilicata. In some areas the dough is made with flour, ricotta, and egg, while in other places they use semolina and water. You can't go wrong either way! Cavatelli are made by flattening a small piece of dough against the tines of a fork or the ridged surface of a* cavatelli *press and then rolling it with the flick of a finger. The small dumplings resemble a bullet with a ridged surface that is perfect for sauce to cling to. A skilled chef or a Campanese nonna can flick hundreds of* cavatelli *off a press in an hour. You can find* cavatelli *at any Italian market, or you can make them yourself. Give it a try!*

2 lbs. whole-milk ricotta cheese
1 tsp. salt
1 extra-large egg
1 extra-large egg yolk
5 to 5½ cups all-purpose, pre-sifted flour
Olive oil, for brushing and drizzling

Drain off any excess liquid from the ricotta. Place the ricotta in a large mixing bowl and beat in the salt, egg, and egg yolk. Add the flour one cup at a time until the dough pulls together. Depending upon the moisture content of the ricotta, you will need 5 to 5½ cups of flour. Turn the dough onto a floured work surface and knead it until smooth. Cut the dough into quarters, roll each into a ball, cover them with plastic wrap, and allow them to rest for 1 hour.

Roll the dough into ½ inch diameter cords and then cut them into ½ inch pieces. Press each piece of dough against the concave side of a fork and roll it gently off the tines until it curls. This will create dumplings with a ridged surface on one side and curled edges on the other.

Fill a 12 quart pot ¾ of the way with water, add 3 tablespoons of salt, and bring to a boil. Drop one or two handfuls of *cavatelli* at a time into the boiling water. The *cavatelli* will sink to the bottom. When they rise to the top, allow them to cook for another 30 seconds, and then remove them with a slotted spoon or skimmer.

Place the *cavatelli* in a baking dish that has been brushed with olive oil. As you add *cavatelli* to the baking dish, drizzle them lightly with olive oil to prevent them from sticking. Top with your favorite sauce. Serve hot. Serves 4 to 6 adults.

Gnocchi di Patate (Potato Dumplings)

ABRUZZO/MOLISE

Potato dumplings called gnocchi *are a popular treat throughout Italy.* Gnocchi *are rustic fare of humble, peasant origin. After a long day of hard work, the* contadini, *or farmers of Molise's Apennine region, are sure to fill their stomachs with homemade* gnocchi *topped with a rich lamb or pork* ragu. *In Naples,* gnocchi *are often topped with a light marinara, and in Apulia you might find them tossed with vegetables in a* tiella, *or earthenware dish, and baked in the oven. It is said that the name* gnocchi *is derived from the word* nocca, *which means "knuckle" in Italian. This certainly describes the shape and size of the dumplings, but hopefully not their texture;* gnocchi *should be soft and delicate like a pillow, never as hard as your knuckles! Today,* gnocchi *are available at most supermarkets in the United States. They come refrigerated, frozen, and as a shelf item in a vacuum-sealed package. Although commercially produced* gnocchi *are convenient, they tend to be flavorless and are always rock-hard. Compare my* gnocchi *to ones that are commercially produced and you will see the difference. Mine are light, flavorful, and guaranteed to melt in your mouth!*

2½ lbs. russet potatoes	1½ tsp. salt
1 extra-large egg	2 cups all-purpose, pre-sifted flour
1 extra-large egg yolk	Olive oil, for brushing and drizzling

Peel the potatoes, slice them into 2 inch chunks, and boil them in water until soft (about 30 minutes). Transfer the potatoes to a colander and let them sit for 10 minutes to drain. Then set the potatoes on a tray to cool.

Beat together the egg, egg yolk, and salt. Pass the potatoes through a potato ricer. Place the potatoes in a mound on your work surface, make a well in the middle, and add the eggs. Use a fork to mash the eggs into the potatoes. Spread the potato mixture in an even layer on your work surface and sprinkle the flour over top. Use a pastry scraper to gently cut the flour into the potatoes, without over-working, and then form the dough into a ball.

Dust your work surface with additional flour and knead the dough gently until smooth and pliable. Add more flour if the dough is too sticky. Cut the dough into 8 equal pieces and roll them into ½ inch diameter cords. Cut the cords into ½ inch pieces and dust them lightly with additional flour. If you prefer, make fancy, ridged *gnocchi* by pressing each piece of dough against the concave side of a fork and rolling it gently off the tines until it curls. This will create dumplings with a ridged surface on one side and curled edges on the other.

Fill a 12 quart pot ¾ of the way with water, add 3 tablespoons of salt, and bring to a boil. Drop one or two handfuls of *gnocchi* at a time into the boiling water. The *gnocchi* will sink to the bottom. When the *gnocchi* rise to the top, allow them to boil for another 30 seconds, and then remove them with a slotted spoon or skimmer. Place the *gnocchi* in a baking dish that has been brushed with olive oil and cover them. As you add *gnocchi* to the baking dish, drizzle them lightly with olive oil to prevent them from sticking. Top the *gnocchi* with your favorite sauce and serve warm. Serves 4 to 6 adults.

Gnocchi di Semola alla Romana (Roman-Style Semolina Dumplings)

LAZIO

Whenever I travel to Italy, I make it a point to try the local specialties. They say that the cuisine of a region says much about its people—where they have come from and in what direction they are heading. One day in Rome I sat down at a trattoria *near the Spanish Steps that served traditional Roman cuisine. On the menu were Roman-style oxtails, braised tripe, pasta with bacon, stuffed artichokes, and so much more. I could not decide what to eat. When the waiter came to take my order, I told him, "I want to try a very traditional Roman dish! What do you recommend?" He replied, "Certainly, you must order the gnocchi alla Romana! They are made with semolina, not potatoes, and are baked in the oven." He then added, "It is a very ancient dish that dates back to the times of Julius Caesar." It sounded so good I could not resist. And they didn't disappoint. The light and flavorful semolina dumplings were baked with butter and topped with plenty of grated Parmigiano-Reggiano cheese that became crisp and golden. It is the perfect wintertime starch to accompany a hearty stew! If you wish, layer the* gnocchi *in a baking dish, spoon over* besciamella *sauce, and sprinkle shredded fontina cheese over top to create a decadent casserole. Or, simply top them with tomato sauce.*

5½ cups whole milk
1 tsp. salt
2 cups semolina flour
14 tbsp. butter, divided, plus additional for greasing

3 egg yolks
1¼ cups grated Pecorino Romano cheese, divided
Black pepper to taste

Place the milk and salt in a saucepan over medium-low heat. When the milk begins to simmer, turn the heat down to low and whisk in the semolina ½ cup at a time until fully incorporated. Continue whisking constantly (and scraping the sides and bottom of the saucepan) for another 3 minutes or until the dough is smooth, thick, and pulls away from the sides of the saucepan. Remove the saucepan from the heat and let the dough cool for 3 minutes. Meanwhile, melt 5 tablespoons of butter. Once the dough is cool, stir in the melted butter, incorporating it fully into the dough. Fully incorporate the egg yolks and then ¾ cup of grated Pecorino Romano cheese.

Grease a 9 by 13 inch baking dish with additional butter, transfer the dough to the baking dish, and spread it to an even ½ inch thickness using a rubber spatula. If the dough is too sticky, spray the head of the rubber spatula with cooking spray. This will make it easier to spread. Allow the dough to set for 1½ hours.

Preheat the oven to 450 degrees. Cut the dough into squares. Melt the remaining 11 tablespoons of butter. Grease the bottom of a 9 by 11 inch baking dish with some of the melted butter. Arrange the *gnocchi* in the baking dish in overlapping rows, like shingles. Then brush the tops of the *gnocchi* generously with the remaining melted butter and season with black pepper. Sprinkle the remaining ½ cup of cheese over top. Bake for 20 minutes or until crisp and golden. Serve hot. Serves 6 to 8 adults.

Salsa Marinara (Tomato Sauce with Garlic and Fresh Herbs)

CAMPANIA

The town of San Marzano lies at the foot of Mount Vesuvius, but its real claims to fame are the tomatoes that grow on the fertile volcanic slopes. It is believed that the first seed of the San Marzano tomato originated in Peru and was brought to Naples in 1770 by Spanish merchants. The succulent, sweet tomatoes thrived in the soil and climate of the region and have been cultivated there ever since. Today, nearly 250 years later, it is hard to imagine a time when tomatoes did not have a place in Southern Italian cooking! In fact, tomato sauce is now synonymous with Neapolitan cuisine. Head to Naples and you will see that just about anything can be cooked in a tomato-based sauce—from vegetables to fish and meats.

Most Italians will agree that tomatoes from San Marzano are the very best for making tomato sauce. Compared to other varieties, they have better texture, fewer seeds, less acidity, and a bright red color. They always produce a sauce that is thick and flavorful. That being said, imported, canned San Marzano tomatoes are considerably more expensive than their domestic counterparts. But if you ask me, it is money well spent! You can find them at high-end supermarkets and Italian specialty food shops. Here is my recipe for a tasty basic tomato sauce. I use whole, peeled tomatoes but like to throw a can of crushed in too. The crushed tomatoes help make the sauce thick and rich. When I wish to add another layer of flavor, I toss in a handful of diced prosciutto.

Olive oil, for sautéing
½ large Spanish or Vidalia onion, diced
Crushed red pepper flakes to taste
Salt and black pepper to taste
4 cloves garlic, finely chopped
3 ounces prosciutto, minced (optional)
3 cans (28 oz. each) whole, peeled San Marzano tomatoes
1 can (28 oz.) crushed San Marzano tomatoes
2 tbsp. finely chopped, firmly packed basil
2 tbsp. finely chopped, firmly packed oregano

Coat the bottom of a large pot with olive oil and set it over medium-low heat. Add the onion and season with red pepper flakes, salt, and pepper. Sauté the onion until soft and then add the garlic and prosciutto. Continue sautéing for another minute.

Pulse the whole tomatoes and the juice from the cans in a food processor to achieve a pulpy consistency and add them to the pot. Add the can of crushed tomatoes (without pulsing) and the basil and oregano. Allow the sauce simmer over low heat for 45 minutes, stirring frequently. Adjust the seasoning, if necessary. Makes 3½ quarts.

Mollica di Pane (Toasted Bread Crumb Topping for Pasta Dishes)

SICILY

In the hills of Agrigento, pasta dishes are often topped with toasted bread crumbs—mollica di pane—instead of grated cheese. In the past, topping pasta with bread crumbs was a matter of necessity for poor farmers who did not have cheese and would not dare to waste even a crumb of bread. Today, it is a delicious and unexpected way to add flavor and texture to any pasta dish. Modern chefs have caught on to this tasty invention of peasant frugality. A few years back, my wife and I dined at an upscale restaurant and were surprised to see pasta with olive oil, garlic and toasted bread crumbs on the menu, as this is something we make at home for a quick meal. "Would you order this?" my wife asked. "Not at that price!" I replied. We proceeded to order something fancy. But later that night when we returned home, I set the water to boil for pasta and my wife got out the frying pan to toast bread crumbs!

½ loaf country-style Italian bread or 2 cups finely ground dry bread crumbs
Olive oil, for drizzling or sautéing

Mollica di Pane can be made with fresh Italian bread or packaged, dry bread crumbs purchased at the supermarket. If you are using fresh bread, grate enough in a food processor for 2 cups of firmly pressed crumbs. Transfer the bread crumbs to a mixing bowl, drizzle lightly with olive oil, and toss so that the crumbs are evenly coated. Preheat the oven to 375 degrees. Spread the bread crumbs evenly on a baking tray and bake for 5 to 7 minutes or until crisp and golden. Stir the bread crumbs every few minutes so that they toast evenly.

If you are using packaged, dry bread crumbs, coat the bottom of a frying pan with olive oil, set it over low heat, and add the bread crumbs. Stir the bread crumbs so that they are evenly coated with the olive oil. Gently toast the bread crumbs until golden brown, stirring continuously to ensure that they toast evenly and do not burn. Serve as a topping for pasta.

Spaghetti con Pomodori Secchi, Capperi, e Peperoncino (Spaghetti with Olive Oil, Garlic, Sundried Tomatoes, Capers, and Crushed Red Chili Flakes)

BASILICATA

For a dish that captures the signature flavors of Basilicata, toss perfectly cooked al dente *pasta with olive oil, sautéed garlic, a few grinds of black pepper, and plenty of crushed red chili flakes. This will create the ideal flavor base for a Southern Italian-style dish. From there, you can add just about anything else! However, in order for your dish to really shine, you must cook the pasta properly. Nothing is more disdained in Southern Italy than pasta that is improperly salted or cooked* scotta *(mushy). Here are a few tips any Basilicatese grandmother would be happy to pass along:*

First, be sure to cook the pasta in a large pot with a copious amount of water. The water should be seasoned with salt, which will add flavor to the pasta. Otherwise, it is certain to taste flat. Add the pasta to the pot after the water has reached a hard boil, and stir it frequently and vigorously to prevent the pasta from sticking together and to the bottom of the pot. Prepare your condiment or sauce ahead of time in a large 5 ½ quart frying pan. When the pasta is ready, transfer it to the frying pan with a skimmer, toss it with the condiment or sauce, and simmer it on the stove top for two minutes so that the pasta absorbs the flavors. Finally, if you prefer or need to strain your pasta in a colander, never rinse it. Rinsing the pasta will remove the starch and destroy the flavor. Now that you know how to cook pasta perfectly, here is a delicious and easy recipe from the heart of Basilicata!

½ cup Sicilian capers preserved in salt

1 lb. spaghetti

Olive oil, for sautéing

4 large cloves garlic, sliced

6 green onions, chopped

1 heaping tsp. crushed red pepper flakes (or more if you prefer)

Salt and black pepper to taste

1½ cups sliced jarred sundried tomatoes preserved in olive oil

2 tbsp. finely chopped, firmly packed oregano

2 tbsp. finely chopped, firmly packed basil

Grated or shaved Pecorino Romano cheese, for topping (optional)

Toasted bread crumbs, for topping (optional) *(see page 122)*

Remove the salt from the capers by soaking them in warm water for 15 minutes and then rinsing them under running water. Fill a 12 quart pot ¾ of the way with water, add 3 tablespoons of salt, and bring to a boil. Add the pasta.

Coat the bottom of a 5½ quart frying pan generously with olive oil and set it over medium-low heat. Add the garlic, green onions, and crushed red pepper flakes. Season with salt and black pepper and sauté until the garlic and green onions are soft. Toss in the sundried tomatoes, capers, oregano, and basil and remove the frying pan from the heat.

When the pasta is *al dente*, set the frying pan back over low heat and transfer the pasta to the frying pan. Toss everything together and sauté for two minutes to marry the flavors of the sauce to the pasta. If necessary, add some pasta cooking water or olive oil to moisten and adjust the seasoning. Serve hot, topped with grated or shaved Pecorino Romano cheese or toasted bread crumbs. Serves 4 to 6 adults.

Penne alla Palermitana (Penne with Cauliflower, Pine Nuts, Raisins, and Saffron)

SICILY

Exactly how saffron was introduced to Italian cuisine is up for debate. Some historians say it was brought to Southern Italy by the Arabs in the eleventh century and that its popularity spread up the peninsula. Others say that Venetian merchants brought it back from the Middle East and that its popularity spread down the peninsula. Regardless of what is fact or fiction, one thing is certain: saffron adds wonderful exotic flavor to many regional Italian dishes. Of all the regions in Italy, Sicily and Abruzzo are perhaps the best known for using saffron in delicious and ingenious ways. In Abruzzo, saffron-infused water is used to make pasta dough, and in Sicily a pinch of saffron threads are added to poached fish in sweet fennel broth. Today, modern chefs are even adding saffron to sweet desserts such as custards and gelato!

My friend Anna in Palermo has mastered the art of cooking with saffron. It is a skill that has been passed down in her family since the days when ancient Arab cultures settled on the island. For pasta dishes, she adds a few generous pinches to the boiling pasta water. When it's done, the pasta has absorbed the wonderful, exotic flavor of the saffron and is tinged yellow! Here is recipe straight from Anna's kitchen. Saffron and a touch of orange zest add intrigue to pasta tossed with sautéed cauliflower, pine nuts, and raisins. Anna serves it topped with toasted bread crumbs because, according to her, "that is how it should be eaten." Truth be told, it's also good topped with grated cheese, and that's how I serve it at home. But please don't tell Anna!

4 generous pinches saffron
Olive oil, for sautéing
1 medium Spanish or Vidalia onion, diced
1 large red bell pepper, seeded and diced
5 cloves garlic, sliced
Zest of 1 large California navel orange
3 tbsp. finely chopped, firmly packed Italian flat leaf parsley
8 fillets Italian jarred anchovies in olive oil, finely chopped
½ cup raisins
⅓ cup pine nuts, toasted
1 head cauliflower, chopped
1 lb. penne pasta
Salt and black pepper to taste
Grated or shaved Pecorino Romano cheese for topping (optional)
Toasted bread crumbs for topping (optional) *(see page 122)*

Fill an 8 quart pot ¾ of the way with water and add 1 tablespoon of salt. Set the water to boil and add the saffron. After a few minutes, the water will turn bright yellow. If the water does not turn bright yellow, add another pinch of saffron. Coat the bottom of a 5½ quart frying pan generously with olive oil and set it over medium-low heat. Sauté the onions and peppers until soft. Add the garlic and continue sautéing for another minute. Stir in the orange zest, parsley, anchovies, raisins, and pine nuts. Add a ladle of the saffron-infused water to the frying pan, sauté for 2 minutes to create a sauce, and then remove the frying pan from the burner.

When the water reaches a boil, drop the cauliflower into the pot and blanch it for 1 minute or until tender but still quite firm. Transfer the cauliflower to the frying pan using a skimmer and toss it gently with the sauce. Drop the pasta into the pot of saffron water. When the pasta is *al dente*, transfer it to the frying pan. Toss everything together with another ladle of the pasta cooking water and sauté for 2 minutes over low heat to marry the flavors of the sauce to the pasta. Season with salt and black pepper. Serve hot, topped with grated or shaved Pecorino Romano cheese or toasted bread crumbs. Serves 4 to 6 adults.

Spaghetti con Capelli di Zucchini (Spaghetti with Zucchini Strands, Garlic, and Herbs)

LAZIO

Tossing pasta with sautéed vegetables is a common practice in Italy. It is simple and quick, and just about any fresh vegetable will do! Pasta with zucchini is a dish you are sure to encounter while traveling through Lazio in springtime, when the zucchini are young and tender. Several varieties of squash are indigenous to Southern Italy. There are long, thin Sicilian squash called cucuzza *and sweet Italian pumpkins called* zucca. *But the very best of all are zucchini Genovesi. A native of the Liguria region, these tender, mild-flavored squash are not only tasty but also versatile. They are delicious stuffed with rice or meat, thinly sliced and fried, and chopped into cubes and tossed into soups, stews, and pasta dishes.*

What makes my version of pasta with zucchini truly unique is the method for preparing the zucchini. Instead of chopping it into cubes, I slice it into long, paper-thin strands using a potato peeler or mandolin. Yes, this takes more time. But it's well worth the effort! The zucchini strands become married to the spaghetti when they are tossed together. Talk about a match made in heaven! Each twirl of the fork captures a mouthful of mild, uncomplicated zucchini flavor. If you have zucchini flowers on hand, tear them into shreds and toss them in too! Serve this dish with a glass of dry white Orvieto wine from Umbria or a refreshing white Casteldaccia from Sicily.

8 medium zucchini (about 6 to 8 inches long)	Salt and black pepper to taste
Olive oil, for sautéing	1 lb. spaghetti
4 cloves garlic, finely chopped	Grated or shaved Parmigiano-
3 tbsp. finely chopped, firmly packed Italian flat leaf parsley	Reggiano cheese, for topping
2 tbsp. finely chopped, firmly packed basil or oregano	Toasted bread crumbs, for topping *(see page 122)*

Cut the zucchini in half lengthwise and scoop out the seeds with a spoon. Use a potato peeler or mandolin to slice the zucchini into long, paper-thin strands. Coat the bottom of a 5½ quart frying pan generously with olive oil, set it over medium-low heat, and sauté the garlic until soft. Add the zucchini, parsley, and basil or oregano and season with salt and black pepper. Continue sautéing for another 3 minutes or until the zucchini is soft. Then remove the frying pan from the burner.

Fill a 12 quart pot ¾ of the way with water, add 3 tablespoons of salt, and bring to a boil. Add the pasta. When the pasta is *al dente*, set the frying pan back over medium-low heat and transfer the pasta to the frying pan. Toss everything together and sauté for two minutes to marry the flavors of the sauce to the pasta. If necessary, add some pasta cooking water or olive oil to moisten and adjust the seasoning. Serve hot, topped with grated or shaved Parmigiano-Reggiano cheese or toasted bread crumbs. Serves 4 to 6 adults.

Tagliatelle con Funghi di Bosco (Tagliatelle with Mushrooms, Green Onions, and Herbs)

ABRUZZO/MOLISE

I once took a stroll through a bustling produce market in Rome. I stopped by a vendor who was selling only mushrooms—baskets of mushrooms set proudly on display next to small bags of dried ones. There were cremini and porcini mushrooms, expensive chanterelles, and many other types that I had never seen before. I'm sure many of these mushrooms came from the Apennine Mountains of Abruzzo, an area known for producing fungi of the highest quality! Oh, if I only had a kitchen in my hotel room! I resisted the urge to buy the lovely fresh ones, but I did leave with a small bag of dried porcini. Here is the perfect recipe for which only the best Abruzzese mushrooms will do. It calls for mushroom varieties that are readily available in most high-end supermarkets in the United States. Quick and delicious, it highlights the wonderful, earthy flavor of mushrooms. It pairs well with both a hearty Sangiovese wine from Tuscany or a sophisticated Gavi from Piedmont.

Olive oil, for sautéing
5 green onions, chopped
4 cloves garlic, sliced
3⅓ lbs. assorted mushrooms (porcini, cremini, and oyster), sliced
Salt and black pepper to taste
¾ cup white wine
5 tbsp. butter
2 tbsp. finely chopped, firmly packed Italian flat leaf parsley
2 tbsp. finely chopped, firmly packed thyme
1 lb. *tagliatelle*
Grated or shaved Parmigiano Reggiano cheese, for topping

Coat the bottom of a 5½ quart frying pan generously with olive oil, set it over medium-low heat, and sauté the green onions and garlic until soft. Add the mushrooms and season with salt and black pepper. Continue sautéing until the mushrooms are soft. Add the wine, butter, parsley, and thyme and continue sautéing until the liquid has reduced to a sauce. Remove the frying pan from the burner.

Meanwhile, fill a 12 quart pot ¾ of the way with water, add 3 tablespoons of salt, and bring to a boil. Add the pasta. When the pasta is *al dente*, set the frying pan back over low heat and transfer the pasta to the frying pan. Toss the pasta well and sauté for two minutes to marry the flavors of the sauce to the pasta. If necessary, add some pasta cooking water or olive oil to moisten and adjust the seasoning. Serve hot, topped with grated or shaved Parmigiano-Reggiano cheese. Serves 4 to 6 adults.

Cavatelli e Broccoli (Cavatelli with Broccoli, Sundried Tomatoes, and Pine Nuts)

BASILICATA

Cavatelli and broccoli is an old family recipe. The first time my wife tried it was also the first time she met my mother. We were invited to my brother's house for dinner. My mother was late, as usual. She had been cooking all morning, got stuck in traffic, and had a migraine. Needless to say, when she stepped in the door of my brother's house carrying five pounds of cavatelli and broccoli, she was not smiling. The only words out of my brother's mouth were "uh oh!" We all knew to stay out of mom's way, but there was an important introduction that had to be made. My brother whispered to my wife, "Run while you can!" My wife stood her ground with a big, heart-warming smile. They said hello, and my mother cracked a smile back. My brother and I both sighed with relief. Thereafter, my wife and mother warmed up to each other nicely. Now, whenever we eat cavatelli and broccoli, we laugh about the fateful day when they first met!

In Basilicata and Campania, cavatelli are traditionally eaten on holidays, festive occasions, and at Sunday dinners—when the entire family gathers around the table to eat and be merry. The cavatelli would no doubt be made fresca, *or fresh that morning, and laid on a linen table cloth until it was time for them to take a plunge into a pot of boiling water. Two minutes later, they would be tossed into the* scula pasta, *or strainer, and quickly dressed. In Basilicata, cavatelli are usually topped with tomato sauce and served with* polpette *(meatballs). However, in springtime, they're likely to be tossed with vegetables sautéed in plenty of olive oil with garlic. No matter what the condiment, a good sprinkle of shaved pecorino cheese is the perfect finishing touch!*

Olive oil, for sautéing
5 cloves garlic, sliced
Crushed red pepper flakes to taste
Salt and black pepper to taste
⅓ cup pine nuts, toasted
¾ cup sliced jarred sundried tomatoes preserved in olive oil
2 tbsp. finely chopped, firmly packed oregano

2 tbsp. finely chopped, firmly packed basil
2 large heads broccoli (without the stem), chopped into florets
1 lb. cavatelli *(see page 117)*
Grated or shaved Pecorino Romano cheese, for topping

Fill a 12 quart pot ¾ of the way with water, add 3 tablespoons of salt, and bring to a boil. Meanwhile, coat the bottom of a 5½ quart frying pan generously with olive oil and set it over medium-low heat. Add the garlic, season with red pepper flakes, salt, and black pepper, and sauté until the garlic is soft. Remove the frying pan from the heat and stir in the pine nuts, sundried tomatoes, oregano, and basil.

When the water comes up to a boil, blanch the broccoli for 1 minute or until tender but still firm. Transfer the broccoli to the frying pan using a skimmer, toss everything together, and season with salt.

Prepare the cavatelli and add them to the pot of boiling water according to the instructions on page 117. When the cavatelli are done, transfer them to the frying pan and toss again. If necessary, drizzle with olive oil to moisten and adjust the seasoning. Serve hot, topped with grated or shaved Pecorino Romano cheese. Serves 4 to 6 adults.

Penne con Pomodorini (Penne with Sautéed Cherry Tomatoes, Garlic, and Herbs)

CALABRIA

One afternoon, I strolled through the back streets of Lipari, a charming port town on an enchanting island off the coast of Calabria. While most people were at the beach, I was meandering along the walls of the old citadel, which rises above the tiny port. I soon found myself on a quiet street of pastel houses with small front gardens enclosed by walls. I strolled past one house whose owner had quite the green thumb. Neatly arranged alongside the house and walkway were pots from which vegetables and plump, red cherry tomatoes were growing. The clusters of tomatoes were so plentiful, I thought, "Surely a handful would not be missed." Were it not for a dog sleeping with one eye open, I would have hopped the wall to snatch a few! In Calabria, sweet cherry tomatoes are cultivated almost year round in rows of greenhouses that stretch across the coastal plains near Santa Eufemia. Calabresi love to cook with their prized pomodorini. *I like them best sliced and tossed with pasta or baked on a pizza. Here is a quick and easy recipe that I make in the summer with cherry tomatoes and herbs picked straight from my garden. It's bright, fresh, and bursting with flavor. Toss in some Kalamata olives, capers, and chopped anchovies for a great take on* puttanesca!

1 lb. penne pasta	3 tbsp. finely chopped, firmly packed oregano
Olive oil, for sautéing	
5 cloves garlic, sliced	Crushed red pepper flakes to taste
1¾ dry quarts cherry tomatoes, sliced in half	Salt and black pepper to taste
3 tbsp. finely chopped, firmly packed basil	Grated or shaved Pecorino Romano cheese, for topping

Fill a 12 quart pot ¾ of the way with water, add 3 tablespoons of salt, and bring to a boil. Add the pasta. Meanwhile, coat the bottom of a 5½ quart frying pan generously with olive oil, set the frying pan over medium-low heat, and sauté the garlic until soft. Add the cherry tomatoes, basil, and oregano and season with red pepper flakes, salt, and black pepper. Continue sautéing for another 3 to 5 minutes or until the cherry tomatoes start to pucker and release some of their juices. Then remove the frying pan from the heat.

When the pasta is *al dente*, set the frying pan back over medium-low heat and transfer the pasta to the frying pan. Toss everything together and sauté for 2 minutes to marry the flavors of the sauce to the pasta. If necessary, add some pasta cooking water or olive oil to moisten and adjust the seasoning. Serve hot, topped with grated or shaved Pecorino Romano cheese. Serves 4 to 6 adults.

Trenette con Acciughe, Cipolle, e Mollica di Pane (Trenette with Anchovies, Sautéed Onions, and Toasted Bread Crumbs)

SICILY

In Sicily, any discussion about anchovies is sure to end in a heated debate. Some say the best anchovies come from the port of Sciacca, and others argue that the best come from the nearby town of Licata. As debates in Sicily might go, I wonder if any thought is ever given to the fact that both towns get their anchovies from the very same sea! Whether you choose anchovies from Sciacca or Licata for this dish is up to you. But be sure to use high quality, Italian, jarred anchovies in olive oil. The anchovy fillets should be thick, meaty, and deep reddish-brown in color. The tiny, mushy fillets that come in small pull-top tins are no substitute and will only ruin your dish. It is my family's tradition to serve this simple dish of pasta with anchovies and onions on Christmas Eve. As my wife will tell you, the pleasant nutty flavor of the anchovies, the sweetness of the sautéed onion, and the pungent bite of garlic and black pepper create a taste sensation beyond compare. Be sure to serve this dish with a glass of white Sicilian wine from Casteldaccia.

1 lb. *trenette*
Olive oil, for sautéing
2 jumbo Spanish onions, chopped
5 cloves garlic, sliced
1 jar (4 oz.) Italian anchovies in olive oil, chopped, divided

Black pepper to taste
Toasted bread crumbs, for topping
(see page 122)

Fill a 12 quart pot ¾ of the way with water, add 3 tablespoons of salt, and bring to a boil. Add the pasta. Meanwhile, coat the bottom of a 5½ quart frying pan generously with olive oil, set it over low heat, and sauté the onions until soft. Add the garlic and half of the chopped anchovies, season with black pepper, and continue to sauté for another minute or until the garlic is soft and the anchovies have melted.

When the pasta is *al dente*, add it to the frying pan along with the remaining chopped anchovies and toss everything together. Serve hot, topped with toasted bread crumbs. Serves 4 to 6 adults.

Spaghetti Primavera Romana (Spaghetti with Artichokes, Fava Beans, and Peas)

LAZIO

If you love artichokes, then head to the coastal town of Ladispoli in April for the annual Sagra del Carciofo, or artichoke festival. The festival is a perfect day trip when spending time in the Eternal City! Halfway between the port of Civitavecchia and Rome, Ladispoli is easily accessible by autostrada *and train. So be forewarned, there is sure to be a hoard of day-trippers pushing their way through the streets and standing in line in front of the food stands. Ladispoli is just one of several towns in Lazio that pays homage to the artichoke each spring—and rightly so! The best artichokes in Italy are grown on Lazio's fertile coastal plain, including the purple Roman variety known as* Romanesco. *If you attend one of Lazio's artichoke festivals, you will see artichokes prepared in both traditional and inventive, modern ways. You may even see artichoke ice cream!*

Tender, young artichokes, fava beans, and sweet peas herald the beginning of springtime in the coastal regions of Lazio that stretch from Rome north to the border of Tuscany. This is a prime agricultural region where the fertile soil has produced plentiful crops since the days of the ancient Etruscans. A welcome departure from the heavy foods of winter, this is a dish that can simply be called Primavera Romana. If you cannot find fresh fava beans in your local market, try asparagus tips instead. Top this light pasta dish with a sprinkle of shaved Pecorino Romano cheese and serve it with a glass of white Vernaccia wine from nearby Tuscany and you will have a meal straight from the heart of Lazio!

Juice of 2 lemons

2 lbs. baby artichokes (about 2½ inches long)

Olive oil, for roasting and sautéing

Salt and black pepper to taste

2 lbs. fava beans in the pod (yields 1½ cups beans)

1 lb. spaghetti

4 green onions, chopped

4 cloves garlic, sliced

1½ cups frozen peas, thawed

1½ tbsp. finely chopped, firmly packed Italian flat leaf parsley

1½ tbsp. finely chopped, firmly packed oregano

1½ tbsp. finely chopped, firmly packed basil

Grated or shaved Pecorino Romano cheese, for topping

Squeeze the lemon juice into a large bowl of cold water, enough to cover the artichoke hearts entirely. Remove the outer leaves of the artichokes until you reach the soft, pale inner cone. Remove the top ⅓ of the cone and peel the stems. Cut the artichokes in half and drop them into the acidulated water to prevent browning.

When all of the artichokes have been prepared and you are ready to roast them, drain them in a colander and pat them dry. Preheat the oven to 415 degrees. Place the artichokes in a large mixing bowl, drizzle with olive oil, season with salt and black pepper, and toss well. Spread the artichokes evenly on a baking tray, cover it with aluminum foil, and roast for 15 minutes. Remove the aluminum foil and continue baking for another 10 to 12 minutes or until lightly crisp and golden.

Shell 1 cup of fava beans. Fill a 4½ quart pot ⅔ of the way with water, add 2½ teaspoons of salt, and bring to a boil. Boil the beans for 20 minutes or until tender. Allow the beans to cool and then remove the skins. Fill a 12 quart pot ¾ of the way with water, add 3 tablespoons of salt, and bring to a boil. Add the pasta. Coat the bottom of a 5½ quart frying pan generously with olive oil, set it over medium-low heat, and sauté the green onions and garlic until soft. Add the peas, artichokes, fava beans, parsley, oregano, and basil and season with salt and black pepper. Toss well and remove the frying pan from the burner.

When the pasta is *al dente*, set the frying pan back over medium-low heat and transfer the pasta to the frying pan. Toss everything together and sauté for two minutes to marry the flavors of the sauce to the pasta. If necessary, add some pasta cooking water or olive oil to moisten and adjust the seasoning. Serve hot, topped with grated or shaved Pecorino Romano cheese. Serves 4 to 6 adults.

Ziti alla Norma (Ziti with Eggplant, Tomatoes, Mozzarella, and Dry Ricotta)

SICILY

Pasta with fried eggplant is the tasty signature dish of Catania. You may ask: Who is Norma and how was this dish named? As the story goes, Norma is not a person. This ziti was actually named in honor of the famous opera Norma, *which was written by composer Vincenzo Bellini in the early 1800s. Bellini was a native of Catania, but no one can say for sure whether pasta with eggplant was his favorite dish. Regardless, he was greatly admired by his native city, and they could not have chosen something more delicious to commemorate his achievement. Even if you're not a fan of the opera, you will sing the praises of this dish! The condiment for the pasta is the perfect marriage of mild eggplant and tangy, sweet tomatoes. A sprinkle of briny, shredded ricotta salata cheese and pungent fresh basil add contrasting, bold flavors that are typical of Sicily's vibrant cuisine. For my signature touch, I add cubes of creamy young* caciocavallo *or mozzarella cheese that melt into the hot pasta. It is decadent and delicious. For an authentic treat, serve it with a glass of Sicilian Nero d'Avola red wine.*

2 lbs. large, plump purple eggplants
Olive oil, for brushing and sautéing
Salt and black pepper to taste
½ large Spanish or Vidalia onion, diced
5 cloves garlic, sliced
2½ cans (28 oz. each) whole, peeled San Marzano tomatoes, diced (juice reserved)

3 tbsp. finely chopped, firmly packed basil
2 tsp. dried oregano
Crushed red pepper flakes to taste
1 lb. ziti
¾ lb. fresh mozzarella cheese, cubed
Ricotta salata cheese, for topping

Preheat the oven to 400 degrees. Slice the eggplants into ½ inch thick rounds, brush them with olive oil, and season them with salt and black pepper. Place the rounds on baking trays that have been lightly brushed with olive oil. Roast the rounds for 15 minutes, flip, and continue roasting for another 10 to 15 minutes or until soft and golden on both sides.

Coat the bottom of a 5½ quart frying pan generously with olive oil and set it over medium-low heat. Sauté the onion until soft, add the garlic, and continue sautéing for another minute. Add the tomatoes and their juice, basil, and oregano. Season with salt and red pepper flakes. Reduce the heat to low and simmer for 15 minutes.

Fill a 12 quart pot ¾ of the way with water, add 3 tablespoons of salt, and bring to a boil. Add the pasta. When the eggplant rounds are done, slice them into strips, add them to the frying pan, toss everything together, and continue simmering on low heat for another 10 minutes. If the sauce becomes too thick, add a ladle of pasta cooking water to the frying pan.

When the pasta is *al dente*, transfer it to the frying pan, toss, and adjust the seasoning if necessary. Fold the mozzarella into the pasta and quickly transfer it to individual serving plates before the mozzarella melts. Top with plenty of shaved ricotta salata cheese. Serve hot. Serves 4 to 6 adults.

Ziti con Verdure Verde e Fagioli (Pasta with Sautéed Mixed Greens, Chickpeas, Cannelini Beans, and Prosciutto)

CAMPANIA

One summer, my friends Rita and Salvo came to the United States for a visit. I invited them to my home for a Sunday dinner feast. They arrived at noon for a meal that would last all day long. We started with antipasto and then moved on to pasta. Next, I brought out roasted pork, potatoes, vegetables, and salad. When I placed a bowl of sautéed Swiss chard and cannellini beans on the table, Salvo exclaimed, "Napoletano!" I smiled and replied, "Vero!" He then explained to everyone that Neapolitans are known throughout Italy for stewing greens with beans. "They make it the very best and eat it all the time," he said. I told Salvo that I know this to be true, as my grandmother's family was from Campania; what I prepared for everyone was her family's recipe. Rita then commented, "I thought you were all Sicilian, but now I learn that you also have Neapolitan blood. No wonder you make such marvelous tomato sauce, too!"

Fresh leafy greens and beans are staples of the Campanese countryside. It therefore stands to reason that they are often prepared with pasta. Here is a rustic pasta dish from the heart of Campania. You can use whatever combination of greens and beans you like best. My favorites for mixing and matching are escarole, spinach, Tuscan kale, or Swiss chard with chickpeas, cannellini, borlotti, or kidney beans. Choose whatever combination you prefer or simply buy whatever is freshest in the market that day. I love using Swiss chard or Tuscan kale picked fresh from my vegetable garden.

Olive oil, for sautéing
5 cloves garlic, sliced
4 oz. slab prosciutto, diced
1 lb. Tuscan kale, stalks removed and chopped
2 cups water
Crushed red pepper flakes to taste (optional)
Paprika to taste
Salt and black pepper to taste

1½ lbs. Swiss chard, stalks removed and chopped
1 jar (10 oz.) sundried tomatoes preserved in olive oil, sliced into strips
1 can (15 oz.) cannellini beans, drained
1 can (15 oz.) chickpeas, drained
1 lb. *ziti* or *rigatoni*
Grated or shaved Pecorino Romano cheese, for topping

Coat the bottom of a 5½ quart frying pan generously with olive oil, set it over medium-low heat, add the garlic and prosciutto, and sauté until the garlic is soft. Add the kale and the water, which will allow the greens to steam. Season with red pepper flakes, paprika, salt, and black pepper and sauté the kale for 10 minutes or until wilted and tender. Add the Swiss chard and continue sautéing for another 5 minutes or until it is wilted and tender. Stir in the sundried tomatoes, cannellini beans, and chickpeas and remove the frying pan from the burner.

Fill a 12 quart pot ¾ of the way with water, add 3 tablespoons of salt, and bring to a boil. Add the pasta. When the pasta is *al dente*, set the frying pan back over low heat and transfer the pasta to the frying pan. Toss everything together and sauté for two minutes to marry the flavors of the sauce to the pasta. If necessary, add some pasta cooking water or olive oil to moisten and adjust the seasoning. Serve hot, topped with grated or shaved Pecorino Romano cheese. Serves 4 to 6 adults.

Ziti con Baccala, Pomodorini, e Olive (Ziti with Salted Cod, Cherry Tomatoes, and Gaeta Olives)

BASILICATA

The mighty Atlantic cod has earned a prominent place in Italian cuisine, even though it is not native to the Mediterranean Basin. In fact, the chances of ever catching cod off the coast of Southern Italy are quite slim. Cod is more likely to arrive in Italy preserved in salt and packed in a box! This most beloved fish of the Italian people actually comes from the far ends of the North Atlantic. Needless to say, it must be transported many miles before reaching its final destination in kitchens across Italy—hence the salt. Salted cod, or baccala, *was introduced to the Italian peninsula by Northern European merchants many centuries ago, before the advent of modern refrigeration. When the abundant fishing grounds of the new world were discovered, it became even more widely available in Southern Europe. The Italians embraced* baccala *as a safe, nonperishable food source and devised creative and tasty ways to prepare it. Today, many centuries later, it is still a favorite. What would a traditional Christmas Eve dinner in Southern Italy be without at least one* baccala *dish? Try this recipe and you will understand why it is still so popular! Chunks of flaky* baccala *are sautéed with cherry tomatoes, red bell pepper, olives, and briny capers and then tossed with perfectly cooked* ziti. *Plenty of garlic and crushed red chili flakes give this dish the bold character of Basilicatese cuisine.*

2 lbs. salted cod fillets	1 cup pitted, halved Gaeta or Kalamata olives
⅓ cup Sicilian capers preserved in salt	
Olive oil, for sautéing	2 tbsp. finely chopped, firmly packed basil
½ Spanish or Vidalia onion, diced	
1 large red bell pepper, seeded and diced	2 tbsp. finely chopped, firmly packed oregano
4 large cloves garlic, sliced	Crushed red pepper flakes to taste
¾ dry quart cherry tomatoes, sliced in half	Salt and black pepper to taste
	1 lb. *ziti* or *rigatoni*

Soak the *baccala* in plenty of cool water for at least 48 hours and change the water at least 3 times daily. The fillets will rehydrate and become soft and pliable. When the *baccala* is ready, remove the fillets from the water, cut them into 1 inch chunks, and set them to simmer in a pot of water for 10 minutes. Meanwhile, remove the salt from the capers by soaking them in warm water for 15 minutes and then rinsing them under running water.

Coat the bottom of a large 5½ quart frying pan generously with olive oil, set it over medium-low heat, and sauté the onion and red bell pepper until soft. Add the garlic, cherry tomatoes, olives, capers, basil, and oregano and season with red pepper flakes, salt, and black pepper. Continue sautéing for another 5 minutes or until the cherry tomatoes have softened and released their juices. When the *baccala* is ready, drain it well, break it into large flakes, add it to the frying pan, toss everything together, and sauté for another 2 minutes to marry the flavors. Remove the frying pan from the burner.

Fill a 12 quart pot ¾ of the way with water, add 3 tablespoons of salt, and bring to a boil. Add the pasta. When the pasta is *al dente*, set the frying pan back over low heat and transfer the pasta to the frying pan. Toss everything together and sauté for two minutes to marry the flavors of the sauce to the pasta. If necessary, add some pasta cooking water or olive oil to moisten and adjust the seasoning. Serve hot. Serves 4 to 6 adults.

Perciatelli con le Sarde (Perciatelli with Sardines and Sicilian Fennel Sauce)

SICILY

Saint Joseph has long been the patron saint of Sicily's poor. In Santa Margherita and other towns in the Val di Belice, Saint Joseph's Day is celebrated on March 19 with a glorious meal that is sure to include grilled fish, fried vegetables, stewed fava beans, stuffed artichokes, and pasta with sardines and fennel. The food is typically displayed on a long table called "la tavola di San Giuseppe," which is set before a tiered altar bearing a statue of Saint Joseph and fancy, decorative breads shaped into rings and crosses. My Sicilian grandparents made their Saint Joseph's table in the basement of their home in Newark, New Jersey, and they always invited children from the local orphanage to dine with them. What a treat it must have been for the kids! Here is my grandmother's recipe for pasta with sardines and fennel. We call it Pasta San Giuseppe. The sauce is an exotic mix of sardines, Sicilian fennel, chopped tomatoes, pine nuts, and raisins. It is tossed with a tubular pasta called perciatelli and then topped with plenty of toasted bread crumbs. It is a dish straight from the heart of the Val di Belice. For a truly authentic taste, be sure to use an imported Sicilian fennel condiment called Condimento Completo per Pasta con le Sarde. It is widely available at Italian markets in the United States, especially around Saint Joseph's Day.

Olive oil, for sautéing
½ small Spanish onion, diced
3 cloves garlic, finely chopped
3 cans (28 oz. each) whole, peeled San Marzano tomatoes (juice reserved)
2 cans (14.5 oz. each) Sicilian fennel condiment
1 tin (4.5 oz.) boneless sardine fillets in olive oil

2 tbsp. pine nuts, toasted
⅓ cup firmly packed raisins
Salt and black pepper to taste
1 lb. *perciatelli*
Toasted bread crumbs, for topping
(see page 122)

Coat the bottom of a saucepan with olive oil, set it over medium-low heat, and sauté the onion until soft. Add the garlic and sauté for another minute. Place the tomatoes and their juice in a food processor or blender and pulse a few times until you achieve a pulpy sauce. Add the tomato sauce to the pot along with the fennel condiment, sardines, pine nuts, and raisins. Season with salt and black pepper and simmer over low heat for 45 minutes.

Meanwhile, fill a 12 quart pot ¾ of the way with water, add 3 tablespoons of salt, and bring to a boil. Add the pasta. When the pasta is *al dente*, drain it well and toss it with a few ladles of sauce to moisten. Serve hot, topped with more sauce and toasted bread crumbs. Serves 4 to 6 adults.

Spaghetti con Vongole e Prosciutto (Spaghetti with Clams, Prosciutto, and Red Bell Pepper)

CAMPANIA

Who doesn't love spaghetti and clams? This popular combination is enjoyed all over Italy. In Sicily, it is made with olive oil and garlic. In Campania, they throw diced San Marzano tomatoes into the mix, and Venetians add a few pats of butter and a splash of white wine. This is my version, which truly stands apart. Red bell pepper adds sweetness that contrasts nicely with the briny clams. A handful of diced prosciutto adds delicious pork flavor that gives the dish extra character. It is the sort of dish you might find along the chic Costiera Amalfitana, where the elite of Rome and Naples spend their summers. Along this stretch of magnificent, rugged coastline, you will find some of Italy's most luxurious hotels and top restaurants where inventive chefs prepare the local dishes in tasty and extravagant ways. If you prefer, try this recipe with fresh Atlantic mussels or create a grand *mare chiara by adding mussels, shrimp, and squid. Adding more seafood is simple! Just peel and devein the shrimp and slice the squid into rings. After the shellfish have steamed opened, toss in the shrimp and squid and let it simmer for another 5 minutes or until they are firm.*

Olive oil, for sautéing
5 green onions, diced
1 red bell pepper, diced
5 cloves garlic, sliced
4 oz. slab prosciutto, diced
3 or 4 dozen littleneck clams, or other small variety (depending on size)
1 cup white wine
Crushed red pepper flakes to taste (optional)

Salt and black pepper to taste
1 lb. spaghetti
3 tbsp. butter
2 tbsp. finely chopped, firmly packed Italian flat leaf parsley
2 tbsp. finely chopped, firmly packed thyme or oregano

Fill a 12 quart pot ¾ of the way with water, add 3 tablespoons of salt, and bring to a boil. Meanwhile, coat the bottom of a 5½ quart frying pan generously with olive oil, set it over medium-low heat, and sauté the green onion and red bell pepper until soft. Add the garlic and prosciutto and continue sautéing for another minute. Add the clams and wine and season with red pepper flakes, salt, and black pepper. Cover the frying pan and sauté for 5 to 7 minutes or until all of the shells have opened.

Meanwhile, drop the pasta in the boiling water. When the shells are open, stir in the butter, parsley, and thyme or oregano and then remove the frying pan from the burner. If any clams do not open, discard them.

When the pasta is *al dente*, set the frying pan back over low heat and transfer the pasta to the frying pan. Toss everything together and sauté for two minutes to marry the flavors of the sauce to the pasta. If necessary, add some olive oil to moisten and adjust the seasoning. Serve hot. Serves 4 to 6 adults.

Orecchiette con Salsiccia e Bietola (Orecchiette with Pork Sausage, Swiss Chard, Leeks, and Green Olives)

APULIA

The plain of northern Apulia is called le Tavoliere, which means "the table." It stretches between the foothills of the Apennine Mountains and the Adriatic Sea. This area has long been referred to as the "granary of Italy" because here, wheat is king! If you travel to le Tavoliere, I recommend staying at an agriturismo housed in a traditional masseria, which is a fortified country estate. In a typical masseria the main house and outbuildings are clustered around a courtyard and are protected by a perimeter wall. These historic structures were built during the sixteenth century by wealthy landowners and nobility who controlled vast acres of wheat fields and olive groves. Many of the masseria have been meticulously restored and converted into bed and breakfasts or small boutique hotels. They are a true step back in time!

In le Tavoliere, pasta is always made with flour milled from the finest locally grown durum wheat. A traditional masseria will include a mulino, a building with a mill to grind kernels of wheat into flour. The flour is then used to make the finest spaghetti and hand-rolled short pasta. In this recipe, the traditional pasta of the region, orecchiette, is tossed with sautéed pork sausage, Swiss chard, leeks, and briny green olives from Cerignola. Topped with flakes of sharp, aged pecorino cheese, this dish is Pugliese cooking at its finest! It is the sort of homestyle fare you are sure to be served at an agriturismo in le Tavoliere. Pair it with a glass of assertive, red Primitivo wine from the region.

Olive oil, for sautéing
1¼ lbs. Italian pork sausage, removed from the casing
½ Spanish or Vidalia onion, diced
2 leeks, trimmed and diced
Salt and black pepper to taste
5 cloves garlic, sliced
2 lbs. Swiss chard, stalks removed and chopped

2 cups water
¾ cup pitted, halved green Cerignola or Castelvetrano olives
2 tbsp. butter
1 lb. *orecchiette*
Grated or shaved Pecorino Romano cheese, for topping

Brush the bottom of a 5½ quart frying pan with olive oil and set it over medium-low heat. Brown the sausage, breaking it up with the back of a wooden spoon. When the sausage is fully cooked, drain off any excess grease and set the sausage to the side.

Coat the bottom of the frying pan generously with olive oil and set it over low heat. Add the onions and leeks, season with salt and black pepper, and sauté for 10 minutes or until soft and caramelized. Add the garlic and continue sautéing for another minute. Add the Swiss chard and the water, which will allow the greens to steam. Raise the heat to medium and continue sautéing for 7 minutes or until the Swiss chard is wilted and tender. Then stir in the olives, sausage, and butter and remove the frying pan from the heat.

Fill a 12 quart pot ¾ of the way with water, add 3 tablespoons of salt, and bring to a boil. Add the pasta. When the pasta is *al dente*, set the frying pan back over low heat and transfer the pasta to the frying pan with a skimmer. Toss everything together and sauté for two minutes to marry the flavors of the sauce to the pasta. If necessary, add some pasta cooking water or olive oil to moisten and adjust the seasoning. Serve hot, topped with grated or shaved Pecorino Romano cheese. Serves 4 adults.

Tagliatelle con Ragu alla Napoletana (Tagliatelle with Neapolitan Meat Sauce)

CAMPANIA

Each region of Italy has its own version of meat sauce, or ragu. *Most recipes call for a combination of two or more ground meats such as beef, pork, and veal. In some places, diced celery, carrots, and onions are used as an aromatic base, and in other places a few good splashes of red wine lend flavor. In Emilia Romagna, they add a touch of cream to soften the tangy bite of the tomatoes for a classic* ragu alla Bolognese. *In Tuscany, rosemary is always the herb of choice, whereas in Calabria, no meat sauce would be complete without a few generous pinches of crushed red chili flakes. The variations are truly endless, and each version is as delicious as the next! My version of* ragu *is simple, quick, and tasty. It is flavored with herbs and spices typical of southern Campania, as they go best with San Marzano tomatoes. I use ground sirloin and a high-quality Italian pork sausage. I skip the ground veal and toss in some finely minced prosciutto instead. The wonderful flavor of the prosciutto adds an extra depth of rich pork flavor that always has my dinner guests saying "Bravissimo!" Be sure to pair it with a bold Montepulciano d'Abruzzo red wine.*

Olive oil, for sautéing
1 small Spanish or Vidalia onion, diced
3 oz. thinly sliced prosciutto
4 cloves garlic, finely chopped
5 cans (28 oz.) crushed San Marzano tomatoes
2½ tbsp. finely chopped, firmly packed basil
2½ tbsp. finely chopped, firmly packed oregano
Crushed red pepper flakes to taste
Salt and black pepper to taste
1½ lbs. Italian pork sausage
2 lb. ground sirloin (93% lean)
1 lb. *tagliatelle*
Grated or shaved Pecorino Romano cheese, for topping

Coat the bottom of a large pot with olive oil, set it over medium-low heat, and sauté the onion until soft. Mince the prosciutto and add it to the pot. Add the garlic and sauté for another minute. Add the crushed tomatoes, basil, and oregano, season with red pepper flakes, salt, and black pepper, and turn the heat to low.

Remove the sausage from the casing. Brush the bottom of a frying pan with olive oil and set it over medium-low heat. Brown the sausage, breaking it up with the back of a wooden spoon. When the sausage is fully cooked, drain off any excess grease and add the sausage to the sauce. Then season the ground sirloin lightly with salt, brown it in the frying pan, and add it to the sauce.

Simmer the *ragu* for 1 hour, stirring frequently and adjusting the seasoning if necessary. Meanwhile, fill a 12 quart pot ¾ of the way with water, add 3 tablespoons of salt, and bring to a boil. Add the pasta. When the pasta is *al dente*, drain it well and toss it with a few ladles of the *ragu*. Serve hot, topped with more *ragu* and plenty of grated or shaved Pecorino Romano cheese. Serves 4 to 6 adults with plenty of sauce left over for another meal.

Rigatoni con Ragu di Cinghiale Finto (Rigatoni with Faux Wild Boar Sauce)

ABRUZZO/MOLISE

Spend some time meandering through the hill towns of Abruzzo's Gran Sasso National Park and you are sure to see wild boar on the menu at the local restaurants. Gran Sasso is the largest preserve of natural forest and rugged alpine terrain in the Apennines. Here, wild game is plentiful—including boar, which roam the wooded slopes surrounding ancient towns such as Pietracamela. Wild boar is a favorite from the northern reaches of Tuscany south to Lazio and Abruzzo. The Umbrians, however, are said to prepare it best—in a hearty ragu *that is then tossed with large tubular pasta. But don't mention this to a proud Abruzzese nonna from Pietracamela! She'll be inclined to argue that her* ragu *is much better.*

I enjoyed a wonderful wild boar ragu *while travelling through the Apennines. It was made with plenty of diced porcini mushrooms and flavored with a bold red wine and fresh herbs. When I returned home, I was determined to re-create the dish. But there was just one dilemma. Where do I get wild boar? It is not available at the supermarkets where I live in rural Virginia. Unless I head into the woods with a shotgun, the chances of me finding wild boar are slim to none! That being said, here is my best shot at reproducing the amazing* ragu *that I enjoyed in the mountains of Abruzzo. I use boneless country pork ribs. Hence the term* finto, *or faux boar sauce! It is almost as good as the real thing. Toss the* ragu *with a substantial pasta such as* rigatoni *or* buccatini *and you will have the ultimate Apennine meal!*

5 cans (28 oz. each) whole, peeled San Marzano tomatoes	2 tbsp. finely chopped, firmly packed basil
Olive oil, for sautéing and drizzling	2 tbsp. finely chopped, firmly packed oregano
1 carrot, peeled and diced	Salt and black pepper to taste
1 rib celery, diced	2.5 lbs. boneless country pork ribs
½ large Spanish or Vidalia onion, diced	2 lbs. cremini mushrooms, sliced
5 cloves garlic, finely chopped	2 lbs. *rigatoni* or *buccatini*
¾ cup red wine	Grated or shaved Pecorino Romano cheese, for topping
1 tbsp. finely chopped, firmly packed rosemary	

Pulse the tomatoes and all of the juice from the cans in a food processor to achieve a pulpy consistency and set aside. Coat the bottom of a large pot with olive oil, set it over medium-low heat, and sauté the carrot, celery, and onion until soft. Add the garlic and sauté for another minute. Add the wine, tomatoes, rosemary, basil, and oregano, season with salt and black pepper, and allow the sauce to simmer over low heat.

Cut the meat into 4 inch chunks and season with salt and black pepper. Coat the bottom of a frying pan with olive oil and set it over medium heat. Brown the meat on all sides and then add it to the sauce. Allow the sauce to simmer for 3 hours, stirring frequently.

Meanwhile, preheat the oven to 425 degrees. Toss the mushrooms with a drizzle of olive oil, season them with salt, and place them in a baking dish. Tent the baking dish with aluminum foil and roast the mushrooms for 40 minutes or until tender. Add the mushrooms and their juice to the sauce.

After the sauce has simmered for 3 hours, remove the meat from the pot, slice the chunks into smaller pieces, and then shred the pieces with a fork. Return the shredded meat to the pot and allow the *ragu* to simmer for another 10 minutes. Adjust the seasoning if necessary.

Meanwhile, fill a 12 quart pot ¾ of the way with water, add 3 tablespoons of salt, and bring to a boil. Add the pasta. When the pasta is *al dente*, toss it with some of the *ragu*. Serve hot, topped with more *ragu* and grated or shaved Pecorino Romano cheese. Serves 6 to 8 adults with plenty of sauce left over for another meal.

Ziti con Melanzane e Salsiccia in Forno (Baked Pasta Casserole with Ricotta, Pork Sausage, and Roasted Eggplant)

CALABRIA

Who doesn't love ricotta cheese? Whether tossed with pasta, baked in a calzone, or sweetened with sugar for the ultimate cannoli filling, ricotta is always creamy and delicious. So what exactly is this wonderful cheese? In Italian, ricotta *means "re-cooked." As the name implies, ricotta is made by re-cooking the whey that is separated from the curds during the cheesemaking process. The re-cooked whey produces a second curd that is then turned into the soft, creamy ricotta that everyone loves. Today, ricotta is produced in whole milk, part skim, and fat free varieties. Unless eating healthy is an obsession, stick with whole milk or part skim. Fat-free ricotta just isn't the same!*

This is my family's recipe for a baked pasta casserole. I use plenty of creamy ricotta flavored with grated Parmigiano-Reggiano cheese and fresh parsley. A crisp topping and gooey mozzarella that pulls into strings when the pasta is scooped make this dish irresistible. With strips of flavorful roasted eggplant and crumbled sausage, it is a hearty one-dish meal typical of the rustic cooking in Calabria, Basilicata, and Campania. If you prefer a less extravagant dish, leave out the eggplant and sausage. For a more substantial dish, add hard-boiled eggs as they do in the countryside near Cosenza. A good sprinkle of crushed red pepper flakes adds even more Calabrese flavor! This is another rustic recipe that you can make all your own, so toss in whatever you like. Prepare it in one large casserole or smaller baking dishes for individual servings.

Olive oil, for brushing
1 large plump, purple eggplant
Salt and black pepper to taste
¾ lb. Italian sausage
1¾ lbs. *ziti*
3½ quarts Salsa Marinara *(see page 121)*

1 lb. mozzarella cheese
2 lbs. ricotta cheese
1 extra-large egg
2 tbsp. finely chopped, firmly packed Italian flat leaf parsley
1¼ cups grated Parmigiano-Reggiano cheese, divided

Preheat the oven to 400 degrees. Brush a baking sheet with olive oil. Slice the eggplant into ½ inch thick rounds. Brush the eggplant rounds on each side with olive oil, season them with salt and black pepper, and place them on the baking sheet. Bake the rounds for 15 minutes, flip, and then continue baking for another 10 to 15 minutes or until they are soft and golden.

Meanwhile, remove the sausage from the casing. Brush the bottom of a frying pan with olive oil and set it over medium-low heat. Brown the sausage, breaking it up with the back of a wooden spoon. When the sausage is fully cooked, drain off any excess grease and set it to the side. When the eggplant rounds are done, cut them into small pieces and set them to the side.

Fill a 12 quart pot ¾ of the way with water, add 3 tablespoons of salt, and bring to a boil. Add the pasta. Meanwhile, heat the Salsa Marinara over low heat and shred the mozzarella. In a mixing bowl, combine the ricotta, egg, parsley, and ¾ cup of grated cheese and season the mixture with salt and black pepper.

When the pasta is *al dente*, drain it well, transfer it to a large mixing bowl, and toss it with the eggplant, sausage, and enough marinara sauce to moisten.

Preheat the oven to 400 degrees. Brush the inside of a 3 inch deep, 10 by 14 inch casserole dish lightly with olive oil. Spread some sauce on the bottom, and then add ½ of the pasta mixture in an even layer. Next, spread over all of the ricotta mixture in an even layer and sprinkle with half of the mozzarella. Spoon some sauce over top and then spread over the remaining pasta. Top the casserole with more sauce, the remaining mozzarella, and the grated cheese. Tent the casserole with aluminum foil and bake for 40 minutes. Remove the foil and bake for another 15 to 20 minutes or until the top is crisp and golden. Serve hot with the remaining marinara sauce on the side. Serves 6 adults.

Gnudi di Spinaci e Ricotta in Forno (Spinach and Ricotta Dumplings Baked with Tomato Sauce and Mozzarella)

LAZIO

The name gnudi *derives from the word* nudo, *which means "nude" in Italian. These soft dumplings are made with ricotta, which is a common filling for ravioli and other stuffed pastas. As there is no pasta covering the dumplings, they are indeed nude, at least by Italian standards.* Gnudi *are popular throughout Italy and are prepared in a variety of ways. They are not only tossed into soups but also baked into tasty casseroles. In many places, they are served as a first course, just like pasta. That is why I have included them in this section. Here is my version, which includes fresh spinach. The soft pillows of sweet ricotta and mild spinach will melt in your mouth. When dressed with tomato sauce and baked in the oven with Mozzarella cheese, they are simply irresistible! For a taste of Northern Italy, try them also baked with* beschamel *sauce and creamy fontina cheese.*

For the dumplings:
9 ounces spinach
1½ cups ricotta cheese
1 cup grated Parmigiano-Reggiano cheese
1 extra-large egg
½ tsp. garlic powder
¼ tsp. black pepper
¼ tsp. salt

¾ cup flour
Olive oil, for brushing

To accompany:
1½ quarts Salsa Marinara *(see page 121)*
½ lb. mozzarella cheese, shredded
Grated Parmigiano-Reggiano cheese, for topping

Fill a 6 quart pot ⅔ of the way with water, add 2 teaspoons of salt, and bring to a boil. Add the spinach and boil until wilted. Drain the spinach in a colander, allow it to cool, squeeze out all of the liquid with your hands, and then finely chop it. Place the ricotta, grated cheese, egg, garlic powder, black pepper, and salt in a large mixing bowl and beat everything together. Stir in the spinach, and then add the flour ¼ cup at a time to form a soft, smooth dough.

Brush a cookie sheet with olive oil and set it next to your stove. Fill a 12 quart pot ¾ of the way with water, add 3 tablespoons of salt, and bring to a low boil. Use two spoons to scoop and shape round dumplings, and then drop them into the boiling water. The dumplings will sink to the bottom. When they float to the top, let them continue boiling for another 45 seconds and then remove them with a skimmer. Transfer the *gnudi* to the cookie sheet and let them rest for 10 minutes.

Preheat the oven to 425 degrees. Coat the bottom of a 10 by 13 inch baking dish with Salsa Marinara, nestle the *gnudi* in the dish, and then spoon more sauce over them. Top the *gnudi* with shredded mozzarella and then sprinkle with plenty of grated Parmigiano-Reggiano. Bake for 15 minutes or until bubbly and golden on top. Serve hot, with marinara sauce on the side. Serves 4 adults.

Crespelle al Forno (Crepes Filled with Ricotta Cheese and Baked with Mozzarella and Tomato Sauce)

ABRUZZO/MOLISE

Crespelle are crepes that are rolled around a savory filling and baked in the oven with plenty of sauce and cheese melted over top. They are a specialty of the Abruzzo and Molise regions. Crespelle are much lighter than cannelloni, which is a similar treat made by rolling sheets of pasta around the filling. In the United States, crespelle are most widely referred to as "manicotti," which is a peculiar name of Italian American origin. Rumor has it that early Italian immigrants started using the term manicotti, which means "sleeve," to describe how the crepe holds the filling. The name caught on, and today, over a century later, manicotti is a popular menu item in most Italian American restaurants. That being said, when you travel through the countryside of Abruzzo, you will not find manicotti on the restaurant menus. You must order Crespelle al Forno instead!

Crespelle can be filled with just about anything and topped with a variety of sauces. At the wedding of Salvo and Rita's daughter in Sicily, they served wonderful crespelle filled with a ragu of veal, pork, and peas and topped with beschamel sauce and fontina cheese. It was a decadent treat, more typical of Northern Italian cuisine than Sicilian. Here is my favorite recipe that is typical of Abruzzo, Molise, and Campania. The delicate crepes are wrapped around creamy ricotta cheese and topped with tomato sauce. For an extra decadent treat, I sometimes top them with mozzarella too!

For the crepes:
1 cup all-purpose, pre-sifted flour
2 eggs
½ cup milk
¾ cup water
1 tbsp. vegetable oil
¼ tsp. salt
Cooking spray

For the filling and to accompany:
2 lbs. ricotta cheese
½ cup grated Parmigiano-Reggiano cheese (plus additional for topping)
1 egg, beaten
1½ tbsp. finely chopped, firmly packed Italian flat leaf parsley
3½ quarts Salsa Marinara (see page 121)
½ lb. mozzarella cheese, shredded

First prepare the crepes: Combine the flour, eggs, milk, water, vegetable oil, and salt and beat until smooth. Allow the batter to rest for 10 minutes. Every so often, stir gently to release any air bubbles. Spray a 10 ½ inch, non-stick frying pan with cooking spray, add ¼ cup of batter, and swirl it around to evenly coat the bottom of the pan. Place the frying pan over low heat. The crepe is done when the batter is firm and completely dry. The crepe only needs to be cooked on one side and does not need to be flipped. Remove the crepe from the frying pan, allow the frying pan to cool for a few minutes, and then continue making crepes.

Prepare the filling. Beat together the ricotta, grated cheese, egg, and parsley. Place a crepe on your work surface, spoon some filling across the middle of the crepe and then roll it up like an eggroll, tucking in the edges so that the filling will not escape. Coat the bottom of a baking dish with Salsa Marinara, nestle the *crespelle* in the baking dish, spoon more sauce over top, and sprinkle with shredded mozzarella and the remaining grated cheese.

Preheat the oven to 375 degrees. Cover the baking dish with aluminum foil and bake for 40 minutes. Then, if you wish, remove the foil and bake a few minutes longer until the cheese on top is golden. Serve hot with more sauce on the side. The batter will make 9 crepes. The filling is enough for 18 crepes. As it is better not to have the batter sit too long, make a second batch of batter to complete the recipe. Serves 9 adults.

To experience the heart and soul of Italy, head to the open air vegetable market. There is one in every city.

VI

Verdure e Contorni (Vegetables and Accompaniments)

Lemons, Hand Gestures, and a Quick Payoff in Sorrento

A Rambling in Campania

One morning, my grandfather took me for a walk in the countryside near Sorrento. I was twelve years old. This was my first trip outside of New Jersey, where we lived. We headed down a quiet road flanked by low stone walls that enclosed neatly planted vegetable gardens, fruit trees, and rows of grape vines clinging to trellises. As we walked, my grandfather pointed out all of the different fruits and vegetables. I enjoyed our stroll in this unfamiliar place. It was nothing like the suburbs of New Jersey. In the distance were small towns clinging to green hills, and beyond the hills were craggy mountain peaks. Rows of palms or tall, slender cypress trees pointed the way from the road to farmhouses, each surrounded by colorful oleander trees and bougainvillea.

We continued our stroll farther away from town. Eventually, we came upon a glorious grove of lemon trees full of bright fruit. I had never seen a lemon tree before, and my grandfather sensed my curiosity. He smiled and then said, "Go ahead and pick some lemons!" I hopped over the low stone wall and ran over to the trees. As I reached for a lemon, I heard a quick, sharp whistle. I looked to my side and saw an old man sitting in a chair next to a small shed. With a stern face, he motioned "no" with his finger, without saying a word. I then ran back to my grandfather, who was waiting by the road.

"What is wrong?" my grandfather said.

"There is an old man sitting by the shed," I replied.

My grandfather glanced over at him. The old man sat there with his arms folded looking back at us. His face was stern. He made eye contact with my grandfather, and once again motioned "no" with his finger. My grandfather was neither impressed nor intimidated. "Pay no attention to that old man, go get some lemons for your grandmother," he said. I hesitated for a moment, and my grandfather reassuringly said, "Go on, don't worry."

I hopped back over the wall and walked slowly towards the lemon trees, keeping an eye on the old man. He became angry and got up from his chair. He grabbed his cane and walked hurriedly over to my grandfather. I stopped in my tracks and waited. The old man stood on one side of the wall, and my grandfather on the other. With elevated voices and a rhapsody of hand gestures, they argued back and forth for a minute in Italian. Then, my grandfather reached into his pocket. He pulled out his wallet and handed something to the old man. The old man tucked it into his shirt pocket, tipped his cap to my grandfather, and walked away without looking in my direction.

My grandfather smiled at me and motioned with his hand. "You go ahead and pick any lemon you want from any tree!" he said.

153

I walked between the trees and when I found the biggest, brightest lemons, I plucked them from the branches. They were almost as big as grapefruits and I could only carry four back in my arms. My grandfather was pleased. He helped me back over the wall, and we started on our way back to town. Soon, we passed more garden plots and a vineyard with large clusters of plump grapes hanging from the vines.

"Grandpa, I think I would like to pick some grapes now," I said.

My grandfather smiled, put his hand across my shoulder, and replied, "I think we have picked enough for today!"

The perfect place for a swim in Tropea, Calabria

Hiking in the mountains above Solunto, Sicily

Vineyards in the Foggia Province of Apulia

Terracotta rooftops in Abruzzo

A shady spot in the whitewashed town of Ostuni, Apulia

A sunny summer day in Agira, Sicily

Scarola con Fagioli (Sautéed Escarole with Cannellini Beans, Garlic, and Paprika)

CAMPANIA

If you travel through the countryside of Campania, expect to find cannellini beans on the menu! After all, the Campanese people, like the Tuscans to the north, are referred to as mangia fagioli, *or "bean-eaters." Cannellini beans are a staple of the countryside in this region and many other parts of central and southern Italy. They are dried in the same manner as chickpeas and lentils and then stored for use throughout the year. Once dried, the cannellini beans must be soaked, preferably overnight, before being cooked in soups, stews, and other hearty dishes. Today cannellini beans are available canned, which eliminates the need for soaking and makes them an easy and convenient ingredient. Like chickpeas and lentils, they are a must in any traditional Italian pantry! In this recipe, the mild flavor and creamy texture of cannellini beans pairs well with sautéed escarole and helps to balance any bitterness. Fresh garlic and a pinch of paprika add a burst of flavor typical of the cuisine of southern Campania. If you prefer, use spinach or Swiss chard instead. It is the perfect, healthy side dish alongside grilled chicken or pork sausage.*

3 medium heads escarole (about 2½ lbs.)
Olive oil, for sautéing
4 cloves garlic, sliced
Paprika to taste
Crushed red pepper flakes to taste (optional)

Salt and black pepper to taste
½ cup water
1 can (15 oz.) cannellini beans, drained
½ cup chopped, firmly packed jarred sundried tomatoes preserved in olive oil (optional)

Remove and discard the core of the escarole and the fibrous stem portion of the leaves. Chop the escarole leaves. Coat the bottom of a 5½ quart frying pan with olive oil, set it over medium-low heat, and sauté the garlic until soft. Add the chopped escarole, season with paprika, red pepper flakes, salt, and black pepper, and add the water, which will allow the greens to steam. Cover the frying pan and sauté the escarole for 10 minutes or until wilted and tender. If necessary, add more water.

When the escarole is done, stir in the beans and sundried tomatoes and continue sautéing for another 3 minutes. Serve hot. Serves 4 adults.

Fave Secchi in Brodo (Stewed Dried Fava Beans with Garlic and Rosemary)

CALABRIA

Nothing could be more satisfying on a cold day than a hearty bowl of stewed dried fava beans. For me, this is one of the top comfort foods of winter. When I was a child, my father would make a large pot of stewed fava beans on a cold day and we would eat them as an antipasto *before dinner. We would fill our bowls with plenty of beans and broth and then suck the tender flesh of each bean from its outer skin. After we finished the last bean, we would* inzuppare del pane, *or wipe the bowl clean of the remaining broth with a piece of crusty Italian bread. The bread sopped with the warm, tasty broth was even better than the beans! Favas are a favorite treat in Calabria, where they grow abundantly in the warm climate. The fava beans are dried for use during the cold winter months when fresh vegetables are scarce. They must be soaked for many hours and then boiled for several more until they become tender and release their starches to create a rich broth. Here is my recipe for stewed dried fava beans with a Calabresi flare. The beans and broth are made flavorful with plenty of onion, garlic, and rosemary.*

2 cups dried brown fava beans
1 tsp. dried oregano
1 small sprig rosemary
2 teaspoons salt
Olive oil, for sautéing

½ small Spanish or Vidalia onion, chopped
3 cloves garlic, chopped
Salt and black pepper to taste

Soak the fava beans in lukewarm water for 6 hours. Discard the soaking water and place the fava beans in a saucepan. Add 8 cups of water, the dried oregano, and a whole sprig of rosemary and season with 2 teaspoons of salt. Set the saucepan over low heat and simmer the beans for about 2 hours, stirring occasionally. Add more water as the cooking liquid boils down. The beans are done when they are tender and the cooking liquid has turned into a rich, brown broth.

At this point, remove the saucepan from the burner and discard the sprig of rosemary. Coat the bottom of a small 10 inch diameter frying pan with olive oil, set it over medium-low heat, and sauté the onion until soft. Add the garlic and sauté for one more minute. Then pour the contents of the frying pan into the saucepan and stir everything together. If necessary, adjust the seasoning with salt and black pepper. Serve hot with crusty Italian bread. Serves 4 adults.

Biétola con Pomodorini, Borlotti, e Prosciutto (Sautéed Swiss Chard with Cherry Tomatoes, Borlotti Beans, and Prosciutto)

BASILICATA

Italians love to add the flavor of pork to sautéed greens such as Swiss chard, spinach, and kale. Prosciutto and pancetta are the most popular pork products in Italy and are sure to find their way into sautéed greens! Prosciutto is a cured ham and comes from the hind leg of the pig, whereas pancetta is bacon or pork belly. Prosciutto is typically sliced paper thin and eaten as an antipasto *with fruit and cheese. The ends and scraps of prosciutto are never wasted—they are diced and tossed into sauces, soups, and stews. Pancetta, on the other hand, is typically* crudo, *or raw, and must be sautéed to render the fat. Pancetta, like prosciutto, is also packed with wonderful pork flavor. It adds depth and character to sautéed vegetables, greens, and pasta sauces. But which is better to cook with? Chefs and home cooks disagree on this point. The curing process for prosciutto demands meticulous attention and a great deal of time, which makes it expensive. Although pancetta is a more affordable product, it must still be rendered to extract the fat and flavor.*

Whenever I want to add a layer of pork flavor to a dish, I reach for prosciutto. It has more depth of flavor and less fat than pancetta, so you don't need to use as much. It only takes a few ounces of finely minced or diced prosciutto to add wonderful pork flavor to sautéed greens. Here is a quick and flavorful recipe that is sure to please. It is typical rustic cooking from the heart of Southern Italy where scraps of meat, bacon fat, or the hard ends of a prosciutto never go to waste. Serve this dish alongside any roasted or grilled meat or simply eat it with a piece of crusty Italian bread.

2½ lbs. borlotti beans in the pod (yields 2 cups of beans)	¾ cup water
	Paprika to taste
2½ lbs. Swiss chard	Crushed red pepper flakes to taste
Olive oil, for sautéing	Salt and black pepper to taste
4 cloves garlic, sliced	¾ dry quart cherry tomatoes, sliced
3 oz. slab prosciutto, diced	in half

Remove the beans from the pods. Fill a 4½ quart saucepan ⅔ of the way with water and add 2½ teaspoons of salt. Add the beans and boil for 15 minutes or until tender. Remove and discard the entire stalk from each leaf of Swiss chard and chop the leaves.

Coat the bottom of a 5½ quart frying pan with olive oil, set it over medium-low heat, and sauté the garlic and prosciutto for 1 minute. Add the chopped Swiss chard and the water, which will allow the greens to steam. Season with paprika, red pepper flakes, salt, and pepper and cover the frying pan. Sauté for 7 minutes or until the Swiss chard is wilted and tender. If necessary, add more water.

When the Swiss chard is done, cook off any excess liquid. Stir in the cherry tomatoes and beans. Sauté for another 3 minutes or until the cherry tomatoes begin to pucker. If necessary, adjust the seasoning. Serve hot. Serves 4 adults.

Verdure Verde in Tiella (Sautéed Broccoli Rabe with Sundried Tomatoes, Capers, and Crispy Bread Crumb Topping)

APULIA

Tiella is a traditional earthenware baking dish that the Pugliese people love to cook with. In Bari, baked pasta dishes, vegetable casseroles, and seafood with rice and potatoes are all made in the tiella and then baked to perfection. The tiella is also used to bake greens, which most people are sure to find unusual. The greens are typically blanched, tossed with bread crumbs, placed in the tiella, and then finished in the oven. Any sort of green can be baked in a tiella, but in Apulia, they prefer bitter dandelions or wild chicory. I like broccoli rabe the best! For this recipe, toss in a handful of sundried tomatoes or briny olives for a burst of contrasting flavor and cubes of young caciocavallo cheese that will melt into the greens. If you cannot find caciocavallo, a smoked mozzarella will do just fine. Serve the tiella with roasted leg of lamb and a bold, primitive red wine from Apulia. It is hearty, rustic fare that is sure to please.

½ loaf country-style Italian bread
2 heaping tbsp. grated Pecorino Romano cheese
Olive oil, for drizzling and sautéing
1 large bunch broccoli rabe (about 1½ to 1¾ lbs.), trimmed
3 cloves garlic, sliced
Crushed red pepper flakes to taste (optional)

Salt and black pepper to taste
½ cup water
½ cup sliced jarred sundried tomatoes preserved in olive oil
1 heaping tbsp. capers in brine
⅓ lb. caciocavallo or mozzarella cheese, cubed (optional)

Grate enough bread in a food processor for 2 cups of firmly packed coarse crumbs. Transfer the bread crumbs to a mixing bowl, stir in the grated cheese, drizzle with olive oil, and toss well so that the crumbs are uniformly moist and fluffy. Remove any fibrous stems from the broccoli rabe.

Coat the bottom of a 5½ quart frying pan generously with olive oil and set it over medium-low heat. Add the garlic, let it sizzle in the oil for 30 seconds, and then add the broccoli rabe and season with red pepper flakes, salt, and black pepper. Add the water to create steam and cover the frying pan, as it will splatter. Toss the broccoli rabe every two minutes and continue sautéing until wilted and tender, about 7 to 9 minutes. If necessary, add more water.

Preheat the oven to 425 degrees. Stir the sundried tomatoes and capers into the broccoli rabe. Transfer the sautéed broccoli rabe to a 9 by 11 inch earthenware baking dish, leaving any excess cooking liquid in the frying pan. Sprinkle with cubed cheese if desired and then sprinkle the bread crumbs evenly over top. Bake for 7 to 10 minutes or until golden brown and crispy on top. Serve hot.

Cavolo Nero con Patate e Ceci (Sautéed Tuscan Kale with Roasted Potatoes and Chickpeas)

ABRUZZO/MOLISE

In springtime, the countryside of Abruzzo is painted in shades of vibrant green with the snowcapped peaks of the Gran Sasso rising in the distance. As the winter snows melt, small streams run deep and swift, carrying milky-blue waters rich in minerals off to the distant Adriatic Sea. With fertile soil thanks to these mineral-rich waters, the countryside of Abruzzo is the perfect place to grow vegetables of every kind. The small garden plots of paesani, *the country folk, are sure to be overflowing with leafy greens such as Swiss chard and Tuscan kale, which is my favorite. I find that the Tuscan variety of kale is more tender and milder in flavor than its curly American cousin. Any type of greens can be used in this dish, but I like Tuscan kale best because it is hearty and substantial. Its flavor pairs well with earthy roasted potatoes and mild, nutty chickpeas. I am sure you will agree! Pair it with grilled pork sausage and a glass of Montepulciano d'Abruzzo wine for a true taste of the Abruzzese countryside.*

Olive oil, for roasting and sautéing	2½ lbs. Tuscan kale
2 large russet potatoes (about 1¼ lbs.)	4 cloves garlic, sliced
Paprika to taste	¾ cup water
Salt and black pepper to taste	¾ cup chickpeas, drained

Coat the bottom of a 9 by 13 inch baking dish with olive oil. Peel the potatoes and chop them into 1 inch thick chunks. Pat the potatoes dry with a dish towel and place them in a mixing bowl. Drizzle with olive oil, season with paprika, salt, and black pepper, and toss well so that the potatoes are evenly coated.

Preheat the oven to 425 degrees. Spread the potatoes evenly in the baking dish and roast them for 15 minutes Stir the potatoes and use a spatula to loosen any that are sticking to the bottom of the baking dish. Then continue roasting the potatoes for another 35 to 40 minutes or until crisp and golden brown.

Meanwhile, remove the entire stalk from each leaf of kale, discard the stalks, and chop the leaves. Coat the bottom of a 5½ quart frying pan with olive oil and sauté the garlic until soft. Add the kale, season with paprika, salt, and black pepper, and add the water, which will allow the greens to steam. Cover the frying pan and continue sautéing for another 10 minutes or until the kale is wilted and tender. If necessary, add more water.

When the kale is done, cook off any excess liquid and stir in the chickpeas. When the potatoes are done, transfer them to the frying pan with a slotted spoon and toss everything together. If necessary, adjust the seasoning. Serve warm. Serves 4 adults.

Farro con Funghi Arrostiti e Cipollato (Farro Cooked Risotto Style with Roasted Mushrooms, Green Onions, and Fresh Herbs)

ABRUZZO/MOLISE

In Abruzzo and Molise, farro *is cultivated alongside wheat and barley in fields that ripple in warm Adriatic breezes.* Farro *is typically eaten as a whole grain and rarely milled into flour for bread and pasta—no doubt because it is inferior to the fine durum wheat grown in the region. That being said, the best attributes of* farro *are the fine texture and nutty flavor of the grains when boiled or sautéed. They are a wonderful alternative to rice or pasta if you're looking for a starchy side dish. In this recipe, the distinct, bold flavor of* farro *is the perfect match for earthy cremini mushrooms. Green onions, parsley, and thyme add the fresh flavors of springtime in the mountains near L'Aquila, where the antique shops display ancient sickles and other grain-harvesting implements of the Abruzzese countryside. If you head to L'Aquila, be sure to stroll through the* Antiquariato e Artigianato in Piazza, *the antiques flea market that is held the second weekend of each month in the Piazza Santa Maria Paganica. You are certain to find a few treasures! Cooked in the style of* risotto, *this dish is creamy and delicious. For a hearty winter meal, serve it alongside roasted pork, beef, or lamb with a glass of red Montepulciano d'Abruzzo or a red Sangiovese from Tuscany.*

1¾ lbs. cremini mushrooms, sliced	5 cups chicken broth
4 green onions, chopped	3 cups *farro*
3 cloves garlic, finely chopped	3 tbsp. butter
2 tbsp. finely chopped, firmly packed thyme	2 tbsp. finely chopped, firmly packed Italian flat leaf parsley
2 cups white wine, divided	½ cup grated Parmigiano-Reggiano cheese
Olive oil, for drizzling and sautéing	
Salt and black pepper to taste	

Preheat the oven to 425 degrees. Place the mushrooms, green onions, garlic, and thyme in a baking dish along with ½ cup of white wine and a few drizzles of olive oil. Season with salt and black pepper, and toss everything together. Cover the baking dish with aluminum foil and bake for 40 minutes or until the mushrooms are tender. Remove the mushrooms from the baking dish with a slotted spoon, set them to the side, and retain the cooking liquid.

Set the broth to simmer in a saucepan. Coat the bottom of a deep frying pan with olive oil, set it over medium-low heat, and sauté the *farro* for 2 minutes, stirring constantly. Then season it with salt and black pepper. Add ½ cup of wine to the *farro.* Stir constantly until the wine is absorbed. Then add the remaining wine ½ cup at a time. Continue stirring constantly, making sure the wine has been absorbed before more is added

Add the cooking liquid from the mushrooms in the same manner, followed by ladles of hot broth. This process, which will takes about 25 to 30 minutes, will tenderize the *farro.* Depending upon the desired tenderness and consistency of the *farro,* you may or may not use all of the broth.

Whisk the butter, parsley, and grated cheese into the *farro.* Then stir in the roasted mushrooms and transfer the *farro* to a serving dish. Serve hot. Serves 4 adults.

Patate e Cipolle Arrostite (Roasted Potatoes, Onions, and Garlic)

BASILICATA

Potatoes are a staple crop of Southern Italy. In Basilicata, they are roasted with baby onions, whole cloves of garlic, and plenty of dried oregano. They are then served alongside grilled lamb and savory pork sausages. My mother has a knack for roasting potatoes to perfection. She always tosses in plenty of onion wedges and cloves of garlic that become crisp and caramelized, just like the potatoes. When I was a child, the crispy bits of onion were always my favorite. I would sneak them from the roasting pan before the rest of the family sat down for dinner. Inevitably, I was caught. Today, my wife and I fight over them! I always season roasted potatoes with black pepper and whatever dried herbs best compliment my main course. Dried oregano and parsley go well with just about anything and are the preferred herbs in Basilicata. For beef, pork, and lamb, I also add a few whole sprigs of fresh rosemary that I nestle between the wedges. There is no right or wrong way to flavor them. Just be sure to follow my roasting instructions so that everything is caramelized, crisp, and delicious.

Olive oil, for roasting	2 heaping tsp. dried oregano
4 large russet potatoes, peeled and chopped	2 heaping tsp. dried parsley
2 medium Spanish or Vidalia onions, cut into wedges	Paprika to taste
	Salt and black pepper to taste
6 cloves garlic, sliced in half	4 small sprigs rosemary (optional)

Coat the bottom of a 10 by 14 inch baking dish with olive oil. After chopping the potatoes, pat them dry with a dish towel. Place the potatoes, onions, and garlic in a large mixing bowl, drizzle with olive oil, add the oregano and parsley, and season with paprika, salt, and black pepper. Toss gently so that everything is evenly coated.

Preheat the oven to 425 degrees. Spread the potatoes, onions, and garlic evenly inside the baking dish. If you prefer, nestle the rosemary in between. Bake for 15 minutes. Stir the potatoes and use a spatula to loosen any potatoes that are sticking to the bottom. Continue roasting the potatoes for another 35 to 40 minutes or until crisp and golden brown. Serve hot. Serves 4 adults.

Fritto Misto di Verdure (Mixed Fried Vegetables—Done Two Ways)

SICILY

One afternoon, I went for a hike through the hills above the small town of Scopello. Along the way, I came across an old man tending his garden. He had a long, thin face and strong chin like my grandfather, and he wore the same sort of cap that my grandfather always donned when he left the house. I was intrigued and stopped to have a chat. The old man asked if I was American, and I said yes. He then told me that he lived in Brooklyn for fifty years but moved back to Sicily after his wife died. While in Brooklyn, he lived in an apartment, and had no yard to plant a vegetable garden. That was why he returned to Sicily. Although most immigrants of his generation adapted to the big city, he always longed for a simple, rustic lifestyle. Now, he lives off of his small pension from the union and eats the vegetables and fruits that he grows. He seemed quite content! I told him that I too had a vegetable garden back in United States, but surely mine was not as well tended as his!

In Sicily, a fritto misto, *or mixed fry of seasonal vegetables, is often served as part of a holiday meal alongside roasted lamb or pork. A* fritto misto *platter served with Easter dinner in Scopello and other towns in western Sicily will include springtime vegetables, such as zucchini, artichokes, cauliflower, broccoli, and cardoons. The cardoons are always the first thing to disappear from the* fritto misto *platter at my home! You can prepare your* fritto misto *by dipping the vegetables in beaten egg and then dredging them in either flour or a mixture of bread crumbs, grated cheese, and herbs. Try it both ways and see which your family likes better. I always arrange mine on a large platter with plenty of lemon wedges. The extra squeeze of fresh lemon adds brightness for a true taste of the sun-kissed Sicilian countryside near Scopello.*

Mixed vegetables for 6 to 8 people
8 extra-large eggs
4 cups all-purpose flour or bread crumb coating (see opposite)
3 quarts corn oil
Salt to taste
4 lemons, cut into wedges

For the bread crumb coating:
4 cups finely ground dry bread crumbs
¾ cup grated Pecorino Romano cheese
2 tbsp. finely chopped, firmly packed Italian flat leaf parsley
Black pepper to taste

Use any combination of fresh vegetables, including zucchini, cauliflower, broccoli, cardoons, artichokes, eggplants, bell peppers, and mushrooms. Chop the vegetables into 3 inch chunks. If using cardoons, remove the feathery leaves, peel the stringy fibers from the stalks, and boil them in lightly salted water for 7 minutes before frying. If using artichokes, remove all of the leaves from the artichoke with a paring knife, and then remove the inner choke. Use a potato peeler to peel the stringy outer fibers of the stem and then cut the artichoke into quarters.

Beat the eggs with a splash of water. For the bread crumb coating, simply combine the bread crumbs, grated cheese, and parsley in a mixing bowl and season with black pepper.

Place one inch of oil in a 5½ quart frying pan and set it over medium heat. When the oil is hot, dip the vegetables in the beaten egg, dredge them in either the flour or the bread crumb mixture, and fry until golden brown on both sides. Place the vegetables on paper towels to absorb the excess oil and sprinkle lightly with salt. Serve hot accompanied by wedges of fresh lemon. Serves 6 to 8 adults.

Peperoni Ripieni (Stuffed Peppers—Done Two Ways)

SICILY

Many of the recipes in this cookbook are the legacy of wonderful home cooks, some of whom died more than twenty years ago. Today, their children and grandchildren continue to pass on their recipes and food traditions, many of which originated in the small mountain towns of rural Campania and Sicily. The first stuffed pepper recipe below is the legacy of my Sicilian grandmother. Everyone loved her stuffed cubanelle peppers baked in tomato sauce, and no one could make them as delicious as she. She had a knack for making the filling so soft and delicious that they melted in your mouth. Like most Italian nonnas she cooked by instinct and never from written recipes. Fortunately, she passed her techniques on to me, and now I can share them with you! The second recipe is one of my very own that incorporates the classic Sicilian cooking style of combining sweet and salty flavors. I stuff sweet red bell pepper halves with bread crumbs, pine nuts, and raisins and bake them until crisp on top. Your family is sure to love both recipes, and perhaps someday, they will be your legacy too!

Stuffed Cubanelle Peppers Baked with Tomato Sauce:

1 loaf country-style Italian bread
Olive oil, for sautéing
½ medium Spanish or Vidalia onion, diced
3 cloves garlic, finely chopped
1½ tbsp. finely chopped, firmly packed Italian flat leaf parsley
1½ tbsp. finely chopped, firmly packed oregano or basil
¾ cup grated Pecorino Romano cheese
Salt and black pepper to taste
10 cubanelle peppers (at least 6 inches long)
1½ quarts Salsa Marinara *(see page 121)*

Grate enough bread for 6 cups of firmly pressed crumbs and transfer them to a mixing bowl. Coat the bottom of a frying pan generously with olive oil, set it over medium-low heat, and sauté the onion until soft. Add the garlic and sauté for another minute. Add the sautéed items, parsley, oregano or basil, and cheese to the mixing bowl with the bread. Season with salt and black pepper and toss well so that the crumbs are uniformly moist and fluffy. If necessary, add a few extra drizzles of olive oil.

Preheat the oven to 375 degrees. Remove the tops from the peppers and scoop out the seeds. Stuff each pepper generously with bread crumbs and then put the top back to seal the opening. Coat the bottom of a deep baking dish with Salsa Marinara. Place the stuffed peppers in the baking dish, and then top them with more sauce. Cover the baking dish with aluminum foil and bake for 45 minutes or until the peppers are soft. Serve hot. Serves 6 to 8 adults.

Red Bell Pepper Halves Stuffed with Bread Crumbs, Pine Nuts, and Raisins:

Olive oil, for sautéing
½ Spanish or Vidalia onion, diced
4 cloves garlic, finely chopped
1 loaf country-style Italian bread
4 tbsp. finely chopped, firmly packed Italian flat leaf parsley
¾ cup grated Pecorino Romano cheese
⅓ cup pine nuts, toasted
½ cup raisins
Salt and black pepper to taste
6 large red bell peppers

Coat the bottom of a frying pan generously with olive oil, set it over medium-low heat, and sauté the onion until soft. Add the garlic and sauté for 1 more minute.

Grate enough bread for 4 cups of firmly pressed crumbs. Place the bread crumbs in a mixing bowl, add the parsley, grated cheese, pine nuts, raisins, and sautéed onion and garlic. Season with salt and black pepper. Toss everything together and, if necessary, add a few drizzles of olive oil so that the bread crumbs are uniformly moist and fluffy.

Preheat the oven to 415 degrees. Brush the bottom of a baking tray with olive oil. Cut the peppers in half and remove the ribs and seeds. Season the insides of the pepper halves with salt. Stuff the pepper halves generously with the bread crumb mixture and place them on the baking tray. Add a thin layer of water to the bottom of the tray, which will allow the peppers to steam. Then tent the tray with aluminum foil. Bake for 40 minutes or until tender, and then remove the foil. Continue baking for another 7 to 10 minutes or until crisp and golden on top. Serve hot. Serves 8 adults.

Friatelli con Aglio e Olio (Fried Cubanelle Peppers with Olive Oil and Garlic)

SICILY

My friend Salvo sells produce from a mobile cart in Bagheria, Sicily. He drives slowly through the narrow streets yelling out his selection for the day: "Oggi, cocuzza lunga! Fichi freschi! Peperoni dolci!" The women come to their doors, lean over balcony railings, and stick their heads out windows, waving and shouting for him to stop. It is quite a scene, especially when a traffic jam builds behind him! If Salvo has a good day, most of his produce will be sold, and early the next morning he will drive to Palermo to pick up more. At seventy years old, Salvo does not intend to retire. He will tell you, "I have been doing this for fifty-five years. I have only a small pension. Many of my customers are too old to walk to the market. What will they do without me?"

Fresh vegetables are an important part of Sicilian cuisine. In fact, many Sicilians buy their produce fresh every day from mobile produce vendors like Salvo or from the market. Storing vegetables in the refrigerator for a week is simply unheard of. After all, how can something be fresh if it has been sitting around for a few days? This is a traditional Sicilian recipe for which only the freshest sweet cubanelle peppers will do. The peppers are fried until tender and then dressed with garlic that has been sautéed in extra virgin olive oil. A good sprinkle of sea salt from Trapani gives this dish even more Sicilian character!

Olive oil, for frying	4 cloves garlic, sliced
1 dozen large cubanelle peppers	Sea salt and black pepper to taste
Extra virgin olive oil, for sautéing	

Coat the bottom of a 5½ quart frying pan with ¼ inch of olive oil and nestle the peppers inside. Set the frying pan over medium-low heat and cover it with a splatter guard. Fry the peppers on all sides until soft, using tongs to gently turn them without piercing about every 3 to 5 minutes. The peppers are done with they are uniformly soft, have turned from a bright green to a pale green, and the skins have puckered. At this point, transfer them to a serving platter and discard the cooking oil.

Coat the bottom of a small 10 inch frying pan generously with extra virgin olive oil, set it over medium-low heat, and let the garlic sizzle gently in the oil for 1 minute. Pour the oil and garlic over the peppers and season with sea salt and black pepper. Serve warm or at room temperature alongside grilled pork sausage or chicken, or serve as an *antipasto* atop grilled Italian bread. Serves 4 to 6 adults.

Fagiolini, Patate, e Pomodorini (Sautéed Italian Flat Beans with Potatoes and Cherry Tomatoes)

CAMPANIA

On my Campanese grandmother's ninetieth birthday, I asked her, "How is it that you have lived so long and stayed so healthy?" She smiled and answered, "Because I eat lots of greens and fresh vegetables!" She then added, "I eat escarole or spinach every week, and string beans with potatoes instead of pasta. If you eat pasta every day, you will get fat!" There must be some truth in Grandma's thinking. At ninety years old, she is thin and beautiful and often mistaken to be my mother!

String beans with potatoes is a popular combination in Italy. If you want to limit the starches in your diet, cut out the pasta during the week, except for Sunday dinner, and make string beans with potatoes instead. Limiting your carbs during the week will help you to stay thin and healthy, just like Grandma. Here is Grandma's favorite preparation for this tasty combination of vegetables. It is fresh, rustic cooking from the Diano Valley in the heart of Campania's Salerno Province.

2 lbs. russet potatoes (or small red potatoes)
Olive oil, for roasting and sautéing
Salt and black pepper to taste
1½ lbs. Italian flat beans or string beans
½ medium Spanish or Vidalia onion, diced
4 cloves garlic, sliced
1 dry quart cherry tomatoes, sliced in half
1½ tbsp. finely chopped, firmly packed basil
1½ tbsp. finely chopped, firmly packed oregano
Crushed red pepper flakes to taste

Preheat the oven to 425 degrees. Coat the bottom of a 9 by 13 inch baking dish with olive oil. Peel the potatoes and chop them into 1½ inch chunks. (If you are using small red potatoes, leave the skins on and slice them in half.) Pat the potatoes dry with a dish towel and place them in a mixing bowl. Drizzle with olive oil, season with salt and black pepper, and toss well so that the potatoes are evenly coated. Spread the potatoes evenly inside the baking dish and bake for 15 minutes. Stir the potatoes and use a spatula to loosen any that are sticking to the bottom of the baking dish. Continue roasting the potatoes for another 35 to 40 minutes or until crisp and golden brown.

Meanwhile, fill an 8 quart pot ⅔ of the way with water and add 1 rounded tablespoon of salt. Add the beans and boil for 2 minutes or until tender but still firm. Remove the beans from the pot with a skimmer and set them to the side. Coat the bottom of a 5½ quart frying pan with olive oil, set it over medium-low heat, and sauté the onion until soft. Add the garlic, sauté for another minute, and then add the cherry tomatoes, basil, and oregano. Season with red pepper flakes, salt, and pepper and continue sautéing for another 5 to 7 minutes or until the cherry tomatoes have puckered and released some of their juices. Add the beans and potatoes to the frying pan and gently toss everything together. Serve hot. Serves 4 to 6 adults.

Asparagi con Mollica e Peperoncino (Asparagus with Garlic, Crushed Red Chili Flakes, and Bread Crumbs)

CALABRIA

One morning my friend Salvo took me to the garage where he keeps his produce. He lifted up the metal garage door and inside there were many large crates full of fresh vegetables and fruit. I helped him load the produce onto his mobile vending cart. There were Sicilian squashes that were close to four feet long, baskets of bright red tomatoes, bundles of long, thin asparagus, and large, plump purple figs. After lifting a few boxes, I worked up a sweat. Oh, how basic and wonderful life is in Italy!

Asparagus is a favorite springtime vegetable in most regions of Italy, and in Calabria it is sure to be served al diavolo—*spicy. Here is a quick and easy recipe for asparagus flavored with crushed red chili flakes and garlic-infused olive oil. It is an unexpected, rustic preparation for a vegetable that is most always served steamed with a drizzle of butter. Just be sure to use the freshest asparagus possible. My friend Salvo will tell you, "Only buy asparagus that is bright green and snaps in half when you try to bend it. Rubbery asparagus is just no good."*

½ loaf country-style Italian bread
2 tbsp. grated Pecorino Romano cheese
Olive oil, for drizzling
1 large bunch asparagus, trimmed

1½ cups water
3 cloves garlic, sliced
Crushed red pepper flakes to taste
Sea salt and black pepper to taste

Preheat the oven to 400 degrees. Grate enough bread in a food processor for 1½ cups of firmly pressed crumbs and then transfer the crumbs to a mixing bowl. Add the grated cheese, drizzle with olive oil, and toss well so that the crumbs are uniformly moist and fluffy. Spread the bread crumb mixture on a baking tray and bake for 7 minutes or until golden brown. Stir the bread crumbs occasionally so that they toast evenly.

Place the asparagus in a frying pan, add the water, and set the frying pan over medium heat. Cover the frying pan and steam the asparagus for 3 minutes or until

tender but still firm. Then set the asparagus to the side. Coat the bottom of the frying pan generously with olive oil, set it over low heat, add the garlic, and season with red pepper flakes, salt, and black pepper. Sauté the garlic until soft and then remove the frying pan from the heat. Add the asparagus back to the frying pan and toss gently so that all of the spears are coated with the seasoned oil. Arrange the asparagus on a serving platter, drizzle some seasoned oil over top, and then sprinkle with toasted bread crumbs. Serve hot. Serves 4 adults.

Carciofini al Forno (Roasted Baby Artichokes with Fresh Herbs and Garlic)

CALABRIA

I once travelled the coastal road from Naples to Reggio, Calabria, stopping every so often to snap photos of the enchanting mountain and sea vistas. As I approached the small town of Gizzeria, the mountains gave way to a vast plain. On both sides of the roadway were farmlands, olive groves, and greenhouses full of flowers. At one point, I drove past fields of silvery green artichoke plants swaying in the wind. The thorny buds stood proud and tall above the lush foliage, as if they were reaching upwards to be kissed by the warm Mediterranean sun! It was a beautiful sight one could only find in Southern Italy! Certainly, it was worthy of a photograph, so I stopped for a moment. If only I could have picked a few. I imagine the hearts of the young buds were tender and delicious!

What we call an artichoke is actually the bud of the artichoke plant, which blooms into a purple flower. Native to the Mediterranean, artichokes have been cultivated in Italy since the days when the Greek philosopher Archimedes walked the streets of ancient Syracuse in Sicily. Today, artichokes are cultivated in all but the alpine regions. That being said, it is no wonder that they have earned a prominent place in Italian cuisine and that Italians have mastered the techniques for cooking them—batter-fried in Palermo, stuffed in Rome, or roasted in Calabria. Here is a country-style preparation from countryside of Calabria. The baby artichokes are roasted with fresh herbs, garlic, and fine Calabrian olive oil. The flavors are fresh and delicious!

Juice of 2 lemons	1½ tbsp. finely chopped, firmly packed basil or thyme
2½ dozen baby artichokes (about 2½ inches long)	1½ tbsp. finely chopped, firmly packed oregano
Olive oil, for drizzling	Coarse salt and black pepper to taste
3 cloves garlic, finely chopped	

Squeeze the lemon juice into a large bowl of cold water, enough to cover the artichoke hearts completely. Remove the outer leaves of the artichokes until you reach the soft, pale inner cone. Remove the top ⅓ of the cone and peel the stems. Cut the artichokes in half and drop them into the acidulated water to prevent browning.

Preheat the oven to 415 degrees. When all of the artichokes have been prepared and you are ready to roast them, drain them in a colander and pat them dry. Place the artichokes in a large mixing bowl, drizzle generously with olive oil, add the garlic, basil, and oregano, season with salt and black pepper, and toss well. Spread the artichokes evenly on a baking tray, cover it with aluminum foil, and bake for 15 minutes.

Remove the aluminum foil and continue baking for another 10 to 12 minutes or until crispy on top. Serve hot or at room temperature. Serves 4 to 6 adults.

Carciofi Chini (Artichokes Stuffed with Bread Crumbs, Parmigiano-Reggiano Cheese, and Herbs)

LAZIO

According to the ancient Romans, artichokes were an aphrodisiac! Regardless of whether this is fact or fiction, one thing is certain: modern Romans cannot get enough of the tasty thistle. Today, the artichoke enjoys elite status in Roman cuisine, which certainly begs the question: Were the ancient Romans right? These days, stuffed artichokes are a popular dish at the restaurants in Rome's Trastevere District. This is one of Rome's oldest residential neighborhoods, where narrow cobblestone streets meander past medieval houses with terracotta rooftops. In Trastevere, you are sure to find plenty of small, family-owned restaurants that prepare traditional Roman cuisine—some of which are sure to date back to the days of Julius Caesar. The next time you head to Rome, make it a point to enjoy a traditional Roman meal in Trastevere. And if Roman-style artichokes are on the menu, give them a try!

Stuffing artichokes is a favorite preparation in Rome. Locals hollow out the centers of the artichokes, stuff them with bread crumbs and anchovies, and roast them in the oven. I like to cook my stuffed artichokes in a large pot on the stovetop. This is a method that I was taught by my Sicilian grandmother. She carefully stuffed the bread crumbs between the leaves and then let the artichokes steam for at least an hour. If you use this method, your stuffed artichokes will be tender and moist every time. If you prefer stuffed artichokes with a true Roman flare, then place them in a casserole dish tented with aluminum foil and roast them at 375 degrees until tender.

½ loaf country-style Italian bread
Olive oil, for sautéing
½ large Spanish or Vidalia onion, diced
3 cloves garlic, finely chopped
1½ tbsp. finely chopped, firmly packed Italian flat leaf parsley

1½ tbsp. finely chopped, firmly packed oregano or basil
¾ cup grated Parmigiano-Reggiano cheese
Black pepper to taste
6 large globe artichokes
Salt to taste

Grate enough bread for 4 cups of firmly pressed crumbs and transfer them to a mixing bowl. Coat the bottom of a frying pan with olive oil, set it over medium-low heat, and sauté the onions until soft. Add the garlic and sauté for another minute.

Add the onions, garlic, parsley, oregano or basil, and cheese to the bread crumbs. Season with black pepper and toss well so the crumbs are uniformly moist and fluffy. If necessary, add a few extra drizzles of olive oil.

Remove the stems from the artichokes so that they stand upright. Peel the stems with a potato peeler. Discard the peelings and set the stems to the side. Cut off the top ¼ of the artichokes and snip the spiny tops of the remaining leaves with scissors. Spread open the leaves and stuff the bread crumb mixture between them.

Place 1½ inches of water in a large, wide pot, sit the artichokes upright in the pot, and nestle the stems between them. Drizzle some olive oil over the artichokes and cover the pot. Simmer over low heat for 45 to 60 minutes, adding more water as needed. The artichokes are done when the leaves are soft and pull off easily from the choke. Serve hot. Serves 4 adults.

Cavolfiore alla Palermitana (Baked Cauliflower with Pine Nuts, Raisins, and Crispy Bread Crumb Topping)

SICILY

The flavor combination of sautéed sweet onions, garlic, pine nuts, and raisins is classically Sicilian and often referred to as alla Palermitana, *or Palermo style. I use it to flavor many different dishes. I even use it as a condiment for* spaghetti *and then finish the dish with a generous sprinkle of toasted bread crumbs. It is a tasty little trick that I learned from my Sicilian grandmother. A sprinkle of crispy* mollica di pane *is always a great way to add texture and intrigue to any dish! That is why I always keep bread crumbs on hand in my kitchen. I grate a loaf or two of fresh Italian bread in the food processor and then freeze the bread crumbs in resealable plastic bags. They will last in the freezer for up to two months. Then, I whenever I want, I grab a handful and fry them up on the stove top or sprinkle them over a casseroles for a crunchy topping.*

The last time I visited my friends Salvatore and Anna in Palermo, Anna asked, "Do you like cauliflower?" I responded, "Only if it is prepared alla Palermitana!" With that being said, Anna proceeded to the Ballero Market in the bustling heart of the city center, where she always does her daily shopping. She returned an hour later with a large head of cauliflower and other fresh vegetables. Later that evening, we feasted on cauliflower roasted to perfection with pine nuts and raisins and topped with bread crumbs. Here is my version of Anna's delicious cauliflower casserole. I like to serve it for Thanksgiving dinner as it pairs well with other side dishes typical of autumn, such as roasted butternut squash, sweet potatoes, and hearty sautéed farro *with mushrooms.*

1 loaf country-style Italian bread	½ large Spanish or Vidalia onion, diced
¾ cup grated Pecorino Romano cheese	4 cloves garlic, finely chopped
Olive oil, for drizzling and sautéing	⅓ cup firmly packed raisins
Salt and black pepper to taste	Zest of 1 California navel orange
1 large head cauliflower	2 tbsp. finely chopped, firmly packed Italian flat leaf parsley
2 rounded tbsp. pine nuts	3 tbsp. butter

Grate enough bread for 2½ cups of firmly pressed crumbs. Place the bread crumbs in a mixing bowl, stir in the grated cheese, drizzle with olive oil, season with salt and black pepper, and toss well so that the bread crumbs are uniformly moist and fluffy. Set aside.

Chop the cauliflower into 2 inch florets. Fill an 8 quart pot ⅔ of the way with water and add 1 rounded tablespoon of salt. Add the cauliflower florets and blanch them for 1 minute or until tender but still quite firm. Drain the cauliflower and transfer it to a mixing bowl.

Place the pine nuts in a small frying pan and toast them over medium heat until golden. Coat the bottom of a large frying pan generously with olive oil and sauté the onion until soft. Add the garlic, raisins, pine nuts, orange zest, parsley, and butter and continue sautéing for 1 more minute.

Preheat the oven to 425 degrees. Pour the contents of the frying pan over the cauliflower, season it with salt and black pepper, and toss well. Transfer the cauliflower to a baking dish and sprinkle an even layer of the bread crumb mixture over top. Bake for 10 minutes or until crisp and golden on top. Serve hot. Serves 4 to 6 adults.

Involtini di Melanzane (Eggplant Roulades Stuffed with Ricotta and Baked Parmigiana Style)

CAMPANIA

A Sunday stroll through one of Naples' old residential neighborhoods will reaffirm that here the tomato is king. As neighbors chat from their window perches above the noisy streets, the wafting aroma of simmering tomato sauce fills the air; there is sure to be a pot of sauce simmering on the stove in every home. If only we could have a taste! Tomato sauce has found its place in many Neapolitan dishes, and not just as a condiment for pasta. It is layered in casseroles, baked atop crispy pizzas, and used to braise vegetables, meats, and seafood. Here is a homestyle dish you are sure to find at any Sunday dinner or family gathering in Naples. Thin slices of delicately fried eggplant are rolled with a scoop of creamy ricotta in the middle, placed in a casserole dish, and then topped with plenty of flavorful tomato sauce and mozzarella cheese. The eggplant rolls are then baked in the oven until the cheese has melted and the tomato sauce is hot and bubbly. I like to serve them alongside Milanese-style cutlets, meatballs, roasted sausage, and beef braciole. For such a wonderful dish, only the best homemade tomato sauce will do. So be sure to make yours with imported San Marzano tomatoes!

4 large, plump, purple eggplants
Salt and black pepper to taste
Flour, for dredging
Olive oil, for frying
1½ quarts Salsa Marinara *(see page 121)*
1½ lbs. ricotta cheese

½ cup grated Pecorino Romano cheese, plus more for topping
1½ tbsp. finely chopped, firmly packed Italian flat leaf parsley
¾ lb. mozzarella cheese, shredded

Slice the eggplants lengthwise into ⅜ inch thick slices. Season the eggplant slices on both sides with salt and black pepper, and then dredge them in flour. Coat the bottom of a frying pan with olive oil, set it over medium heat, fry the eggplant slices until soft and golden, and then place them on paper towels to drain the excess oil.

Preheat the oven to 375 degrees. Coat the bottom of a 10 by 14 inch baking dish with a layer of Salsa Marinara. Combine the ricotta, Pecorino Romano, and parsley in a mixing bowl. Place a scoop of ricotta on one end of an eggplant slice and roll it up. Continue until all of the eggplant slices have been rolled. Nestle the eggplant rolls in the baking dish, top them with sauce, and then sprinkle with shredded mozzarella. Cover with aluminum foil and bake for 15 minutes. Makes about 12 rolls. Serve hot, topped with grated Pecorino Romano cheese. Serves 6 to 8 adults.

Funghi Ripieni con Spinaci (Mushroom Caps Stuffed with Sautéed Spinach, Prosciutto, and Parmigiano-Reggiano Cheese)

CAMPANIA

Cusano Mutri is an atmospheric hill town with charming cobblestone streets, winding alleyways, and flower-filled terracotta pots resting peacefully on window ledges. If you enjoy outdoor adventures and love mushrooms, then visit Cusano Mutri in late September. You can go mountain climbing and zip lining through the deep gorges of the Matese Mountains. The scenery is breathtaking! After working up an appetite, head to the town's annual Sagra dei Funghi Porcini, or mushroom festival. There you will find food stalls serving mushrooms cooked in every way imaginable! Listen to traditional Neapolitan songs, dance a Tarantella, have a few glasses of wine, and indulge in tasty mushroom dishes!

Here is one of my favorite recipes for roasted, stuffed mushroom caps. It is a dish you might just find at the Sagra dei Funghi Porcini in Cusano Mutri. Any mushroom large enough to stuff will do, including portabella and cremini, but I prefer white mushrooms. Roasting is a great way to prepare mushrooms and other vegetables. My secret is to add a thin layer of water to the bottom of the roasting pan and then tent it with aluminum foil. This will allow the mushrooms to steam and become tender without drying out. In the last few minutes of cooking, I remove the foil so that the mushrooms get crisp on top. They are a perfect side dish for your favorite roasted or grilled meats.

2½ dozen large white mushrooms (about 2½ inches diameter)
Olive oil, for drizzling and sautéing
3 cloves garlic, minced
3 oz. slab prosciutto, finely diced
Black pepper to taste

1½ lbs. spinach, chopped
¾ cup grated Parmigiano-Reggiano cheese, divided
Salt to taste
½ loaf country-style Italian bread

Remove the stems from the mushrooms and use a spoon to hollow out the caps. Set the caps aside and dice the stems. Coat the bottom of a frying pan with olive oil, set it over medium-low heat, and sauté the garlic until soft. Add the prosciutto and mushroom stems and season with black pepper. Sauté until the mushroom stems are soft. Add the spinach and then continue sautéing until the spinach is wilted and tender. Cook off or drain any excess liquid, transfer the spinach mixture to a mixing bowl, allow it to cool, and then stir in ¼ cup of grated cheese. If necessary, season lightly with salt.

Grate enough bread for 2 cups of firmly pressed crumbs. Place the bread crumbs in a mixing bowl, add the remaining grated cheese, drizzle with olive oil, and toss well so that the bread crumbs are uniformly moist and fluffy.

Preheat the oven to 415 degrees. Brush the bottom of a baking dish with olive oil. Season the insides of the mushroom caps lightly with salt and black pepper. Place some spinach mixture in the cap, but do not overstuff. Then press a small mound of

bread crumbs on top. Place the stuffed mushrooms in the baking dish and add a thin layer of water to the bottom of the tray, which will allow them to steam. Tent the baking dish with aluminum foil and bake for 40 minutes or until tender. Remove the foil and bake for another 7 to 10 minutes or until golden brown on top. Serve hot. Serves 8 adults.

Boats along the Bay of Naples

VII

Frutti di Mare (Seafood)

Intimidation by Octopus in Palermo

A Rambling in Sicily

One day when I was in Palermo, my friend Anna decided to cook a seafood feast for the entire family. She left the apartment early in the morning with her small collapsible shopping cart and returned an hour later with a bounty of wonderful fish from the nearby Ballaro Market. There were clear plastic bags full of mullet, sardines, anchovies, shrimp, squid, and a very large octopus. I watched as she and Salvatore cleaned the seafood. I had never seen such a large octopus and was curious about how it would be prepared. I marveled at the fresh fish and thought, "What a glorious dinner I will be eating tonight!"

Later that afternoon, the cooking frenzy began. Seafood was simmering in pots on every burner of Anna's kitchen stove. A second stove on the covered balcony was also put to use. This stove was always reserved for frying, as Anna did not want to splatter grease on her new American-style kitchen. I sat at the table and watched as Anna ran back and forth between the kitchen stove and the balcony, where Salvatore was frying the fish. With a bead of sweat on her brow, she hurriedly chopped vegetables, stirred the pots, and tended to items baking in the oven. At sixty years old and standing just 5 feet tall, she was a force to be reckoned with in her kitchen. And Salvatore certainly knew his place! He was the sous chef and dared not make a fuss as she shouted at him to chop, stir, or fry.

Anna then pulled the large octopus from a pot of boiling water and placed it on a platter. She set the platter on the table in front of me along with a two-pronged meat fork and a knife. "Go ahead, you slice it," she said. She then hurried off to the balcony to check on Salvatore. I grabbed the fork and knife, one in each hand. I sat there for a moment and looked down upon the octopus. It was lying upright with its long rubbery tentacles curled in one direction or another. I examined my foe curiously. I have sliced many turkeys and roasts, but this was outside of my comfort zone. But, with Anna and Salvatore so busy, I dared not ask, "How do you slice an octopus?"

I then decided upon a course of action. With surgical precision, I cut off each tentacle, and then I placed the fork and knife down. Surely, I hadn't screwed this up! Anna then came over to the table. "No! Slice the whole thing," she shouted. Before I could say a word, she hurried off to the stove. Once again, I picked up the fork and knife. I reexamined my foe. Then, with surgical precision, I sliced each tentacle into a few pieces and put the knife and fork down. Thank God my job was done! Surely, I hadn't screwed this up!

Anna then turned from the stove, glanced my way, and shouted in a stern voice, "No, slice it all!" I sat there for a moment, looked down at my foe a third time, and analyzed the situation. I did not know how to go about slicing the octopus' large, round head. I was suddenly overwhelmed and intimidated. This task was turning into a battle, and I did not want to lose. I needed to take an aggressive approach to get the job done. Again, I picked up the fork and knife. I mentally prepared myself for combat, and then plunged the knife right in. Black ink immediately splattered all over and filled the bottom of the platter. This was completely unexpected. Now, for sure, I had screwed up! The platter was a mess and there was a splatter of ink on the white tablecloth and my shirt.

I finished slicing the octopus and set the fork and knife down. I cringed at the thought of what Anna was going to say. A number of thoughts ran through my mind: How did I not realize that there would be ink inside the octopus? Was I supposed to remove the ink sac first? Did I ruin the octopus that she spent so many hours cooking? Will she be upset that I soiled her table? Anna saw my predicament. She grabbed a dish towel, moistened it in the sink, and hurried over. She quickly cleaned the tablecloth and the edges of the platter. She then cracked a quick smile and said, "Oh, what a beautiful octopus! There is plenty of ink. Good job!"

She hurried back to the stove, seemingly unaffected by the aftermath of my battle. I gave a sigh of relief. Despite the pressure and unexpected mess, I defeated my worthy opponent! And now, I had bragging rights. I quickly changed my battle-soiled shirt. When I returned to the kitchen, everyone gathered to eat. I celebrated my victory over the mighty octopus with a wonderful seafood dinner and the company of dear friends!

Eating sea urchins plucked fresh from the sea in Cefalu, Sicily

The port of Lipari in the Aeolian Islands

Fresh seafood proudly displayed at a neighborhood pescheria

Aquaculture ensures an abundant supply of Adriatic shellfish in Italy

The ancient tonnra in Scopello, Sicily

The hills of Molise are a patchwork of colors in the summer

The colorful houses of Procida, Campania

Insalata di Baccala (Salted Cod Salad with Capers, Green Olives, and Lemon Dressing)

CAMPANIA

In the mountainous heart of Basilicata, salted cod is a favorite treat. Hilltop towns such as Avigliano are very far from the sea. Before the advent of modern refrigeration, fresh seafood was simply not possible for the Aviglianesi. However, salted cod was easy to store and transport to the mountain towns of the interior, and it soon became a viable alternative to the usual meat dishes. For the Aviglianesi, the arrival of salted cod many centuries ago was a truly wonderful thing. They incorporated it into the local cuisine, and eventually it became part of the cultural heritage. Today, salted cod is celebrated at an annual festival each summer called La Sagre di Baccala. If you are travelling through the mountains of Basilicata in August, be sure to stop in! There will be plenty of food stalls where you can sample baccala *recipes from the region. The event also includes music, dancing, and exhibitions of local crafts. It is sure to be a tasty and festive occasion. And if you happen to get lost along the way, just follow your nose! The smell of fish will take you there!*

At the Sagre di Baccala, salted cod is cooked in many different ways. Among the best-known preparations is ciauredda, *or cod soup with tomato broth, peppers, and onions.* Baccala *is also pureed into a spread for* crostini, *deep fried in tasty croquettes, stewed with potatoes, and tossed into salads. Here is my recipe for an Aviglionese-style* baccala *salad. It is the perfect summertime treat on a warm August afternoon in the mountains of Basilicata. Chunks of* baccala *are tossed with green olives, capers, and chopped, fresh red bell pepper. Dressed with fresh-squeezed lemon and a high-quality olive oil, this salad is vibrant and delicious. Be sure to pair it with a fine Pinot Grigio from Veneto.*

2 lbs. salted cod fillets	¾ cup pitted, halved green
½ small Spanish or Vidalia onion, diced	Castelvetrano or Ascolane olives
2 ribs celery, diced	⅓ cup capers in brine
1 small red bell pepper, seeded and diced	Olive oil, for dressing
3 cloves garlic, finely chopped	Juice of 3 lemons, divided
3 tbsp. finely chopped, firmly packed Italian flat leaf parsley	Salt and black pepper to taste

Soak the salted cod fillets in plenty of cool water for at least 48 hours, changing the water at least 3 times daily. The fillets will rehydrate and become soft and pliable. Boil the fillets for 10 to 15 minutes (depending upon thickness), remove them from the pot, and allow them to cool. When the fillets have cooled, break them into large flakes and place them in a mixing bowl. Add the onion, celery, bell pepper, garlic, parsley, olives, and capers. Drizzle generously with olive oil, squeeze over the juice of 2 lemons, season with salt and black pepper, and toss well. If you prefer more acidity, squeeze over the juice of the third lemon. Serve at room temperature or slightly chilled. Serves 4 to 6 adults.

Insalata di Mare (Seafood Salad with Diced Red Bell Pepper, Black Olives, and Lemon Dressing)

CALABRIA

From the mountainous shores of Calabria to the shallow lagoon of Venice, Italy's diverse coastlines produce a wide variety of seafood. Clams are gathered on sandy Adriatic beaches, sea urchins, lobsters, and crabs are plucked from rocky shoals, and giant swordfish are pulled from the depths of a clear, blue sea. The nets of pescatori, who practice traditional fishing methods from small boats, pull in squid, sardines, red mullet, and anchovies. Today, mussels and oysters are also farmed along the Ionian coast of Apulia. The possibilities for seafood in Italy are truly endless! Insalata di mare, *or seafood salad, is a popular dish in all coastal regions of the country—and certainly in Calabria, which is blessed by the bounties of two seas, the Tyrrhenian and the Ionian. It is a favorite first course at the restaurants in Calabria's seaside resorts. While most recipes for* insalata di mare *start by boiling the seafood, I roast mine instead. Roasting enhances the delicate sweet flavor of the seafood and keeps it succulent and tender. After all, nobody likes rubbery shrimp and squid! With plenty of fresh squeezed lemon juice, good quality olive oil, and garlic, this dish captures the quintessential flavors of Calabria. Be sure to serve it with a glass of white Verdicchio wine from Le Marche.*

2 lbs. lobster tails
Olive oil, for dressing and brushing
Dried oregano to taste
Paprika to taste
Salt and black pepper to taste
1¾ lbs. squid (pre-cleaned, tubes and tentacles)
1½ lbs. peeled and deveined shrimp
½ small Spanish or Vidalia onion, diced
2 ribs celery, diced

1 small red bell pepper, seeded and diced
3 cloves garlic, finely chopped
3 tbsp. finely chopped, firmly packed Italian flat leaf parsley
¾ cup pitted, halved black Cerignola olives
Juice of 3 lemons, divided

Preheat the oven to 400 degrees. Cut the lobster tails in half lengthwise and place them cut side up on a baking tray. Drizzle with olive oil, sprinkle with oregano, and season lightly with paprika, salt, and black pepper. Tent the baking tray with aluminum foil and roast for 20 minutes. Remove the foil and continue roasting for another 5 to 7 minutes or until the flesh is firm and opaque.

Cut the squid tubes into 1 inch wide rings; the squid tentacles should be left whole. Pat the shrimp and squid dry with a dish towel and place them in separate bowls. Drizzle each with olive oil, sprinkle with oregano, season with paprika, salt, and black pepper, and toss well so that everything is coated. Brush two baking trays lightly with olive oil. Place the shrimp on one baking tray and the squid on the other. Roast the shrimp and squid at 400 degrees for 15 to 20 minutes, or until firm and opaque.

Transfer the shrimp and squid to a mixing bowl using a slotted spoon and discard any cooking liquid remaining in the baking trays. Extract the lobster meat from the shells, chop it into chunks, and add it to the mixing bowl. Allow the seafood to cool to room temperature.

Add the onion, celery, bell pepper, garlic, parsley, and olives to the mixing bowl. Drizzle generously with olive oil, and squeeze over the juice of 2 lemons. Season with salt and black pepper and toss well. If you prefer more acidity, squeeze over the juice of the third lemon. Serve at room temperature or slightly chilled. Serves 4 to 6 adults.

Tonno in Agrodolce (Tuna in Sweet and Sour Sauce with Onions and Capers)

SICILY

Tuna migrate from the Atlantic Ocean to the deep waters off of Sicily's northwest coast every spring. Here, a traditional method of net fishing called mattanza *has been practiced since the Middle Ages. Each morning, the tuna fishermen set sail in groups of small, wooden boats in search of the migrating tuna. When they locate a school, the tuna are corralled into a net trap that is dropped into the water between the boats. The trap is referred to as the* camera della morte, *the "chamber of death." Once the tuna enter the so-called chamber, the net is raised and they are forced to the surface and harpooned. Today, only fishermen from the islands of Favignana and Marettimo still practice* mattanza, *as modern fishing methods are more practical.*

Here is a traditional tuna recipe from Sicily that has been handed down in my family for generations. In late summer, when tuna migrate to the waters off New Jersey, my father always set out on his boat, the Charluzza, *to catch them. When he returned with tuna, my mother always cooked them as my Sicilian grandmother did, in* agrodolce, *smothered with onions in a sweet and sour sauce. It is a tasty dish that has its roots in the coastal towns of western Sicily, where locals still hang on to ancient traditions. I like to add a handful of briny capers for a burst of contrasting flavor and plenty of garlic. When you have the freshest tuna, no other preparation will do! It's a bright and flavorful dish that is perfect when served slightly chilled in the summer.*

½ cup Sicilian capers preserved in salt
2½ lbs. tuna steaks (½ inch thick)
Salt and black pepper to taste
All-purpose, pre-sifted flour, for dredging
Olive oil, for frying

3 large Spanish or Vidalia onions, sliced into strips
6 cloves garlic, sliced
2 tbsp. sugar
¾ cup red wine vinegar

Remove the salt from the capers by soaking them in warm water for 15 minutes and then rinsing them under running water. Meanwhile, cut the tuna steaks into 3 inch pieces, season them with salt and black pepper, and dredge them in flour. Coat the bottom of a frying pan with olive oil, set it over medium-low heat, and fry the tuna for 2 minutes on each side or until firm but still slightly pink in the middle. Place the tuna in a casserole dish and set it to the side.

Coat the bottom of a deep frying pan generously with olive oil, set it over medium-low heat, and sauté the onions until soft. Add the garlic and continue sautéing for another minute. Stir in the sugar, vinegar, and capers, season with salt and black pepper, and remove the frying pan from the heat. Allow the onions to cool and then pour all of the onions and sauce over the tuna. Allow the tuna to marinate for at least 4 hours in the refrigerator before serving. Serve slightly chilled or at room temperature. Serves 4 to 6 adults.

Gamberi in Padella (Sautéed Head-On Shrimp with Tomatoes, Garlic, and Fresh Herbs)

SICILY

One afternoon in Italy I had a seafood lunch with my friend Salvo. We were at a small restaurant on a mountain above Bagheria with a fine view of the distant blue sea. The waiter brought us a platter of sautéed shrimp. They were cooked whole, with the heads intact. These shrimp were certainly plucked fresh from the sea that morning. What a treat! Salvo grabbed one, twisted off the head, and sucked out the juices. He motioned for me to grab a shrimp too. "Go on, take one!" He said. I took a shrimp and started to peel the shell. Salvo interrupted me, "No. Spupa!" he exclaimed. "You must suck the head! The juice is sweet and delicious!" I did as Salvo suggested and soon realized that there is simply no better way to eat shrimp. In America, shrimp are most always served stripped of their shells and deveined. How unfortunate! Look what I have been missing all these years! Here is a quick and easy recipe for sautéed head-on shrimp. A handful of diced fresh tomatoes and a splash of white wine creates a wonderful sauce for mopping with a piece of crusty bread. But be forewarned, eating them can be messy! There is sure to be a few squirts and splatters as you pick the meat and suck the juices from the heads. So roll up your sleeves and tuck a dish towel into your shirt as Salvo does!

2 lbs. jumbo, head-on shrimp
Olive oil, for sautéing
½ small Spanish or Vidalia onion, diced
4 cloves garlic, sliced
½ cup white wine
6 large tomatoes, diced

1½ tbsp. finely chopped, firmly packed basil
1½ tbsp. finely chopped, firmly packed oregano
Crushed red pepper flakes to taste
Salt and black pepper to taste

Leave the shells and heads of the shrimp intact, trim the antennas, and cut off the tips of the swimmerets with scissors. Coat the bottom of a 5½ quart frying pan generously with olive oil and set it over medium-low heat. Sauté the onion until soft, add the garlic, and continue sautéing for another minute. Add the wine, diced tomatoes, basil, and oregano and season with red pepper flakes, salt, and black pepper. Sauté the tomatoes for 5 to 7 minutes or until they have released their juices to create a sauce.

Add the shrimp. Cover the frying pan and sauté the shrimp, stirring occasionally, for 10 to 12 minutes or until firm and opaque. Serve hot with a piece of crusty Italian bread to mop up the sauce. Serves 4 to 6 adults.

Frutti di Mare alla Tarantina (Mixed Ionian Seafood with Fresh Herbs, Garlic, and White Wine)

APULIA

Aquaculture is now practiced in many parts of Italy. In the coastal lagoons of Veneto and Emilia Romagna, fish farms raise Mediterranean sea bass called branzino, *and along the rivers of Trentino-Alto Adige and Friuli-Venezia-Giulia, trout hatcheries produce fish with firm white flesh that is perfect for roasting. The center of aquaculture in Southern Italy is the region around Taranto. Here you will find a large sandy lagoon called Mare Piccolo, or the small sea. The clean, brackish waters of Mare Piccolo are perfect for raising mussels, oysters, and clams. If you travel the coastal road that winds around the Mare Piccolo, you are sure to see fishermen in small boats tending to their cages and traps, each marked by a buoy that bobs in the water. The rows of buoys seem to go on for miles!*

Taranto is a working-class port where simple dishes highlight the freshness of the local ingredients. If you head to a seafood restaurant in Taranto, chances are your dinner was plucked fresh from the Mare Piccolo that morning. Here is my take on Taranto-style sautéed mixed shellfish. With a splash of white wine and plenty of fresh herbs and garlic, it is flavorful and delicious. Be sure to serve it with a slice of crusty Italian bread to mop up the tasty sauce and a glass of chilled Frascati from Lazio. If you prefer, serve it over spaghetti.

2-3 dozen littleneck clams, or other small variety (depending on size)	4 cloves garlic, sliced
2 lbs. mussels (about 3 dozen medium mussels)	2 cups white wine
	Salt and black pepper to taste
1¾ lbs. squid (pre-cleaned, tubes and tentacles)	1½ lbs. peeled, deveined shrimp
Olive oil, for sautéing	4 tbsp. butter
½ small Spanish or Vidalia onion, diced	1½ tbsp. finely chopped, firmly packed oregano or thyme
	1½ tbsp. finely chopped, firmly packed Italian flat leaf parsley

Rinse the clams and mussels, remove the beards from the mussels, and cut the squid tubes into 1 inch rings. Leave the tentacles whole. Coat the bottom of a large pot with olive oil, place it over medium-low heat, and sauté the onion until soft. Add the garlic and sauté for another minute. Add the clams and mussels to the pot, pour in the wine, and season lightly with salt and black pepper. Cover the pot and simmer, stirring occasionally, for 5 to 10 minutes or until all of the shells have opened.

Add the shrimp, squid tubes, and tentacles. Continue simmering with the pot covered for another 7 to 10 minutes, stirring occasionally. The seafood is done when the shrimp and squid are firm and opaque. Use a skimmer to transfer the seafood to a large serving bowl, and then cover it with aluminum foil.

Reduce the heat to low, stir the butter and herbs into the sauce, and adjust the salt if necessary. Allow the sauce to simmer for another 2 minutes and then pour it over the seafood. Serve hot with crusty Italian bread. Serves 4 to 6 adults.

Vongole Oreganato (Clams Stuffed with Bread Crumbs, Prosciutto, and Red Bell Pepper)

CAMPANIA

Growing up in New Jersey in the 1970s, there were plenty of restaurants and pizzerias serving Italian American fare. Baked clams oreganato was a popular menu item back then and one of my favorites. It is a simple preparation of clams baked in a garlicky sauce and topped with crispy bread crumbs. This style of cooking was no doubt brought the United States by the wave of immigrants from Naples and other parts of Southern Italy who arrived in the early part of the twentieth century. Today, it is an Italian American classic! Here is my version of baked clams inspired by the dish I loved as a child. I mince the clams and stir them into seasoned bread crumbs with diced prosciutto, sweet red bell pepper, fresh herbs, and a splash of clam broth. Then I stuff the filling into half-shells and bake them until crisp on top and moist and delicious inside. If you head to the seaside towns on the Bay of Naples, such a tasty dish just might be on the menu! Roasted fish and seafood are always made with plenty of garlic, and sometimes a good sprinkle of pangrattato, *fresh-ground bread crumbs, is added for extra texture. This recipe is an Italian American classic derived from old-style flavors and techniques.*

½ loaf country-style Italian bread
Olive oil, for sautéing and brushing
½ small Spanish or Vidalia onion, diced
½ red bell pepper, seeded and diced
2 cloves garlic, finely chopped
2 tbsp. prosciutto, finely diced
3 tbsp. butter
1½ dozen cherrystone or top neck clams (2 to 2½ inches wide)

¾ cup white wine
¾ cup water
Black pepper to taste
2½ tbsp. finely chopped, firmly packed Italian flat leaf parsley
2 rounded tbsp. grated Parmigiano-Reggiano cheese
Salt to taste
4 lemons, cut into wedges

Grate enough bread for 2 cups of firmly packed crumbs. Set aside. Coat the bottom of a frying pan generously with olive oil, set it over medium-low heat, and sauté the onion and bell pepper until soft. Stir in the garlic, prosciutto, and butter, sauté for another minute, and set the frying pan to the side.

Place the clams in a pot and add the wine and water. Cover the pot and set it over medium-high heat for 3 minutes or until the clam shells have opened. Transfer the clams to a bowl using a skimmer and retain the cooking liquid.

Remove the clams from the shells, chop them, add them to the frying pan, and season with black pepper. Stir in the parsley, bread crumbs, and grated cheese. Add as much cooking liquid from the clams as is necessary to achieve a mixture that is moist and fluffy. If necessary, season with salt.

Preheat the oven to 425 degrees. Brush the insides of 16 half-shells lightly with olive oil and stuff them with the filling. Place the stuffed clams on a baking tray and bake for 15 minutes or until crisp and golden on top. Serve hot with lemon wedges. Serves 4 adults.

Zuppa di Vongole e Fagioli (Sautéed Clams and Cannellini Beans in Tomato Broth Served Over Grilled Roman Bread)

LAZIO

Northern Lazio feels more like part of Tuscany than the hinterland of Rome. The coastal plains of the Tuscan Maremma give way to the sandy beaches and fertile farmlands of Lazio, where wheat, beans, and artichokes are grown in a patchwork of fields. If you wish to experience the feel of Tuscany, then head to the medieval town of Montalto di Castro. Set on a low hill with views of the nearby mountains of Tuscany and a glimpse of the blue Tyrrhenian Sea, Montalto di Castro is full of Renaissance charm. The centro storico, *or old town, is surrounded by crenelated defensive walls made of ancient red brick and stone. After you walk through the arched entrance to the* centro storico, *you will find a network of cobblestone streets, arch-covered alleys, and medieval buildings with dark green shutters and terracotta pots filled with geraniums on every windowsill. In the central piazza, there is a grand Renaissance-style palazzo with vines of ivy growing up its walls to the very top. It is the sort of place one could envision a chance encounter with the likes of Leonardo da Vinci or Michelangelo.*

Fresh clams plucked from the sandy shores of Montalto Lido and cannellini beans from neighboring Tuscany make this dish an extra-special treat. It is a dish that combines the bounties of the fields with the bounties of the sea from this region. The tender, briny clams are tossed with the beans in a hearty tomato-based broth. Sautéed aromatics, fresh herbs, and a splash of white wine add even more depth of flavor to the broth, which is reminiscent of a hearty Manhattan clam chowder. Served atop a slice of grilled bread and accompanied by a glass of white Tuscan Vernaccia, it is the ultimate treat from northern Lazio.

Olive oil, for sautéing
1 large carrot, peeled and diced
½ Spanish or Vidalia onion, diced
1 rib celery, diced
4 cloves garlic, sliced
2 tbsp. tomato paste
1½ cups white wine
1 cup water
1½ tbsp. finely chopped, firmly packed Italian flat leaf parsley
½ tbsp. finely chopped, firmly packed rosemary
1 large bay leaf
Crushed red pepper flakes to taste (optional)
Salt and black pepper to taste
3 or 4 dozen littleneck clams, or other small variety (depending on size)
1 can (28 oz.) whole, peeled San Marzano tomatoes, diced (juice reserved)
24 oz. canned cannellini beans, drained
1 loaf country-style Italian bread

Coat the bottom of a 5½ quart frying pan generously with olive oil, set it over medium-low heat, and sauté the carrot, onion and celery until soft. Add the garlic and sauté for another minute. Push the vegetables to one side of the frying pan, tilt the frying pan to pool the oil on the other side, and fry the tomato paste for 1 minute.

Add the white wine, water, parsley, rosemary, and bay leaf. Season with red pepper flakes, salt, and black pepper and bring the sauce up to a simmer. Add the clams. Cover the frying pan and simmer for 7 to 10 minutes or until all of the shells have opened. Transfer the clams to a bowl using a skimmer, and cover the bowl with aluminum foil.

Add the diced tomatoes and their juices to the frying pan. Add the cannellini beans and simmer over low heat for 10 minutes, stirring occasionally. If the broth becomes too thick, add some water or more wine. Return the clams to the frying pan, gently toss everything together, and simmer for another minute. If necessary, adjust the seasoning. Remove the bay leaf before serving.

Slice the Italian bread into ½ inch thick slices, brush them lightly with olive oil, and grill them over a medium flame or toast them in a preheated, 425 degree oven for 7 minutes or until crisp and golden. Place a slice of grilled bread on each serving plate and then spoon plenty of clams, beans, and broth over top. Serve hot. Serves 4 to 6 adults.

Cozze Grattinate (Baked Mussels with Crispy Bread Crumb Topping)

APULIA

If you want to explore a coastal area of Italy that is off the radar of most international tourists, then head to the southern coast of Apulia. Small sandy beaches are tucked into the indents of the rocky coast, and there are beautiful sea caves, such as Grotta Zinzulusa, which are exciting to explore. You can enter Grotta Zinzulusa by boat or foot. Once you're inside, take a dip! When rays of sunshine peek into the cave, the illuminated water is a vibrant blue. Afterwards, snorkel in the clear Ionian Sea and admire the abundant marine life that lives along the craggy shoreline. With such active pursuits, you are bound to work up an appetite, and nothing could be better than sitting down at a seafood restaurant and snacking on a platter of plump, juicy mussels. Gathered from rocky shoals, mussels are plentiful along Apulia's Adriatic and Ionian coasts, and the Pugliese know just how to cook them. Here is a popular homestyle preparation from the region. Fresh mussels are steamed open and then stuffed with a flavorful bread crumb stuffing. It is simple and delicious. Once you start snacking on these, you won't be able to stop. They are addictive!

1 loaf country-style Italian bread
Olive oil, for sautéing
½ medium Spanish or Vidalia onion, diced
1 red bell pepper, seeded and diced
Salt and black pepper to taste
4 cloves garlic, finely chopped
⅓ cup grated Parmigiano-Reggiano cheese
2½ tbsp. finely chopped, firmly packed Italian flat leaf parsley
2 lbs. mussels (5 to 5½ dozen medium)
1½ cups white wine
3 tbsp. butter
4 lemons, cut into wedges

Grate enough bread for 3 cups of crumbs pressed firm and set aside. Coat the bottom of a frying pan with olive oil, set it over medium-low heat, add the onion and bell pepper, season with salt and black pepper, and sauté until soft. Add the garlic and sauté for another minute.

Place the bread crumbs, grated cheese, parsley, and sautéed items in a mixing bowl and toss everything together with a few drizzles of olive oil so that the mixture is moist and fluffy.

Remove the beards from the mussels. Place the mussels in a 5½ quart frying pan, add the white wine and butter, and season with salt and black pepper. Cover the frying pan and sauté over medium heat for 5 minutes or until the shells have opened. Allow the mussels to cool so that they can be handled.

Preheat the oven to 415 degrees. Drizzle some sauce from the frying pan on each mussel and then press a spoonful of the bread crumb mixture between the shells. Place the mussels on a baking tray and bake for 10 minutes or until the bread crumbs are crisp and golden on top. Serve hot with lemon wedges. Serves 6 adults.

Granchio in Salsa di Pomodoro (Crabs Braised in Tomato Sauce)

APULIA

Crabs are a favorite in Apulia and are considered a delicacy because they are hard to catch. Sweet and succulent, the crabs are tossed into a grand seafood stew or simply braised in fresh tomato sauce. Here on the east coast of the United States, we also have wonderful crabs. When I was a child, my father took me crabbing, and sometimes my Sicilian grandmother came too. We would catch the crabs by tying a chicken leg to a string and tossing it in the water. We would wait for the crabs to grab the chicken leg and then pull them to the surface and scoop them up in a net. We always caught plenty, and when we returned home my mother would toss the crabs into an enormous pot of simmering tomato sauce. The sauce was always the perfect condiment for a bowl of spaghetti, which my mother served alongside the crabs. Picking the crab meat and sucking the sweet juices from the shells and claws was always messy. As young children, there was sure to be sauce on our little chins. But my Sicilian grandmother was always standing nearby with a mapina, *or dish towel. "Come here, let me wipe your* musa," *she would say. And before we could run, Grandma had our chins wiped clean!*

8-10 live, jumbo blue crabs or 4 pre-cleaned and pre-cooked large Dungeness crabs

3½ quarts Salsa Marinara *(see page 121)*

2 bay leaves (optional)

Crushed red pepper flakes to taste (optional)

Salt and black pepper to taste

Prepare the blue crabs by removing and discarding the top shell and innards, snipping off the ends of the legs with scissors, and chopping the crabs in half. Wash the crabs under cool running water and pat them dry.

Prepare the Salsa Marinara following the recipe on page 121. If you wish, add bay leaves and additional crushed red pepper flakes to the sauce.

Before the sauce simmers, add the crabs to the pot and then let the sauce simmer for 1½ hours over low heat, stirring frequently. If you are using Dungeness crabs, simmer for 45 minutes. Remove the bay leaves and adjust the seasoning with salt and black pepper if necessary. Serve hot accompanied by a bowl of spaghetti tossed with the crab sauce. Serves 4 adults.

Aragosta in Forno (Roasted Lobster with Spicy Garlic and Anchovy Sauce)

SICILY

When the people of Palermo want the freshest seafood, they drive fifteen minutes west to the busy fishing port of Sferracavallo, where there are just as many seafood restaurants as there are boats in the harbor. The town bustles with all of the chaos one would expect in Sicily: crowded sidewalks, traffic jams, and plenty of traffic lights and signs that go completely ignored! So when you go to Sferracavallo, don't be surprised when a car driving in the wrong direction down a one way street meets you head on! Just be patient, stay alert, and do not lose sight of the fact that you will soon be eating the best seafood ever! At the end of the day, you'll agree that it was worth it!

I enjoyed wonderful seafood meals in Sferracavallo with my friends Salvatore and Anna. Salvatore always drove us there from Palermo, jamming on the brakes, making illegal turns, honking the horn, and cursing all the way! I always wore a seatbelt. Once we arrived at their favorite restaurant, we would sit for hours as waves of food were brought to the table. Raw shellfish was brought first. Then we feasted on fried anchovies, pasta with sea urchin roe or cuttlefish ink, and broiled swordfish or tuna. If we were lucky, the restaurant had fresh spiny lobsters that day, grilled to perfection and topped with a garlicky sauce. Here is my rendition of Aragosta alla Sferracavallo. The savory sauce is flavored with garlic, anchovies, and crushed red chilies. You can also grill the lobster instead of roasting it in the oven with bread crumbs.

2 thick slices country-style Italian bread (optional)

¾ cup olive oil

4 cloves garlic, finely chopped

6 fillets Italian jarred anchovies packed in olive oil, finely chopped

½ tsp. crushed red pepper flakes (or more if you prefer)

Black pepper to taste

3 tbsp. butter

1 tbsp. finely chopped, firmly packed Italian flat leaf parsley

4 lobsters (1½ to 1¾ lbs. each)

If you prefer a crispy topping, grate the bread in a food processor and moisten the crumbs with a drizzle of olive oil. Set the bread crumb topping aside.

Place the ¾ cup of olive oil in an 8½ inch frying pan, set it over low heat, add the garlic, anchovies, and red pepper flakes, and season with black pepper. Sauté for 1 minute or until the anchovies have melted. Then whisk in the butter and parsley and remove the frying pan from the burner.

Preheat the oven to 425 degrees. Place the lobsters on their backs and use a sharp, sturdy knife to cut them in half lengthwise. Place the lobster halves cut side up on a baking tray and drizzle plenty of spicy sauce over top. If you wish, sprinkle with the bread crumbs. Tent the baking tray with aluminum foil and roast for 15 minutes. Then remove the foil and continue roasting for another 7 to 10 minutes or until the flesh is firm. If using bread crumbs, they should be crisp and golden. Serve hot with more spicy sauce on the side. Serve hot. Serves 4 adults.

Calamari Ripieni di Cuscusu (Squid Stuffed with Couscous and Topped with Spicy Garlic and Anchovy Sauce)

SICILY

What food does Sicily have in common with Morocco and Israel? Couscous! If you want to learn about Sicily's culinary ties to North Africa and the Middle East, then don't miss the International Couscous Festival in San Vito lo Capo. Each September, couscous aficionados descend upon the sleepy town to celebrate couscous traditions from all around the Mediterranean. It is a celebration of the cultural traditions that unite the peoples of the Mediterranean Basin. There is great food, international music, and an international couscous competition, where different countries compete to be crowned "il Capo di Cuscusu," or the master of couscous.

Serve this exotic dish at your next dinner party and your guests will dub you "il Capo" too! This is my favorite recipe for stuffed squid, and in this preparation no part of the squid is wasted. The tentacles are chopped, sautéed until tender, and stirred into couscous that is flavored with fresh herbs. The couscous is then stuffed into whole squid tubes, which are sealed with a toothpick and grilled or roasted to perfection. The finishing touch is a drizzle of spicy garlic and anchovy sauce that is full of bold, Sicilian flavor. It is an inventive, modern dish you might just find at the couscous festival in San Vito. Be sure to serve it with a glass of white Corvo wine from Sicily.

5 cups prepared couscous *(see page 116)*
2½ lbs. squid (pre-cleaned, tentacles and 4-6 inch tubes)
Olive oil, for sautéing
½ medium Spanish or Vidalia onion, diced
4 cloves garlic, finely chopped
3 tbsp. finely chopped, firmly packed Italian flat leaf parsley
Salt and black pepper to taste

For the spicy sauce:
¾ cup olive oil
4 cloves garlic, finely chopped
6 fillets Italian jarred anchovies packed in olive oil, finely chopped
½ tsp. crushed red pepper flakes (or more if you prefer)
Black pepper to taste
3 tbsp. butter

Prepare the couscous following the recipe on page 116 or, if you prefer, use packaged, instant couscous. Chop the squid tentacles.

Coat the bottom of a frying pan with olive oil and sauté the onion over medium-low heat until soft. Add the garlic, tentacles, and parsley and season with salt and black pepper. Continue sautéing until the tentacles are firm and any excess liquid in the frying pan has cooked down.

Preheat the oven to 415 degrees. In a bowl, combine the sautéed items with the couscous. Stuff the squid tubes with the couscous mixture and secure the edges with a toothpick. Brush the stuffed squid with olive oil, season lightly with salt, and set on a baking tray that has also been brushed with olive oil. Bake for 20 minutes or until firm and opaque. Alternatively, grill the squid over a low flame for 3 minutes on each side with the cover down.

Meanwhile, prepare the spicy sauce: Place the olive oil in an 8½ inch frying pan and set it over low heat. Add the garlic, anchovies, and red pepper flakes and season with black pepper. Sauté for 1 minute or until the anchovies have melted. Whisk in the butter and remove the frying pan from the burner.

When the stuffed squid are done, arrange them on a serving platter and drizzle with sauce. Serve hot, with more sauce on the side. Serves 6 to 8 adults.

Polpo in Forno (Citrus Marinated Roasted Octopus)

BASILICATA

I once took a stroll alongside the harbor in the tiny port of Maratea to admire the fishing boats. There was a fisherman with his boat tied up to the quay. He had a bucket, inside of which were three large octopuses. He took one from the bucket and slammed it down repeatedly against the hard cement wall of the quay. I asked, "Why are you doing this to the octopus?" The fisherman smiled and replied, "You must beat the octopus to make it tender—otherwise it will be tough like rubber when it is cooked." I have since come to realize that the wise old fisherman was indeed correct. For octopus to be soft and delicious, it must be either tenderized before cooking or braised for a very long time.

Along Basilicata's tiny stretch of Tyrrhenian coast, grilled octopus is a favorite. It is a tasty treat you are sure to find at one of the restaurants in Maratea. Here is my version. I simmer the octopus in water flavored with white wine, citrus, garlic, and bay leaves. I also throw in the cork from a wine bottle, which helps to tenderize the octopus. This is an old trick that I learned from a friend in Italy. When the octopus is tender, I pull it from the pot and let it rest in a flavorful citrus marinade for at least 4 hours before setting it under the broiler to crisp up.

For the boil:	For the marinade:
1 whole 3 lbs. octopus	2 cloves garlic, finely chopped
1 large California navel orange	2 tbsp. finely chopped, firmly packed
2 large lemons	Italian flat leaf parsley
6 cloves whole garlic	1 tbsp. finely chopped, firmly packed
4 bay leaves	oregano
1 tbsp. whole black peppercorns	Juice of 1 large lemon
2 rounded tsp. Sicilian sea salt	Juice of 1 California navel orange
1 wine bottle cork	½ cup olive oil
4 cups white wine	Salt and black pepper to taste
8 cups water	

Place the octopus in an 8 quart soup pot. Slice the orange and lemons in half and add them to the pot along with the garlic, bay leaves, peppercorns, salt, and cork. Pour over the wine and water. Cover the pot and simmer over low heat for 1½ hours. Drain the octopus and allow it to cool to room temperature.

Meanwhile, prepare the marinade. Whisk together the garlic, parsley, oregano, lemon juice, orange juice, and olive oil and season with salt and black pepper.

Remove the tentacles from the octopus, trim any excess skin from the tentacles, and slice the body in half. Place the octopus in a bowl and pour the marinade over

top. Allow the octopus to marinate in the refrigerator for at least 4 hours.

Preheat the oven to 425 degrees. Transfer the octopus to a roasting pan and drizzle with some marinade. Roast for 7 minutes, then turn the oven up to broil. Broil on high for 3 to 5 minutes or until crisp. Serve hot topped with a drizzle of the leftover marinade. Serves 2 to 4 adults.

Fritto Misto di Trabocchi (Mixed Fry of Mediterranean Seafood)

ARUZZO/MOLISE

Trabocchi *are traditional fishing structures built along the Adriatic coast from Abruzzo to Apulia. They are ingenious devices composed of long outriggers, winches, and nets that stand on piers jutting into the sea. The nets are lowered into the water to scoop up the fish as they swim by. Along the Gargano coast, white limestone outcrops fall into deep, azure waters. It's the perfect spot for* trabocchi. *As you drive the coastal road that winds around pine-clad hills and striking whitewashed towns such as Vieste, you are sure to see many* trabocchi. *Further up the coast in Abruzzo and Molise, the* trabocchi *reach into the sea from wide, sandy beaches that are shared with sunbathing tourists. It is no doubt a curious sight! If you have time, stop and see what the nets bring in. There is sure to be a wide variety of fish, shrimp, squid, and other creatures both big and small.*

This is a recipe that calls for any combination of fresh seafood pulled in by the trabocchi *that day. The idea is to use whatever seafood is freshest, regardless of how big or small. And the more variety the better! Simply dusted in flour and fried until golden and crisp, nothing could be easier than a* fritto misto, *or mixed fry. For a taste of Abruzzo's vibrant port city of Pescara, serve it with a quick, light marinara sauce made with San Marzano tomatoes and plenty of crushed red pepper flakes. For a taste of the Gargano coast, serve the* fritto misto *with plenty of fresh lemon wedges. It is sure to please either way!*

6 lbs. assorted fish and seafood	3 quarts corn oil
Salt to taste	4 lemons, cut into wedges (optional)
All-purpose, pre-sifted flour, for dredging	Salsa Marinara, to accompany (optional, see page 121)

Use a combination of at least 4 of the following: whitebait, anchovies, smelts, red mullet, sole, sea bass, whiting, hake, cod, skate wings, shrimp, and squid. Small fish such as whitebait, anchovies, and smelts should be fried whole. Larger fish should be filleted and cut into large pieces. Whiting and hake can be cut into 3 inch chunks with the bone left in. Shrimp should be peeled and deveined and squid should be cut into 1 inch rings.

Heat the oil in a 5½ quart frying pan. Season the seafood with salt, and then dredge in flour. Fry the seafood until crisp and golden, place on paper towels to absorb the excess oil, and sprinkle lightly with salt. Serve hot, accompanied by lemon wedges or Salsa Marinara. Serves 4 to 6 adults.

Polpette di Sarde Finto (Pan Fried Tuna Cakes)

SICILY

One afternoon, my friend Anna told me about something very unusual that she ate at a restaurant in the heart of old Palermo. She described it to me with such animation and passion that I wished I had a bite! "I ate something so wonderful it brought tears to my eyes," she explained. "They were meatballs so moist and soft that they melted in my mouth, and they were full of such deep flavor that my taste buds cried for joy!" She then asked me to guess what these amazing meatballs were made from. "Surely, they were made from fine-ground veal and pork," I said. "No, they were made from sardines!" she exclaimed. "Certainly you have never eaten anything like this before—it is a very ancient dish from Palermo." I then asked Anna to make the dish for me, but she declined. "It is a very difficult dish to make, and there is only one restaurant in Palermo that makes them so delicious." So the only thing necessary for me to try this tantalizing dish was a reservation!

When I returned home from Sicily, I gave it my best shot to recreate the unusual sardine balls. I searched the local markets for fresh sardines, but unfortunately they were not available. So instead, I improvised and used fresh tuna. I call the recipe Polpette di Sarde Finto, which means "fake sardine balls." If my friend Anna were to try them, I'm sure she would exclaim, "Finto!" Nonetheless, I think she would approve with the disclaimer that they simply are not as good as the real ones served at her favorite restaurant in old Palermo. If fresh sardines are available, by all means use them instead. Other oily fish such as mackerel or salmon would also be a fine substitute. Regardless of which fish you use, serve them with wedges of fresh lemon. For sardines, tuna, and mackerel, a light tomato sauce pairs well too!

3 thick slices country-style Italian bread

2 lbs. tuna steaks

Olive oil, for sautéing and frying

½ small Spanish or Vidalia onion

½ red bell pepper

1 clove garlic, chopped

4 fillets Italian jarred anchovies packed in olive oil, finely chopped

2 eggs, beaten

⅓ cup grated Parmigiano Reggiano cheese

3 tbsp. finely chopped, firmly packed Italian flat leaf parsley

Black pepper and salt to taste

4 lemons, cut into wedges (optional)

Salsa Marinara to accompany (optional, see page 121)

Grate enough Italian bread in a food processor for 1 cup of firmly pressed crumbs. Transfer the crumbs to a bowl and pour over enough water to moisten. Set aside. Grind the tuna in the food processor until you achieve the consistency of ground meat.

Coat the bottom of a frying pan with olive oil, set it over medium-low heat, and sauté the onion and bell pepper until soft. Add the garlic and anchovies and continue sautéing until the anchovies have melted. Remove the frying pan from the heat and allow the sautéed items to cool.

Place the ground tuna, beaten eggs, grated cheese, parsley, bread crumbs, and sautéed items in a large mixing bowl. Season with black pepper and lightly with salt. Combine thoroughly, without overworking. The consistency should be soft and moist. If necessary, add more water to soften.

Form the mixture into palm-sized ovals. Place ½ inch of olive oil in a large, deep frying pan and set it over medium heat. Fry the tuna balls on both sides until golden brown and then set them on paper towels to absorb the excess oil. Serve hot with lemon wedges or topped with Salsa Marinara.

Pescespada alla Ghiotta (Roasted Swordfish with Cherry Tomatoes, Black Olives, and Capers)

CALABRIA

Since the days of antiquity, swordfish have roamed the swirling waters of the Straits of Messina between Sicily and Calabria. In Greek mythology, this treacherous, narrow passage was the home of two sea monsters: Scylla and Charybdis. Ancient Greek sailors would not dare enter the straits for fear of being eaten! Today, the straits are home to car ferries and hydrofoils that transport tourists to and from the island. Nonetheless, the swirling waters of Scylla and Charybdis still produce the finest swordfish in all of the Mediterranean. Be sure to take a late morning stroll along the quayside in Bagnara's port when the fishing boats return. It is sure to be quite a scene with swordfish hanging on display and plenty of locals eagerly waiting for the fishermen to slice them into steaks for the perfect afternoon meal.

Alla ghiotta is a favorite preparation for swordfish in both Calabria and Sicily. Truth be told, it is a wonderful preparation for just about any type of firm saltwater fish. So if swordfish is not available, be inventive! Fresh tuna, Chilean sea bass, or halibut steaks would all be fine substitutes. For a true taste of Messina, use plump black olives. For a true taste of Reggio Calabria, use green olives instead and add a few pinches of crushed red pepper flakes. Pair this dish with a glass of white Verdicchio wine from Le Marche and you have a meal that legends are made of!

Olive oil, for sautéing
4 cloves garlic, sliced
6 fillets Italian jarred anchovies in olive oil, finely chopped
1 dry quart cherry tomatoes, sliced in half
2 tbsp. capers in brine
⅔ cup pitted and halved black Cerignola or Kalamata olives
1½ tbsp. finely chopped, firmly packed oregano

1½ tbsp. finely chopped, firmly packed Italian flat leaf parsley
1 tsp. crushed red pepper flakes (or more if you prefer)
Salt and black pepper to taste
2 tbsp. red wine vinegar
3 tbsp. butter
6 swordfish steaks (about ¾ to 1 inch thick)

Coat the bottom of a frying pan with olive oil, set it over medium-low heat, and sauté the garlic until soft. Add the anchovies. Let the anchovies sizzle in the oil for half a minute and then add the cherry tomatoes, capers, olives, oregano, and parsley. Season with red pepper flakes, salt, and black pepper and continue sautéing for 5 minutes or until the skins of the cherry tomatoes begin to pucker. Then stir in the vinegar and butter and sauté for another minute.

Set your grill to a medium-low flame and grill the fish for 5 minutes on each side with the cover down. If you prefer to roast the swordfish, brush the steaks with olive oil, season them with salt and black pepper, set them in a baking dish that has been brushed with olive oil, and bake in a preheated 400 degree oven for 20 minutes or until firm. Place the swordfish steaks on a serving platter and spoon the sauce over top. Serve hot. Serves 6 adults.

Baccala in Marinara (Salted Cod with Tomatoes, Onions, and Black Olives)

BASILICATA

The Feast of the Seven Fishes, or La Festa dei Sette Pesci, is a traditional dinner served on Christmas Eve in Southern Italy. For seafood lovers like me, this is the most eagerly anticipated meal of the year. The exact origins of this wonderful tradition are unknown. However, one thing is certain: at least seven different fish dishes must be served for the feast. In some places, it is customary to serve even more! The number varies from region to region and from family to family. Some families serve seven dishes to symbolize the seven sacraments, while others serve ten dishes for the Ten Commandments. The families that really love seafood serve thirteen dishes in honor of Jesus and the twelve apostles. Now that's a lot of fish!

Baccala in Marinara is a favorite Christmas Eve dish for many Italians. We serve it every year just as my grandparents and great-grandparents did. The chunks of flaky white cod and plump black olives are smothered in a flavorful sauce made with diced San Marzano tomatoes, onions, and fresh garlic. We always serve it in a soup bowl with a piece of crusty bread for mopping. Here is my menu for La Festa dei Sette Pesci: Insalata di Mare, Insalata di Bacala, Cozze Grattinate, Pasta con Alici, Pasta con Frutti di Mare, Baccala in Marinara, and Fritto Misto di Mare. Choose whatever seafood you like for your feast, but be sure to include Baccala in Marinara! Buon Natale!

2 lbs. salted cod fillets
Olive oil, for sautéing
1 large Spanish or Vidalia onion, sliced into strips
3 cloves garlic, sliced
2 cans (28 oz. each) crushed San Marzano tomatoes
1½ tbsp. finely chopped, firmly packed basil
1½ tbsp. finely chopped, firmly packed oregano
Crushed red pepper flakes to taste (optional)
Salt and black pepper to taste
1½ cups pitted, whole black Cerignola olives

Soak the salted cod in plenty of cool water for at least 48 hours and change the water at least 3 times daily. The fillets will rehydrate and become soft and pliable. Remove the fillets from the water, pat them dry, and cut them into 3 inch pieces.

Coat the bottom of a large, deep frying pan with olive oil, set it over medium-low heat, and sauté the onion until soft. Add the garlic and continue sautéing for another minute. Then add the tomatoes, basil, and oregano and season with red pepper flakes, salt, and black pepper. Slosh ⅔ cup of water in each tomato can and add it to the frying pan. Add the salted cod and olives and simmer over low heat for 40 to 45 minutes or until the salted cod is tender and flaky. Stir gently every few minutes. If the sauce becomes too thick, add more water. Serve hot with a piece of crusty Italian bread. Serves 4 to 6 adults.

Coda Di Rospo con Olive Verde e Caperi (Monkfish Sautéed in White Wine Sauce with Green Olives and Capers)

ABRUZZO/MOLISE

Monkfish live in the deep waters of the Atlantic Ocean and Mediterranean Basin. It is a common catch for the deep-sea fishermen of Pescara on Abruzzo's sandy Adriatic coast. In the United States, monkfish has long been called "the poor man's lobster," and with good reason. The firm, sweet flesh is far superior to other varieties of fish. How the "poor man" got involved, I do not know. Because truth be told, monkfish is quite expensive these days! In fact, where I live in Virginia, it's more expensive per pound than Maine lobster. I am eagerly awaiting the day when the roles are reversed and lobster becomes known as "the poor man's monkfish."

If you have never eaten monkfish, be sure to give it a try. It stands up well to a flavorful sauce and is one of the usual cast of characters in a brodetto, *or stew of mixed fish. Along the Adriatic coast, it is also sautéed with white wine, which is certain to be a Verdicchio from Le Marche. My version of monkfish with white wine sauce includes briny capers, green olives from Ascoli Piceno, and plenty of fresh garlic and herbs. Serve it with a piece of crusty Italian bread to mop up the wonderful sauce!*

2½ lbs. monkfish fillets
Salt and black pepper to taste
All-purpose, pre-sifted flour, for dredging
Olive oil, for frying and sautéing
4 green onions, diced
4 cloves garlic, sliced
1½ cups white wine
1½ cups fish stock
Zest of 1 lemon

1 bay leaf
2 tbsp. finely chopped, firmly packed Italian flat leaf parsley
1 tbsp. finely chopped, firmly packed oregano or thyme
2 tbsp. capers in brine
1 cup pitted, whole green Ascolane or Cerignola olives
3 tbsp. butter

Cut the fillets into 3 inch chunks, season with salt and black pepper, and dredge them in flour. Coat the bottom of a large, deep frying pan with olive oil, set it over medium-low heat, and brown the fish on all sides until lightly golden. Transfer the fish to a bowl and cover with aluminum foil.

Add the green onions to the frying pan and sauté until soft. Add the garlic and continue sautéing for another minute. Stir in the wine, stock, lemon zest, bay leaf, parsley, and oregano. Season with salt and black pepper, and then return the fish to the frying pan and add the capers and olives. Sauté for 12 to 14 minutes or until the fish is firm, turning it every so often. If necessary, add a few additional splashes of wine or broth. When the fish is done, stir the butter into the sauce and remove the bay leaf. Serve hot. Serves 4 to 6 adults.

Grigliata Mista con Salsa Verde (Grilled Seafood with Green Sauce)

CALABRIA

Sicilian salt-cured capers are expensive and hard to find in the United States. You must search them out at Italian specialty shops. The first time I ate salt-cured capers was in Sicily, while visiting my friends Rita and Salvo. When I left, Rita gave me several large bags to take home. I added them to all sorts of dishes but ran out after a few months. I called their daughter Paola, who also lives in the United States, and asked, "The next time your mother sends you a care package, please ask her to put some capers in for me." And so began the great caper connection! Thanks to Rita, for the past twelve years my pantry has remained stocked with the best-quality Sicilian capers cured in Mediterranean sea salt. They are large, plump, and full of flavor.

Salsa verde is a popular sauce throughout Italy. In Northern Italy, it is prepared with chopped cornichons, hard-boiled egg, and tangy mustard, whereas in Calabria bread is used as a binder instead of egg and salt-cured capers are thrown into the mix. Regardless of the preparation, it is a light, refreshing, and flavorful accompaniment to a platter of grilled summer fare. Here is my tasty version. I make it during the summer when my garden is overflowing with Italian parsley, and I always use the capers that Rita sends me. We eat it on just about everything, but I like it best with bold, flavorful fish just as the Calabrese do! The possibilities are endless. Serve salsa verde at your next cookout when grilled fish is on the menu and pair it with a glass of chilled white Sicilian Corvo wine.

½ cup Sicilian capers preserved in salt
4 cups firmly packed whole sprigs Italian flat leaf parsley
½ medium Spanish or Vidalia onion, roughly chopped
½ large red bell pepper, seeded and roughly chopped
½ cup pitted, whole Castevetrano or Calabresi olives
2 cloves garlic
1 cup olive oil
⅔ cup red wine vinegar
Zest of 1 lemon
5 fillets Italian jarred anchovies in olive oil
4 extra-large hard-boiled egg yolks
Salt and black pepper to taste
8 assorted fish steaks (tuna and swordfish)

Soak the capers for 10 minutes in warm water and then rinse them under running water to remove the salt. Pulse the parsley, onion, pepper, olives, capers, and garlic in a food processor until finely chopped and then transfer the mixture to a large mixing bowl. Add the olive oil, vinegar, lemon zest, anchovies, and egg yolks to the food processor and blend until smooth. Add the dressing to the mixing bowl, season with salt and black pepper, and stir well. Allow the salsa verde to sit in the refrigerator for at least 4 hours before serving.

Brush the fish steaks with olive oil, season them with salt and black pepper, and grill them over a medium-low flame for 5 minutes on each side. Serve hot with slightly chilled salsa verde spooned over top. Serves 8 to 10 adults.

Zuppa di Pesce con Cuscusu (Mixed Fish in Saffron Fennel Broth Served with Couscous)

SICILY

From its mountain perch, the fortified town of Erice has a magnificent view of Trapani's bustling harbor and the coastal salt flats where Italy's finest sea salt is produced. My friend Salvatore once told me, "The sweetest seafood in the Mediterranean comes from the waters off Trapani." When I asked why, he explained, "Because the sea is saltier there than anywhere else." I do not know whether Salvatore's theory is true, and I am not here to sort out fact from convenient fiction, but I surmise that this may be a tall tale created by the Trapanese fishermen who want to sell their catch. One thing I do know for certain is that if you head to Erice, you are sure to dine on delicious seafood!

With high defensive walls and a maze of cobblestone streets winding between medieval churches and palazzos, Erice is a throwback to the days when Barbary pirates roamed Sicily's coast. You will find charming restaurants housed in historic buildings that serve traditional Trapanese dishes. Mine and Salvatore's favorite is couscous served with an exotic fish stew flavored with fennel and saffron. In Erice, the fish stew is made with at least four varieties of fish, which may include red mullet, sardines, monkfish, and sea bass. I add chopped almonds and raisins to the couscous for added texture and a touch of sweetness, which gives the dish even more Sicilian flare. It is a truly unique and tasty dish that is always made best with sweet fish plucked fresh from the salty waters of Trapani! Serve it with a bold white Gavi wine from Piedmont.

8 cups couscous, steamed *(see page 116)*
¾ cup slivered almonds
½ cup raisins
Olive oil, for sautéing
½ large Spanish or Vidalia onion, diced
4 cloves garlic, finely chopped
½ cup tomato paste
1 quart fish or seafood broth
3 cups water
½ cup pasteurized orange juice
Zest of 1 California navel orange
3 tbsp. finely chopped Italian flat leaf parsley
1 rounded tsp. dried oregano
2 fresh bay leaves
3 large pinches saffron
1 large bulb fennel, bulb chopped into strips and fronds finely chopped
Crushed red pepper flakes to taste (optional)
Salt and black pepper to taste
3 lbs. mixed fish fillets (monkfish, sea bass, grouper, cod, or other firm fish)

Prepare the couscous according to the instructions on page 116. Toast the almonds in the oven at 375 degrees for 5 minutes or until golden. Stir the almonds and raisins into the couscous before you set it to steam.

Meanwhile, prepare the fish soup. Coat the bottom of a soup pot with olive oil and set it over medium-low heat. Add the onion to the pot and sauté until soft. Add the garlic and continue sautéing for another minute. Push the onions and garlic to one side of the pot, tilt the pot to pool the oil on the other side, and fry the tomato paste for 2 minutes. Add the broth, water, orange juice, orange zest, parsley, oregano, bay leaves, saffron, fennel, and fronds. Season with red pepper flakes, salt, and black pepper and simmer over low heat for 30 minutes or until the fennel is tender.

Slice the fish into large chunks and season them with salt and black pepper. Coat the bottom of a large frying pan with olive oil, set it over medium-low heat, and lightly brown the fish on all sides. Transfer the fish to the soup pot and continue simmering the soup for another fifteen minutes or until the fish is fully cooked and tender. Remove the bay leaves and adjust the seasoning if necessary. Place a heaping mound of couscous on individual serving plates and spoon the fish soup over the couscous so that it absorbs all of the delicious broth. Serve hot. Serves 4 to 6 adults.

Merluzzo in Forno con Piselli (Oven Roasted Whiting with Fresh Herbs and Peas)

CAMPANIA

When I was a child living in New Jersey, my father took me deep-sea fishing every winter for whiting, or merluzzo *as we called them in Italian. He always seemed to pick the coldest and roughest day of the year. We would bundle up in thermal underwear, layers of clothes, and a heavy jacket and head to the Jersey shore to hop on one of the party boats. On a good day, we would catch a hundred or more fish between us. We would share the fish with our family and friends and pack plenty of them in our freezer.*

Italians are quite fond of merluzzo, *which are a bottom fish similar to hake or cod. A similar species caught off the coast of Sicily is called* nasello, *and it is equally delicious. In Palermo, they prepare it in many different ways. After a long, cold day of fishing, my father and I always enjoyed a bowl of* zuppa di merluzzo, *or whiting soup, which is a traditional Sicilian dish that he no doubt learned from his mother. On Christmas Eve, the* merluzzo *was always dredged in flour, fried until crisp and golden, and served as part of a* fritto misto. *For a quick and easy meal, I roast* merluzzo *in the oven with plenty of fresh Mediterranean herbs, just as they do in Palermo. For a nice presentation, I remove the bone, spread out the meat on a serving plate, and top it with sautéed fresh peas. The sweetness of the peas is a perfect match for this delicate, mild flavored fish.*

6 whole whiting (1½ to 2 lbs. each)	2 cloves garlic, finely chopped
Olive oil, for brushing and sautéing	1 can (14.5 oz.) diced tomatoes
Salt and black pepper to taste	½ tbsp. finely chopped, firmly packed basil
3 tbsp. finely chopped, firmly packed Italian flat leaf parsley	1 cup water
3 tbsp. finely chopped, firmly packed oregano	3 cups frozen peas, thawed
4 small sprigs of rosemary	Paprika to taste
½ Spanish or Vidalia onion, diced	Crushed red pepper flakes to taste (optional)

Dress the fish by removing the heads, scales, and innards. Clean the fish under running water and then pat them dry. Brush the outsides and cavities of the fish with olive oil and season them with salt and black pepper. Sprinkle the parsley and oregano inside the cavities of the fish.

Preheat the oven to 425 degrees. Place the fish inside a baking dish that has been brushed with olive oil and nestle the sprigs of rosemary between them. Cover the baking dish with aluminum foil and bake for 30 minutes or until firm and flaky.

Meanwhile, coat the bottom of a saucepan with olive oil, set it over medium-low heat, and sauté the onion until soft. Add the garlic and sauté for another minute. Add the tomatoes, basil, and water to create a broth. If the diced tomatoes are packed in puree, add another ½ cup of water to thin it out. Season the broth with red pepper flakes, salt, and black pepper. Simmer the broth over low heat for 15 minutes. Stir in the peas and simmer for another 3 minutes.

When the whiting are done, place them on individual serving dishes. Remove and discard the spines of the fish, spread open the meat, and spoon the peas and tomato broth over top. Serve hot. Serves 6 adults.

Sarde Beccafico (Baked Sardines with Fennel, Tomatoes, Pine Nuts, and Raisins)

SICILY

"My squid have long legs like an American woman!" "My mullet are as red as the ass of a bad child!" These are just some of the exuberant statements you will hear as you walk through Palermo's Vucciria market. It is quite a scene as fishmongers, produce vendors, and other purveyors shout and sing to get your attention. These vendors know that a catchy pitch is always sure to land a sale! Set in the heart of ancient Palermo, the narrow streets of the Vucciria are always packed with vendors, like Sicilian sardines in a jar. It is a feast for all five senses. Brightly colored fruits and vegetables will catch your eye, the aroma of spices will tickle your nose, and loud shouts will reverberate in your ears as merchants beckon you to taste, sniff, or squeeze. Sicilians have been shopping in markets like these for centuries. With the feel of a Middle Eastern bazaar, they are exotic places, reminiscent of the days when Palermo was called Bal'harm by its Arab rulers. Here is a delicious and intriguing recipe straight from the Vucciria. Bold, flavorful sardines are baked in a casserole with fennel, tomatoes, pine nuts, raisins, and a hint of orange zest. They are then topped with crispy bread crumbs, which add texture and interest. It is a true taste of old Palermo!

½ loaf country-style Italian bread
Olive oil, for drizzling and sautéing
½ medium Spanish or Vidalia onion, diced
1 bulb fennel with fronds, diced (bulb and fronds separated)
Salt and black pepper to taste
3 cloves garlic, finely chopped
1 can (28 oz.) whole, peeled San Marzano tomatoes, diced (juice reserved)
⅓ cup pine nuts, toasted
⅓ cup firmly packed raisins
Zest of 1 California navel orange
12 sardines (8-10 inches long)

Grate enough bread in a food processor for 2 cups of crumbs. Place the bread crumbs in a bowl and drizzle them with olive oil so that the mixture is moist and fluffy. Coat the bottom of a frying pan generously with olive oil and set it over medium-low heat. Add the onion and fennel bulb, season with salt and black pepper, and sauté until soft. Add the garlic and sauté for another minute.

Stir in the tomatoes and their juice, fennel fronds, pine nuts, raisins, and orange zest. Continue sautéing for another 10 minutes to thicken and meld the flavors. If the frying pan becomes too dry, add some water.

Prepare the sardines by removing the heads, scales, and innards. Then pull out the spine and spread the fish open. Brush the bottom of a baking dish with olive oil, place the fillets skin-side down in the dish, and season them with salt and black pepper. Spread a heaping spoonful of the sautéed items on each fillet and top them with bread crumbs.

Preheat the oven to 400 degrees. Cover the baking dish with aluminum foil and bake for 15 minutes. Then remove the foil and bake for another 7 minutes or until crisp and golden on top. Serve hot. Serves 6 to 8 adults.

Where the hills meet the plains in the Foggia Province of Apulia

VIII

Carne (Meats)

Raw Pork in the Countryside of Caltanissetta

A Rambling in Sicily

My friends Anna and Salvatore moved to Palermo from a rural town in the province of Caltanissetta, which is located in the mountains of central Sicily. Like many people of their generation, they moved to the city in the 1980s in search of work. One summer day, we went to their town to visit Salvatore's cousin, a butcher. We left Palermo and headed into the desolate Sicilian interior. We approached the town on a dusty road that we shared with a shepherd moving his sheep. As we rounded a bend, the town stood before us—it was a jumble of old houses huddled on the gentle slope of a mountain. I immediately sensed that this was a provincial town. But I did not mind that at all. I was excited to explore a place seemingly untouched by tourism and modern commercial activities.

Our first stop was to the church of San Giovanni, the town's patron saint who is revered by the townspeople. We paid homage the saint and then strolled through the winding cobblestone streets of the old quarter. They were full of life as women tended their clotheslines, children played ball, and old men sat on wooden chairs and chatted. Anna pointed to the house where she was born and told us stories about her childhood. We then proceeded to the butcher shop to meet Salvatore's cousin. He and his family were anxiously waiting. After many hugs and kisses, everyone sat down at a table for a snack and some wine.

Salvatore's cousin then brought over a platter of raw ground pork. Everyone applauded and quickly reached in with their forks to take some. Everyone, that is, except me! I was always told never to eat raw or undercooked pork. What were these people thinking?

Anna sensed my hesitation and asked, "Why are you not eating?"

I pointed to the piece of bread on my plate and told her that I was just fine.

"No, you must try the raw pork. It is a specialty of our town," Anna told me emphatically.

I shook my head apologetically and told her that I preferred not to eat raw pork.

Salvatore then yelled from across the table with his loud, husky voice, "Don't worry! This pork comes from a special pig that was just slaughtered only minutes ago! You will not get sick!"

The table became silent, and everyone's attention was now focused on me. I smiled politely and again said, "No, thank you."

Everyone else soon weighed in. There was a cacophony of voices coming at me from all directions.

"Really, you will not get sick!"

"It tastes so good!"

"Please, we want you to try some!"

The pressure was mounting. I understood that this was a special dish, and I did not want to insult my friends or the butcher. But I just would not risk getting sick while on vacation. So I took a stance and blurted out, "No! I don't care how special that pig was! I am not eating raw pork."

With that, the table became silent. True to character, my feisty friend Anna was sure to have the last word.

"OK. But, you don't know what you are missing," she replied.

Everyone then continued eating the raw pork. I had some bread and a glass of wine and was perfectly content. As the afternoon progressed, other relatives came to the butcher shop to greet us, and they too ate the raw pork. We spent the entire day there and returned to Palermo after midnight.

The next morning, I went into the kitchen at 8:00 a.m., but nobody else was there. Anna and Salvatore were always up at the crack of dawn. How odd, I thought. Anna is usually cooking and cleaning by this time, and Salvatore is reading the newspaper. I sat at the table and waited for them. Perhaps today they decided to sleep in? A few minutes later, they entered the kitchen.

"Look, I am alive! I did not die last night from eating the raw pork!" Anna exclaimed in joyful animation.

Salvatore laughed and then added, "I am alive too! You should have eaten some!"

I was quick to respond. "Yes, you are both alive! But I was up before you this morning because I slept well, without worrying all night that I might get sick!"

We all laughed and then sat down for an espresso.

I enjoyed rambling through the Sicilian interior with my friends Anna and Salvatore. They showed me what life is like in a rural Sicilian town, and meeting all of their relatives was a special treat. As for the food I ate at the butcher shop, I can tell you the bread was crisp and delicious, and the homemade red wine was bold. With regard to the raw pork, you will just have to take Anna and Salvatore's word that it was delicious too!

Chilies hung to dry on a tree near Catanzaro, Calabria

The rugged coast of Torre del Impiso, Sicily

The rugged Gargano coast of Apulia

Each region of Italy has its own special way to cure meats and sausage

The macelleria, *or neighborhood butcher shop*

Window in the whitewashed town of Ostuni, Apulia

Village scene in Abruzzo

Grigliata Mista con Salsa di Capperi (Mixed Grilled Meats with Caper Condiment)

SICILY

Capers are the flower buds of the capparis *plant, which grows just about everywhere in Italy. It sprouts up amongst rocky crags, alongside stone walls, and even from cracks in city streets! The best capers come from the island of Pantelleria, off the southwest coast of Sicily. Here, the methods for cultivating and curing capers have changed very little over the centuries. First, the capers are picked by hand. It is backbreaking work that is made even more difficult by a hot Mediterranean sun overhead. The capers are then packed in sea salt and allowed to cure for several weeks before they are packaged and shipped to Sicily and the mainland. Once the capers have found their way into a kitchen, they must be soaked to remove the salt. Then they can be tossed into a dish to make it extra special.*

If you go to Pantelleria, rent a motor scooter and take a ride around the island. The landscape is truly unique. The hillsides are crisscrossed with stone walls separating endless fields of capers. With whitewashed cubist houses called dammusi *set against the backdrop of a blue sea, Pantelleria has the feel of a Greek island. But you will not find Zorba here! Instead, you will meet friendly Pantescan men with sun-beaten faces carrying baskets filled with capers from the fields. After your tour, head to a* trattoria *for an authentic Pantescan meal. Be sure to try spaghetti tossed with clams and capers or grilled goat with caper sauce. Here is my version of caper sauce, for which only the best capers from Pantelleria will do. It will add a burst of bright Mediterranean flavor to any type of grilled meat or fish.*

2 cups firmly packed Sicilian capers preserved in salt
½ cup pine nuts
1 cup coarsely chopped, firmly packed Italian flat leaf parsley
2 cloves garlic
4 tbsp. red wine vinegar

Black pepper to taste
1-1½ cups extra virgin olive oil, plus additional for brushing
Assorted meats for 6 adults (pork, lamb, chicken, or beef)
Salt to taste

Remove the salt from the capers by soaking them in warm water for 15 minutes and then rinsing them under cool running water. Place the pine nuts in a small frying pan and toast them over low heat until golden. Place the capers, pine nuts, parsley, garlic, and vinegar in a food processor and season with black pepper. Pulse until everything is finely ground and then continue processing while slowly adding a stream of olive oil. Add enough olive oil to achieve a thick condiment. If necessary, season with salt. Allow the sauce to sit for 8 hours or overnight before serving.

Brush the meat lightly with olive oil, season it with salt and black pepper, and grill it over a medium flame to the desired doneness. Arrange the grilled meats on a serving platter with the caper condiment on the side. Serve the sauce at room temperature. Serves 6 adults.

Salsiccia con Peperonata (Roasted Pork Sausage with Red Bell Peppers, Onions, Olives, and Capers)

APULIA

My uncle Gaetano, whose family hails from Apulia, was a fine butcher. He always provided the whole family with fresh pork sausage. Often, he flavored the sausage with flecks of black pepper and aromatic fennel seeds. Every now and then he added a few pinches of crushed red chili flakes too! In Italy, each region has its own special way of making sausage. My favorite is a thin, traditional sausage from Southern Italy called cervelato, *which is no wider than a finger. It is flavored with a sprinkle of grated pecorino cheese, white wine, garlic, and fresh parsley. I like to roll the* cervelato *into spirals, stick them on skewers, and then grill or roast them in the oven.*

There is nothing better to serve with homemade sausage than peperonata; *it is a favorite accompaniment to all sorts of grilled meats. The preparations vary from region to region. In Tuscany,* peperonata *is prepared as a stew of bell peppers, onions, and tomatoes, whereas in Sicily the peppers are sautéed with a few good splashes of vinegar and a pinch of sugar. Green Pugliese olives, capers, and Spanish onions make my version unique. Instead of sautéing the peppers, I roast them in a flavorful marinade of white wine, olive oil, and garlic. The touch of acidity from the wine, the sweetness of the onion, and briny flavor of the capers make my* peperonata *a true taste sensation. Serve it with sausage, pork chops, or chicken for a tasty, rustic dinner from the countryside of Apulia.*

¼ cup firmly packed Sicilian capers preserved in salt

1 large Spanish or Vidalia onion, sliced

4 large mixed bell peppers (red, green, orange, and yellow), seeded and sliced

¾ cup pitted, halved Castelvetrano or Sicilian olives

5 cloves garlic, sliced

1½ tbsp. finely chopped, firmly packed oregano

1½ tbsp. finely chopped, firmly packed Italian flat leaf parsley

1 cup white wine

Olive oil, for drizzling

2½ lbs. Italian pork sausage

Salt and black pepper to taste

Preheat the oven to 415 degrees. Remove the salt from the capers by soaking them in warm water for 15 minutes and then rinsing them under cold running water. Place the onions, peppers, olives, garlic, oregano, and parsley in a deep 10 by 14 inch baking dish. Add the capers, wine, and a few generous drizzles of olive oil. Season with salt and black pepper and toss everything together.

Cover the baking dish with aluminum foil and roast the *peperonata* for 45 minutes. Remove the foil, stir, and continue baking, uncovered, for another 45 minutes, stirring every 15 minutes or so until the peppers and onions are tender and lightly caramelized.

Meanwhile, rub the bottom of another baking dish with olive oil. Slice the sausage into portion-sized pieces and set them in the baking dish. Roast the sausage at 415 degrees for 25 minutes or until fully cooked. Place the *peperonata* on a serving platter and arrange the sausage on top. Serve hot. Serves 4 adults.

Salsiccia con Lenticchie e Cavolo Nero (Roasted Pork Sausage with Lentils and Tuscan Kale)

ABRUZZO/MOLISE

Roasted pork sausage with lentils is a hearty dish from the southern Apennines. It is also the traditional meal prepared for La Festa di San Silvestro, which is celebrated on New Year's Eve. On this day, families gather to pay homage to San Silvestro and to ring in the New Year with plenty of food and fun. It is said that lentils symbolize money and pork symbolizes the richness of life. Many Italians believe that eating these foods on New Year's Day is sure to bring good health and fortune in the coming year. Sausage and lentils are typically served during the New Year's Eve celebration immediately after the clock strikes midnight. My version of this traditional dish is sure to please a hungry New Year's Eve crowd. I simmer the lentils with diced vegetables, Tuscan kale, and plenty of spices. A small handful of diced prosciutto adds an extra layer of flavor to the lentils that is beyond compare. Be sure to use a fresh, high-quality pork sausage laced with fennel seeds. Serve this dish for your next New Year's Eve celebration with a bold Montepulciano wine from Abruzzo. It is the perfect, hearty wintertime dish that is packed with bold flavors.

Olive oil, for brushing
2½ lbs. Italian pork sausage
1 batch Lentil Soup with Kale and Diced Vegetables *(see page 85)*

Preheat the oven to 425 degrees. Brush the bottom of a baking dish with olive oil. Cut the sausage into portion-sized pieces and set them in the baking dish. Roast the sausage for 25 minutes or until fully cooked. Place the lentil soup in a deep serving platter and arrange the sausage on top. Serve hot with slices of crusty Italian bread. Note that for this dish the lentil soup must be extra thick, about the consistency of oatmeal. This is achieved by adding less or no water after the initial 3 quarts and cooking the lentils a little longer. Serves 4 adults.

Agnello Arrostito (Roasted Rack of Lamb—Done Two Ways)

LAZIO

Lamb is traditionally served on Easter in most regions of Italy. It is a favorite holiday treat in the rolling hills east of Rome, where they prefer agnello abacchio, *or milk-fed baby lamb that is sure to be tender and delicious.* Agnello abacchio *is always light pink in color and has a mild flavor, which makes the chops perfect for searing. If I am hosting a small dinner party, I like to sear a few petite racks of baby lamb that have been trimmed and French cut. The petite racks make for an elegant presentation and the succulent meat is beyond compare. For Easter dinner when there will be a crowd, I always roast a large leg of lamb that can feed everyone. Regardless of which cut you choose, be sure to serve your lamb while it is piping hot. It always tastes best when served straight from the grill or oven, because after it has cooled the flavor becomes more gamey. The people of Lazio have figured this out; they serve lamb chops piping hot, or* scottadito. *In Roman dialect, this means that they are so hot you will "burn your fingers" when you eat them. Here are my two favorite recipes for marinated roasted rack of lamb. They are so delicious, you will not be able to resist eating the lamb right away—even if it means burning your fingers!*

2 petite racks of lamb, trimmed and French cut
Sea salt and black pepper to taste
Olive oil, for searing and brushing

For the marinade:
3 bay leaves, torn into small pieces
½ tsp. black peppercorns, freshly ground
4 large cloves garlic, chopped
3 large green onions, chopped
1 tbsp. finely chopped, firmly packed rosemary
1 tbsp. finely chopped, firmly packed thyme
2½ cups red wine
1 cup olive oil
1 tsp. coarse salt

Whisk together all marinade ingredients. Transfer the marinade to a gallon-sized resealable plastic bag. Place the petite racks of lamb in the bag and set it in the refrigerator to marinate overnight.

Preheat the oven to 400 degrees. Remove the lamb from the marinade, pat it dry, and season it lightly with sea salt and freshly ground black pepper. Coat the bottom of a large frying pan with olive oil and set it over medium heat. When the frying pan has heated, sear the lamb for 1 or 2 minutes on both sides or until lightly golden. Then

transfer the lamb to a roasting pan that has been brushed with olive oil and roast until it reaches an internal temperature of 154 degrees (about 15 minutes). When the lamb is done, place it on a cutting board and let it rest for 5 minutes before cutting. Serves 4 adults.

| *With red wine and fig sauce:* | 2 tbsp. butter |
| 1 rounded tsp. all-purpose, pre-sifted flour | 2 tbsp. fig jam |

Marinate and prepare the lamb as instructed. While the lamb is roasting, prepare the sauce: Strain the remaining marinade through a fine mesh sieve, and then transfer 2 cups of marinade to a saucepan. Set the saucepan over medium-low heat and bring it to a slow simmer. Whisk in the flour until smooth, and then the butter and fig jam. Continue simmering for another 2 minutes or until the sauce has thickened. Adjust the seasoning if necessary, and add more fig jam if you prefer a sweeter sauce. Serve hot drizzled over the lamb.

Crusted with bread crumbs and Parmigiano-Reggiano cheese:
2 thick slices of country-style Italian bread
¾ cup grated Parmigiano-Reggiano cheese

Grate enough bread for 1 cup of firmly packed crumbs. Mix together the bread crumbs and grated cheese and place in a mound on a baking sheet. After you have marinated and seared the lamb, dredge it on all sides in the bread crumb mixture. Then proceed to roast the lamb as instructed above.

Cosciotto d'Agnello Ripieno (Roasted Leg of Lamb Stuffed with Arugula, Sundried Tomatoes, and Pecorino Cheese)

CALABRIA

One Sunday when I was visiting Italy, my friend Anna invited her whole family over for dinner. "Look at the beautiful baby lamb Salvatore brought home. There is plenty for everyone!" she exclaimed. "How many people will come to dinner?" I asked. "At least twenty, and if my sister comes with her family, then four more!" she replied. I questioned Anna further, "But your apartment is small. Where will everyone sit?" She then laughed. "Oh, don't worry. We always make do!" By noon, a crowd had gathered and it was time for a feast. The adults sat elbow to elbow around the dining room table, some on folding chairs, and others on stools. The young children sat at the kitchen table, and the teenagers gathered around the couch. Everyone had a plate full of food. It was a happy and joyous time made even more wonderful by the succulent roasted lamb that Anna had prepared.

Roasted lamb is the perfect entrée when feeding a large crowd. When Anna and Salvatore are in Palermo, she always prepares the lamb al forno or roasted in the oven. However, when the family gathers at their beach villa in Calabria, they grill the lamb outside. For city-dwellers and career-oriented persons who do not have the time or means for outdoor grilling, here is the next best thing. This is a simple and easy oven-roasting method that captures the hearty flavors of Northern Calabria, where the rugged mountains of the Pollino Massif meet the Tyrrhenian Sea. For easy preparation and great flavor, I use a boneless leg of lamb that I stuff with sundried tomatoes, arugula, green onions, and garlic. The fresh, bold flavors of the filling stand up well alongside the lamb. Serve it with a hearty red Montepulciano wine from Abruzzo.

2 jumbo Spanish or Vidalia onions, cut into wedges

7 cloves garlic, 3 sliced in half and 4 minced

2 sprigs rosemary

1 cup red wine

Olive oil, for drizzling

Coarse salt and black pepper to taste

5 lb. boneless, butterflied leg of lamb

4 green onions, chopped

Grated or shaved Pecorino Romano cheese, for sprinkling

¾ cup chopped jarred sundried tomatoes preserved in olive oil

2 cups chopped and firmly packed arugula

Butcher string, to tie the lamb

Spread the onions and sliced garlic evenly in a deep, 10 by 13 inch roasting pan. Add the whole sprigs of rosemary, pour the red wine over top, drizzle with olive oil, season with salt and black pepper, and set the roasting pan to the side. Lay the lamb fat side down on your work surface. Rub the minced garlic all over the lamb and season it with salt and black pepper. Sprinkle the green onions, grated cheese, sundried tomatoes, and arugula on top of the lamb. Roll up the lamb and tie it securely like a package, tucking in the edges so that the filling does not escape. Rub the outside of the lamb with olive oil and season it with coarse salt and black pepper. Place the lamb on top of the onions.

Preheat the oven to 450 degrees and roast the lamb for 15 minutes. Then baste the lamb with the juices from the bottom of the pan and reduce the temperature to 375 degrees. Continue roasting the lamb, basting every 15 minutes, until it has reached an internal temperature of 145 degrees. (This will produce lamb cooked medium.) The total cooking time should be about 60 minutes.

When the lamb is done, set it on a cutting board, cover it with aluminum foil, and let it rest for 15 minutes. Meanwhile, strain the juices from the roasting pan through a mesh sieve. Slice the lamb, arrange it on a serving platter, and drizzle the juices over top. Serve hot. Serves 4 adults.

Stinco Brassato con Funghi (Braised Lamb Shanks with Mushrooms)

ABRUZZO/MOLISE

When driving in the tranquil countryside of Molise, be wary of traffic jams. Here, motorists share the roadways with our four-legged friends; as you come around a bend, you might just find a few hundred sheep or goats in front of you! Such encounters are common, so be prepared to stop at a moment's notice. If you find yourself in such a situation, just proceed slowly. Chances are the shepherd is nearby and will guide the herd towards the side of the road. If not, the animals will move out of your way as you nudge forward. On one occasion, my wife and I found ourselves driving through a herd of goats five hundred strong. She rolled down the window to take a picture and a curious goat stuck his head right in! We went home with a close-up photograph of his nose.

In Molise, lamb is often braised or cooked in a hearty stew. The Molisani have discovered that slow braising is the best way to prepare lamb shanks. The method for braising shanks is simple; just sear the meat in a frying pan and allow it to slow cook for an hour or more in plenty of wine and stock until the connective tissue breaks down and the meat is so tender that it falls off the bone. Aromatic vegetables, fresh herbs, and spices can be added to the braising liquid to flavor the meat and create a tasty sauce. In my version, cremini mushrooms add an extra depth of rich, earthy flavor. I like to serve the shanks alongside potato gnocchi *with plenty of mushrooms and rich sauce spooned over top. A sprinkle of shaved pecorino cheese is the final touch that truly makes it special.*

4 lamb shanks (1½ lbs. each)	2 tbsp. tomato paste
Salt and black pepper to taste	2 cups red wine
Flour, for dredging	1 lb. cremini mushrooms, sliced
Olive oil, for searing and sautéing	1 tbsp. finely chopped, firmly packed
1 large carrot, peeled and diced	Italian flat leaf parsley
1 large rib celery, diced	1 tbsp. finely chopped, firmly packed
½ large Spanish or Vidalia onion, diced	rosemary
4 cloves garlic, finely chopped	2 cups light beef broth

Season the lamb shanks with salt and black pepper and dredge them lightly in flour. Coat the bottom of a deep, 5½ quart frying pan with olive oil and set it over medium heat. When the oil is hot, brown the shanks on both sides until lightly golden. Remove the shanks from the frying pan and set them to the side.

Add the carrot, celery, and onion to the frying pan and sauté them until tender. Add the garlic and continue sautéing for another minute. Push the sautéed aromatics to one side of the frying pan, tilt the frying pan to pool the oil on the other side, and fry the tomato paste for 2 minutes.

Add the wine, mushrooms, parsley, and rosemary and season with salt and black pepper. Continue sautéing until the mushrooms are fully cooked. Turn the heat down to low and return the shanks to the frying pan. Pour over the broth and enough water so that the braising liquid comes ¾ of the way up the shanks. Cover the frying pan and simmer gently for 2½ hours, turning the shanks every 20 minutes.

As the shanks cook, the braising liquid will reduce. Add more water as needed so that the shanks always remain ¾ submerged by the braising liquid. The shanks are done when the meat pulls away from the bone. Remove the shanks from the frying pan, place them on a serving platter, and cover them with foil. Continue cooking the braising liquid until it has reduced to a thick sauce. Adjust the seasoning if necessary and then spoon it over the shanks. Serve hot. Serves 4 adults.

Involtini di Maiale Ripieni (Roasted Pork Roulades Stuffed with Bread Crumbs, Red Bell Pepper, Pine Nuts, and Raisins)

SICILY

Sometimes getting lost in the countryside of Sicily is a wonderful thing! A few wrong turns and before you know it, each mile is a new adventure. You never know what you will stumble upon! That is how I wound up in the town of Caltagirone one morning. I was on my way from Palermo to the Roman ruins at Villa Casale, but poor signage, a lapse of attention, or perhaps just fate brought me to Caltagirone. This ancient mountain citadel is known for producing the highest-quality ceramics in Sicily. Before I knew it, I was shopping! I spent the better part of a day wandering in and out of ceramic shops, haggling for a bargain, and buying ceramic pieces to adorn my home. It turned out to be quite an unexpected and enjoyable day.

Later that evening, I enjoyed authentic Sicilian cuisine at a small restaurant with an amazing view of Caltagirone's tiled rooftops and church domes. Here is my recreation of the wonderful stuffed pork roulades that I ate that fateful day. The pork loin was sliced into rounds, pounded thin, and then rolled with a delicate bread crumb filling that was flavored with pecorino cheese, fresh herbs, and a hint of orange. Each roll was neatly secured with a skewer and then roasted to perfection. For a true taste of the Caltagirone, serve these pork roulades with a glass of red Nero d'Avola wine from Sicily.

½ loaf country-style Italian bread
⅓ cup pine nuts
Olive oil, for sautéing and drizzling
1 large red bell pepper, chopped
½ large Spanish or Vidalia onion, chopped
3 cloves garlic, finely chopped
⅓ cup raisins
Zest of 1 large California navel orange, divided
½ cup grated Pecorino Romano cheese
1 tbsp. finely chopped, firmly packed oregano

3 tbsp. finely chopped, firmly packed Italian flat leaf parsley, divided
Salt and black pepper to taste
8 pork loin cutlets (¼ lb. each)
Wooden skewers, to secure the roulades
8 bay leaves
6 tbsp. butter
2 tbsp. flour
¾ cup white wine
1½ cups light pork or chicken broth
½ cup pasteurized orange juice

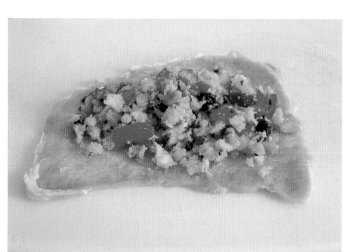

Grate enough bread for 3½ cups of firmly pressed crumbs. Place the pine nuts in a small frying pan and toast them over low heat until golden. Coat the bottom of a frying pan generously with olive oil, set it over medium-low heat, and sauté the pepper and onion until soft. Add the pine nuts, garlic, raisins, and half of the orange zest. Continue sautéing for another minute or until the raisins have plumped.

Place 3 cups of the bread crumbs in

a large mixing bowl and stir in the grated cheese, sautéed items, oregano, and 2 tablespoons of parsley. Season the bread crumb mixture with salt and black pepper and add a few drizzles of olive oil so that the bread crumbs are uniformly moist and fluffy.

Pound the cutlets to ¼ inch thickness, pushing outwards as you pound to expand their size. Season the cutlets on both sides with salt and black pepper. Place some filling on top of each cutlet, roll them up, and secure with a wooden skewer. Brush the *involtini* with olive oil and then roll them in the remaining ½ cup of bread crumbs.

Preheat the oven to 400 degrees. Place the *involtini* in a baking dish that has been brushed with olive oil and nestle the bay leaves between them. Bake for 25 minutes or until the bread crumbs on top are golden.

Meanwhile, prepare the sauce: Melt the butter in a saucepan over low heat and add the flour to make a roux. When the roux is golden in color, add the wine, broth, orange juice, and the remaining orange zest and parsley. Whisk until smooth, season with salt and black pepper, and simmer over low heat for 5 minutes or until the sauce has thickened. Strain the sauce through a mesh sieve. Serve hot with sauce on the side. Serves 4 adults.

Braciolone di Maiale (Roasted Pork Stuffed with Spinach, Prosciutto, and Hard-Boiled Eggs)

SICILY

In Sicily, holidays and festive occasions call for a special meal, and braciolone *always fits the bill.* Braciolone *is a large roulade of veal or pork that is stuffed and then braised or roasted in the oven. The most traditional version of this dish is called* farsumagru *in Sicilian dialect, and it is stuffed with ground pork and whole hard-boiled eggs. However, any assortment of ingredients—including vegetables, cheeses, and cured meats—can be used. There are endless possibilities for stuffing a* braciolone. *I roll up a butterflied pork loin with layers of prosciutto, provolone cheese, sautéed spinach, and pine nuts. When Salvatore and Anna came to visit me in the United States, I prepared this dish for them. Salvatore proclaimed, "Troppo buono!" Anna agreed that it was delicious but could not resist offering some criticism. "You know, the slices would look prettier if you put hard-boiled eggs in the middle," she said. Serve this dish at your next holiday feast with stuffed artichokes and roasted potatoes. If you want a festive presentation, go right ahead and add a few eggs as my friend Anna suggests! Accompanied by a glass of red Barbaresco wine from Piedmont, it is sure to be a hit.*

5-5½ lbs. boneless pork loin, butterflied

Olive oil, for sautéing and drizzling

5 cloves garlic, 2 finely chopped and 3 sliced in half

2½ lbs. spinach, chopped

½ cup water

Salt and black pepper to taste

½ cup grated Parmigiano-Reggiano cheese

¼ cup pine nuts, toasted

4 large Spanish or Vidalia onions, chopped

2 red bell peppers, chopped

3 ribs celery, chopped

3 carrots, peeled and chopped

2 sprigs rosemary

2 bay leaves

1 handful Italian flat leaf parsley

2 cups white wine, divided

½ lb. thinly sliced prosciutto or Genoa salami

½ lb. Fontina cheese, sliced

4 hard-boiled eggs

Butcher string, to tie the loin

2 tbsp. flour, for thickening the sauce, plus additional for dusting

4 tbsp. butter

2 cups pork or chicken broth, plus additional as needed

Ask your butcher to butterfly the roast into a wide, even slab for stuffing. Pound the slab with a mallet, pushing outward as you pound to expand its size. This will allow it to hold more filling and will make it easier to tie.

Coat the bottom of a frying pan with olive oil, set it over medium-low heat, sauté the chopped garlic until soft, and then add the spinach and the water, which will allow the greens to steam. Season the spinach with salt and black pepper and continue sautéing until wilted. Then drain it in a colander and press out any excess cooking liquid with the back of a wooden spoon. Transfer the spinach to a mixing bowl and stir in the grated cheese and the pine nuts.

Place the onions, peppers, celery, and carrots in the bottom of a roasting pan with the rosemary, bay leaves, and parsley. Pour over 1½ cups of white wine, drizzle with olive oil, and season with salt and black pepper.

Lay the pork slab fat side down on a work surface. Season it with black pepper and salt and then place the sliced prosciutto on top. Evenly spread the spinach mixture on top of the prosciutto, followed by the Fontina cheese. Nestle a row of hard-boiled eggs down the middle. Roll up the pork slab and tie it tightly with butcher's string.

Preheat the oven to 375 degrees. Season the outside of the *braciolone* with salt and pepper and then rub it with flour. Coat the bottom of a 5½ quart frying pan with olive oil and set it over medium heat. When the oil has heated, sear the *braciolone* on all sides until lightly golden and then set it in the roasting pan on top of the chopped vegetables. Roast until it reaches an internal temperature of 153 degrees (about 20 minutes per pound). When the *braciolone* is done, place it on a cutting board, cover it with aluminum foil, and let rest for 15 minutes before slicing.

Meanwhile, melt the butter in a saucepan over medium-low heat and add 2 tablespoons of flour to make a roux. When the roux is golden, remove the saucepan from the burner. Place a mesh sieve over the saucepan and pour the vegetables and juices from the roasting pan into the sieve. Use the back of a wooden spoon to press the vegetables into the sides of the sieve to extract all of the juices, and then discard the vegetables. Set the saucepan over low heat, add the remaining wine, and whisk until smooth. Allow the sauce to simmer for 3 minutes and then add the broth, a little at a time, until you achieve the desired consistency. Adjust the seasoning if necessary. Serve hot with sauce on the side. Serves 6 to 8 adults.

Saltimbocca alla Romana con Funghi e Mozzarella (Veal Cutlets Stuffed with Prosciutto, Mushrooms, Mozzarella, and Sage)

LAZIO

Romans are known to give their favorite dishes a catchy name. In the Roman dialect, saltimbocca means "to jump into the mouth." As the name suggests, these veal roulades are so tasty, they will be eaten up very fast. Over the years, this classic Roman dish has been modified and refashioned by inventive chefs. However, no dish can be labeled "Saltimbocca alla Romana" unless it contains two essential ingredients: prosciutto and plenty of salvia, or sage picked fresh from the Alban Hills. There are few places in Italy where aromatic sage is more loved than in Rome. In my version of this classic, strips of sautéed portobello mushrooms and creamy mozzarella cheese are the surprise inside each savory roll. Surely, no Roman would complain! The earthy flavor of the mushroom pairs nicely with the salty prosciutto and sage. Fresh garlic and a sprinkle of Pecorino Romano cheese add extra zing. It is a dish that will "jump into your mouth." Pair it with a glass of white Frascati from the vine covered hills outside of Rome and you have a meal fit for Caesar Augustus!

Olive oil, for sautéing
2 cloves garlic, finely chopped
1½ cups white wine
2 large portobello mushrooms, trimmed and sliced into ½ inch thick strips
Salt and black pepper to taste
1½ cups light beef broth
6 tbsp. butter
2 tbsp. finely chopped, firmly packed Italian flat leaf parsley

8 veal cutlets (¼ lb. each, about 6 inches long)
4 tbsp. finely chopped, firmly packed sage, divided
⅓ lb. thinly sliced prosciutto
½ lb. mozzarella cheese, shredded
Butcher string, to tie the roulades
Flour, for dredging

Coat the bottom of a frying pan with olive oil, set it over medium-low heat, and sauté the garlic until soft. Add the wine and the mushrooms, season with salt and black pepper, and sauté for 2 minutes. Add the broth, butter, and parsley. Continue sautéing for another 3 minutes or until the mushrooms are tender. Remove the mushrooms from the frying pan with a slotted spoon and set the sauce to the side.

Pound the cutlets as thin as possible, pushing outwards as you pound to expand their size. Season them with salt and black pepper and sprinkle each with ½ tablespoon of fresh sage. Place some prosciutto on top of each cutlet, followed by some shredded mozzarella and a few strips of sautéed mushroom. Roll up each veal cutlet and tie it like a package with butcher string, tucking in the edges so that the filling will not escape. Lightly dredge the roulades in flour.

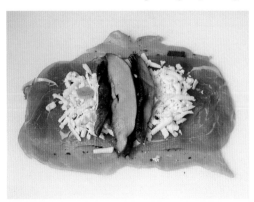
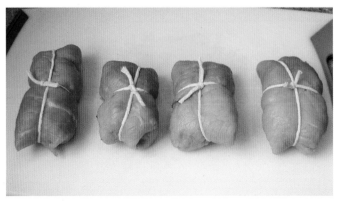

Preheat the oven to 375 degrees. Coat the bottom of a second frying pan with olive oil and set it over medium heat. Brown the veal roulades lightly on all sides, and then place them in a 10 by 14 inch baking dish. Pour the wine sauce over top and bake for 10 minutes. Spoon some sauce over the roulades to baste them, and continue roasting for another 10 minutes. Serve hot topped with sauce. Serves 4 to 6 adults.

Braciole di Manzo Ripiene (Beef Roulades Stuffed with Hard-Boiled Eggs and Soppressata and Braised in Tomato Sauce)

CAMPANIA

Braising meat in tomato sauce is popular in all parts of Southern Italy. Oftentimes meatballs, pork sausages, thick chunks of pork, and stuffed meat roulades will be braised together in one enormous pot of slowly bubbling tomato sauce. The juices from the meat add wonderful flavor to the tomato sauce, which is then used as a condimento, *or condiment to dress a bowl of pasta. This is a typical Sunday dinner in the small town of Boscoreale on the slopes of Mount Vesuvius, where the rich volcanic soil ensures that garden plots overflow with ripe red tomatoes in summertime that are prefect for making sauce. The pasta is tossed with just enough flavorful* condimento *to coat it and is always served as a first course. The succulent braised meats come next! In the home of a proud Campanese, the braised meats are artfully arranged on a large platter and served with vegetables or sautéed greens on the side.*

Braciole is a thin slice of meat, usually beef or pork, that is perfect for making stuffed roulades. Just be sure to pound it thin. Braciole is always my first pick from the platter of braised meats on the Sunday dinner table. Here is a rustic recipe from Boscoreale. A few thin slices of cured pork sausage add great depth of flavor. My recipe calls for soppressata, which is a typical cured sausage of the region. If you prefer, use Genoa salami, capicollo, or prosciutto instead. A bold red Sangiovese wine from Tuscany or a Valpolicella from Veneto is the perfect accompaniment.

1 batch of Salsa Marinara *(see page 121)*
8 hard-boiled eggs
Salt and black pepper to taste
2 tbsp. finely chopped, firmly packed Italian flat leaf parsley
2 tbsp. Parmigiano-Reggiano cheese
Olive oil, for drizzling and frying

4 beef cutlets (preferably top round, 8 inches long and 6 inches wide)
½ lb. thinly sliced soppressata or Genoa salami
½ lb. thinly sliced soft provolone cheese
Butcher's string, to tie the roulades

Prepare the Salsa Marinara following the recipe on page 121. Using a fork, mash the eggs in a mixing bowl to a fine crumble, season them with salt and black pepper, and then stir in the chopped parsley, grated cheese, and a drizzle of olive oil to moisten.

Pound the cutlets to ¼ inch thickness, pushing outwards as you pound to expand their size. Season the cutlets with salt and black pepper. Place a few slices of soppressata and provolone on top of each, followed by a layer of the egg mixture. Roll up the cutlets and tie them securely like a package, tucking in the edges so that the filling does not escape.

Coat the bottom of a frying pan with olive oil and brown the roulades on all sides. Transfer the roulades to the pot of simmering Salsa Marinara and simmer on low for 2 hours, stirring frequently. Serve hot with Salsa Marinara on the side. Serves 4 to 6 adults.

Polpette (Beef and Pork Meatballs)

BASILICATA

No Italian cookbook would be complete without a recipe for polpette. *After all, what could be more Italian than spaghetti and meatballs? Or should I say what could be more American? Today, nearly one hundred years after the massive immigration of Southern Italians to the United States, spaghetti and meatballs is just as popular in the United States as hamburgers, hotdogs, and apple pie. Although* polpette *are predominant in Southern Italian cooking, they are enjoyed throughout Italy and are prepared in many different ways. Most recipes call for ground beef while others call for a combination of several ground meats, including veal, pork, and beef. In Lombardia and Emilia Romagna, ground mortadella is also thrown into the mix for a traditional meatball called Mondigheli.*

If you ask any Italian, they will tell you that their grandmother makes the best meatballs. That being said, here is my version of my Campanese grandmother's recipe for the most delicious meatballs you will ever eat! In the Diano Valley of southern Campania, where my grandmother's family hails from, polpette *are eaten immediately after being fried, while still piping hot. They are crisp and caramelized on the outside and soft and savory in the middle. If you prefer your meatballs in tomato sauce, then brown them lightly without cooking them through and set them to simmer in the sauce for two hours. The sauce will be flavorful and delicious and the meatballs soft and tender!*

2 thick slices country-style Italian bread	½ cup grated Parmigiano-Reggiano cheese
1 cup milk	½ small onion, minced
2 lbs. ground beef (20% fat content)	1 clove garlic, minced
1 lb. ground pork	3 tbsp. finely chopped, firmly packed Italian flat leaf parsley
Crushed red pepper flakes to taste (optional)	2 eggs, beaten
Salt and black pepper to taste	Olive oil, for frying

Use a food processor to grind enough bread for 1 cup of firmly packed crumbs. Combine the bread crumbs and milk in a small bowl and let it sit for a few minutes.

Thoroughly combine the ground beef and pork in a large mixing bowl and season the meat with red pepper flakes, salt, and black pepper. Add the bread crumb mixture, grated cheese, onion, garlic, parsley and beaten eggs. Mix everything together without overworking and roll out palm-sized meatballs.

Add just under ½ inch of olive oil to a 5½ quart frying pan and set it over medium heat. When the oil has heated, fry the meatballs until golden brown on both sides. If you prefer to serve the meatballs in tomato sauce, brown them lightly without cooking them through and transfer them to a pot of simmering tomato sauce. Allow the meatballs to simmer in the sauce over low heat for at least 2 hours. Makes 16 medium-sized meatballs. Serves 6 to 8 adults.

Quaglie in Salmoriglio (Roasted Split Game Hens with Olive Oil and Lemon Marinade)

CALABRIA

High-quality olive oil is the pride of Southern Italy. If you ask my friends Anna and Salvatore, they will tell you that nothing is more wonderful than fresh-pressed extra virgin olive oil drizzled over grilled meats, vegetables, and slices of juicy, fresh oranges. They will also tell you that the best olive oil in Southern Italy comes from the groves near their beach villa in Scalea, Calabria. In Calabria, olive oil is always a matter of local pride. But as far as I am concerned, it all tastes great, regardless of where the olives were grown or who pressed it! If the olive oil is from Calabria, it's going to be spectacular! Cornish game hens are perfect for marinating in a vibrant, tasty Calabrian marinade called salmoriglio. *Olive oil, lemon juice, garlic, onion, and plenty of fresh herbs add wonderful flavor that will make those birds really sing! I like to split the hens and roast them in the oven with plenty of the remaining marinade drizzled over top. Then I serve them with roasted potatoes drizzled with the flavorful pan drippings. In the summertime, I throw them on the grill.*

Zest of 1 lemon
¾ cup fresh lemon juice
⅓ cup finely chopped Spanish or Vidalia onion
⅓ cup finely chopped green onion
2 large cloves garlic, finely chopped
2 tbsp. finely chopped, firmly packed oregano

2 tbsp. finely chopped, firmly packed thyme
½ rounded tsp. Sicilian sea salt
½ tsp. black pepper
½ cup olive oil
2 Cornish game hens

Wisk together the lemon zest, lemon juice, onion, green onion, garlic, oregano, thyme, sea salt, black pepper, and olive oil in a large mixing bowl. Split the hens in half, place them in the mixing bowl, and spoon over the marinade so that they are thoroughly coated. Cover the bowl with plastic wrap and set it to marinate in the refrigerator for at least 8 hours or overnight. Turn the split hens or spoon marinade over them every so often.

Preheat the oven to 375 degrees. Place the split hens skin side up in a baking dish that has been brushed with olive oil and bake for 20 minutes. Baste the split hens with the remaining marinade and continue roasting for another 25 to 35 minutes or until the skin is golden brown and the juices run clear when the tip of a knife is inserted behind the thigh. Serve hot with the pan drippings. Serves 4 adults.

Gatto alla Palermitana (Meat Ragu Casserole with Potatoes and Eggplant)

SICILY

Sicily is a land of many footprints. Although Sicilian cuisine is most known for its Arab influences, many other cultures have also left their mark on the island. Most notable are the Spanish merchants who brought many new ingredients from the Americas to Sicily and the aristocrats of the late eighteenth and early nineteenth centuries who had a fondness for opulent French-style dishes. Here is a traditional Sicilian casserole that was created by French influences in Southern Italy. It is called gatto. *The name is a derivation of the French word* gatteau, *which means "casserole." It is a favorite dish of Palermo that dates back to a time when it was fashionable for Sicilian aristocrats to employ French chefs in their homes. These chefs were called* monzu—*a Sicilian corruption of the word* monsieur. *The great* monzu *of Sicily elevated the island's simple cookery by adding a touch of French extravagance. In Palermo's fine restaurants today, you can still enjoy elaborate dishes that are the legacy of the skilled* monzu *of yesteryear.*

This fancy dish is a one-pot meal large enough for a bourgeoisie banquet. But don't let the grand size deter you—it is guaranteed to disappear! If you are not cooking for a crowd, cut the recipe in half, or make the full dish and have leftovers for the next day. With layers of potatoes, cheese, tender roasted eggplant, and savory meat ragu, *Gatto alla Palermitana is Sicily's version of* cucina ricca, *the opulent cuisine of aristocrats. Be sure to enjoy it with a glass of fine red Nero d'Avola wine from Sicily.*

Olive oil, for sautéing
½ large Spanish or Vidalia onion, diced
4 cloves garlic, finely chopped
3 rounded tbsp. finely diced prosciutto
3 rounded tbsp. tomato paste
1 cup red wine
1 can (28 oz.) crushed San Marzano tomatoes
2 rounded tsp. dried basil
2 rounded tsp. dried oregano
Crushed red pepper flakes to taste
Salt and black pepper to taste
3¾ lbs. ground beef (90% lean)
4 lbs. eggplants (about 4 large)
8 lbs. russet potatoes, peeled and chopped
1¾ sticks butter, melted, divided
3 cups grated Pecorino Romano cheese, divided
1 cup finely ground dry bread crumbs
1½ lbs. low-moisture mozzarella cheese, shredded
1 cup milk

Coat the bottom of a 5½ quart frying pan with olive oil, set it over medium-low heat, and sauté the onion until soft. Add the garlic and prosciutto and continue sautéing for another minute. Push the sautéed items to one side of the frying pan, tilt the frying to the other side to pool the oil, and fry the tomato paste in the oil for 1 minute. Add the wine, followed by the crushed tomatoes, basil, and oregano. Slosh ⅔ cup of water in the tomato can and add it to the frying pan. Season with red pepper flakes, salt, and black pepper, reduce the heat to low, and simmer for 20 minutes.

Meanwhile, brush the bottom of a second frying pan with olive oil, add the ground beef, and season it lightly with salt and black pepper. Set the frying pan over medium-low heat and brown the meat, breaking it up with the back of a wooden spoon. Drain off any excess grease and then add the meat to the tomato sauce. Continue simmering the sauce over low heat for another 40 minutes or until the meat *ragu* has thickened. Adjust the seasoning if necessary.

Preheat the oven to 400 degrees. Slice the eggplants into rounds that are just under ½ inch thick, brush them with olive oil, and season them with salt and black pepper. Place the rounds on baking trays that have been lightly brushed with olive oil. Bake for 12 minutes, flip, and continue baking for another 10 to 15 minutes or until the rounds are soft and golden on both sides.

Set the potatoes to boil in a pot of water for 30 minutes or until soft. Drain the potatoes and transfer them to a large mixing bowl. Mash the potatoes until smooth, stir in 1 stick of melted butter and 2½ cups of grated cheese, and season with black pepper and salt.

Brush the inside of a 3 inch deep, 11 by 16 inch baking dish with some of the remaining melted butter. Add a handful of bread crumbs, tossing them around to coat the bottom and sides of the baking dish with a light, even layer of crumbs. Discard the excess crumbs. Spread ½ of the potato mixture evenly on the bottom of the casserole dish, sprinkle over ½ of the shredded mozzarella, and then place a layer of overlapping eggplant rounds. Spread over all of the *ragu*, and then sprinkle over the remaining mozzarella. Stir the milk into the remaining mashed potatoes and beat until light and fluffy. Spread the potato mixture over top, creating an indented surface with plenty of nooks and crannies. Sprinkle over the remaining grated cheese and drizzle with the remaining melted butter.

Preheat the oven to 375 degrees. Tent the casserole with aluminum foil and bake for 50 minutes. Then remove the foil, turn the temperature up to 425 degrees, and continue baking for another 15 minutes or until the top is golden brown. Serve hot. Serves 12 adults.

Melanzane Ripieni alla Paola (Baked Eggplant Halves Stuffed with Ground Beef and Pork)

CALABRIA

The town of Paola sits on a slope above the Tyrrhenian Sea. The medieval quarter is full of Southern Italian charm with narrow streets that meander between baroque buildings, pastel houses with wrought iron covered windows, and a church dome adorned with colorful majolica tiles that rises above the terracotta rooftops. It is quite an atmospheric place! Here, you will also find the sanctuary of San Francesco. It is said that a miracle took place here during World War II, when the townspeople took refuge in the sanctuary during an air raid. A bomb struck the sanctuary but failed to detonate, and the townspeople were saved. Today, people from all over Italy come to the sanctuary of San Francesco to pray for a miracle.

My visit to Paola was an uplifting experience, but not in the spiritual sense. It was here that I ate my first Calabrian dish that was so spicy it lifted me off of my feet. At first glance, it looked rather innocent; plump eggplant halves neatly stuffed with sautéed ground beef and diced tomatoes. But after a few mouthfuls, only cold water and prayers could save me from the flecks of dried, hot chilies that they were spiked with. Despite the chef's heavy hand with the hot chilies, it was still a tasty dish, and I finished every last bite. Here is my re-creation. Add as much spice as you like, or leave it out entirely! If you prefer, top the eggplants with shredded mozzarella cheese and they will be extra tasty.

1 lb. ground beef (90% lean)
½ lb. ground pork
Olive oil, for sautéing
Salt and black pepper to taste
5 small Italian eggplants (6 to 8 inches long)
½ Spanish or Vidalia onion, chopped
4 cloves garlic, finely chopped
½ cup red wine
Crushed red pepper flakes to taste

1 can (28 oz.) crushed San Marzano tomatoes
1 tbsp. dried oregano
1½ tbsp. finely chopped, firmly packed basil
¾ cup grated Pecorino Romano cheese
½ lb. mozzarella cheese, shredded(optional)

Combine the ground beef and ground pork in a bowl. Brush the bottom of a frying pan with olive oil and set it over medium-low heat. Add the ground meat and season with salt and black pepper. Brown the meat, breaking it up with the back of a wooden spoon, and set it aside. Cut the eggplants in half lengthwise, and use a spoon to scoop out most of the flesh. Set the eggplant shells to the side and chop the flesh of the eggplants.

Coat the bottom of the frying pan with olive oil, set it back over medium-low heat, and sauté the onion and garlic until soft. Add the wine and the flesh of the eggplants. Season with red pepper flakes, salt, and black pepper and continue sautéing for 7 minutes or until the eggplant is soft. Then add the crushed tomatoes. Slosh ⅔ cup of water in the tomato can and add it to the frying pan. Stir in the dried oregano and the basil, reduce the heat to low, and simmer for 5 minutes. Stir in the browned meat and continue simmering for another 10 minutes or until the mixture has thickened. Remove the frying pan from the heat, allow the mixture to cool for 3 minutes, and then stir in the grated cheese. Adjust the seasoning if necessary.

Preheat the oven to 400 degrees. Rub the bottom of a baking dish with olive oil. Season the insides of the eggplant shells with salt and black pepper. Pile the meat filling high inside the eggplant shells and place them in the baking dish. Add a thin layer of water to the bottom of the baking dish, which will allow the eggplants to steam. Cover the baking dish with aluminum foil, and bake for 40 minutes or until the eggplant shells are tender. If you wish, top them with shredded mozzarella and set the baking dish back in the oven, uncovered, for another 3 minutes or until the cheese has melted. Serve hot. Serves 4 to 6 adults.

Trippa alla Romana con Piselli (Beef Tripe Braised in Tomato Sauce with Peas, Onions, and Red Bell Peppers)

LAZIO

Every Italian American of my generation had at least one grandmother who cooked tripe. It was that extra special dish that Nonna made only once in a while, and for good reason. Most aficionados of this underrated dish will tell you that they love to eat tripe but hate to cook it. It must be soaked for hours, boiled for hours, and then stewed for hours before it becomes tender and delicious. Nonetheless, it is a favorite dish of Italian Americans who mostly think of it as peasant fare. After all, tripe is a less desirable cut of meat and should never be served to dinner guests or for a holiday meal. And heaven forbid you order it at a restaurant, because nobody makes it as good as Nonna!

In Italy, however, tripe is held in much higher esteem. In fact, the people of Milan are affectionately referred to by other Italians as busecconi, *or "tripe eaters," because they are quite fond of tripe soup, which is traditionally eaten on Saturday. Rome is another city where tripe is much beloved. Romans prefer their tripe stewed in tomato sauce and topped with a sprinkle of grated pecorino cheese. A true Roman nonna is sure to add a few splashes of white Frascati to the sauce too! My version of Trippa alla Romana includes sweet young peas and diced red bell peppers, which add freshness and a burst of bright flavor. A few pinches of crushed red chilies add even more interest. My Sicilian grandmother, on the other hand, always cooked tripe with chunks of potatoes for a hearty one-dish meal. The possibilities are truly endless. Just be sure to use the best honeycomb beef tripe, and stew it for as long as needed to make it fork-tender.*

2 lbs. beef honeycomb tripe
4 cups of milk
Olive oil, for sautéing
½ Spanish or Vidalia onion, chopped
3 cloves garlic, finely chopped
1 can (28 oz.) crushed San Marzano tomatoes
1 tbsp. finely chopped, firmly packed basil

1 tbsp. finely chopped, firmly packed oregano
Crushed red pepper flakes to taste
Salt and black pepper to taste
1 large red bell pepper, seeded and chopped
2 cups frozen peas, thawed
Grated or shaved Pecorino Romano cheese, for topping

Cut the tripe into 2 inch strips, place it in a bowl, and pour over the milk. Cover the bowl with plastic wrap and let it soak in the refrigerator for at least 6 hours. Fill an 8 quart saucepan ⅔ of the way with water and add 1 rounded tablespoon of salt. Rinse the tripe under running water, transfer it to the saucepan, and simmer it over low heat for 2 hours or until tender.

When the tripe is almost done, prepare the sauce: Coat the bottom of a 6 quart saucepan with olive oil, set it over medium-low heat, and sauté the onion until soft. Add the garlic, sauté for another minute, and then add the crushed tomatoes. Using the can from the tomatoes, add 1 can of water to the pot. Add the basil and oregano and season with red pepper flakes, salt, and black pepper.

Drain the tripe thoroughly and add it to the saucepan. Reduce the heat to low and simmer for 30 minutes. Add the chopped peppers and continue simmering for another 30 minutes. Then stir in the peas and remove the saucepan from the heat. Serve hot, topped with grated or shaved Pecorino Romano cheese. Serves 4 adults.

Padella di Cacciatore (Chicken Braised in White Wine with Cherry Tomatoes, Black Olives, and Capers)

CALABRIA

La Sila is a mountainous region in central Calabria. With tall pine forests, pristine lakes, and babbling streams, it is as close to Switzerland as can you get in Southern Italy! Most of the area is now protected as a national park. It is a great place to go if you wish to escape the summertime heat of the coast. La Sila has always been a paradise for hunters. Wild boar, deer, rabbit, and quail are the hunter's mark. If you travel to La Sila, be sure to stay in a small town like Camigliatello, which sits at the foot of the highest peaks. Here, you will be near the best ski slopes south of Naples and plenty of hiking trails. When it comes time to eat, be sure to sample the local cuisine, which is likely to include the hunter's catch!

Cacciatore means "hunter" in Italian. Any dish prepared alla cacciatore or "hunter's style" will be simple and rustic. Here is a quick and easy stovetop preparation for chicken prepared alla cacciatore in a padella, or frying pan. I use typical Calabrian ingredients that burst with the flavors of the Mediterranean. It is a preparation you are likely to encounter during your ramblings through the beautiful rugged mountains of Calabria. Also try this recipe with small game hens, quail, and rabbit. Whatever meat you choose, be sure to pair it with a glass of white Vernaccia wine from Tuscany.

3 lbs. boneless chicken breasts and thighs (uniform in size)	2 fresh bay leaves
Salt and black pepper to taste	1 tbsp. dried oregano
Flour, for dredging	Crushed red pepper flakes to taste
Olive oil, for sautéing	3 tbsp. butter
½ Spanish or Vidalia onion, diced	2 tbsp. finely chopped, firmly packed basil
4 cloves garlic, sliced	1 dry quart cherry tomatoes, sliced in half
2½ cups white wine	
1½ cups chicken broth	1½ cups whole, pitted black Cerignola olives
½ cup capers in brine	

Cut the chicken breasts and thighs in half, season with salt and black pepper, and dredge lightly in flour. Coat the bottom of a 5½ quart frying pan with olive oil and set it over medium-low heat. When the oil has heated, brown the chicken on all sides until lightly golden. Remove it from the frying pan and set it aside.

Sauté the onion until soft and then add the garlic and continue sautéing for another minute. Return the chicken to the frying pan and add the wine, broth, capers, bay leaves, and dried oregano. Season with red pepper flakes, salt, and black pepper. Reduce the heat to low and braise for 30 minutes, turning the chicken every 10 minutes. As the braising liquid cooks down, add more wine as needed.

After the chicken has braised for 30 minutes, stir in the butter, basil, cherry tomatoes, and olives. Continue sautéing for another 3 to 5 minutes or until the cherry tomatoes have released some of their juice and the skins begin to pucker. Adjust the seasoning if necessary and remove the bay leaves before serving. Serve hot. Serves 4 to 6 adults.

Tacchino Ripieno (Roasted Turkey with Bread and Egg Stuffing)

CAMPANIA

At the turn of the twentieth century, immigrants from Southern Italy landed on the shores of the United States eager to become Americani. *They quickly adapted to American culture while preserving many of their own traditions. They decorated trees on Christmas, gave baskets of candy to their children on Easter, and roasted a turkey with stuffing for Thanksgiving. Like other immigrant groups, the Italians embraced American food traditions but often added their own unique twist. For example, a Thanksgiving dinner prepared in an Italian immigrant's home included not just turkey but also trays of* antipasto, *lasagna, and a stuffing prepared Nonna's way.*

Here is my grandmother's recipe for Italian bread stuffing. It is cucina povera, *or rustic cooking from the heart of Southern Italy and Sicily, where leftover bread and a few eggs can be stretched into a meal by a skilled* casalinga *(housewife) with a large family to feed. Flavored with garlic, fresh herbs, and plenty of grated Pecorino Romano cheese, it is savory and delicious. Sautéed mushrooms and bits of prosciutto or crumbled pork sausage make my version of grandma's stuffing extra special. This stuffing is traditionally used for beef, pork, and pork skin roulades that are braised in tomato sauce. My grandmother thought it would be great stuffed inside a Thanksgiving turkey, too! This recipe is enough to fill the cavity of an 18 to 20 pound bird, but if you wish, cut the recipe in half and try it stuffed in a whole roasted chicken, a butterflied roasted pork loin, or double-cut pork chops.*

1 large loaf country-style Italian bread	Olive oil, for sautéing
¾ cup grated Pecorino Romano cheese	½ large Spanish or Vidalia onion, diced
Salt and black pepper to taste	2 ribs celery, diced
3 tbsp. finely chopped, firmly packed Italian flat leaf parsley	4 cloves garlic, minced
	8 ounces cremini mushrooms, sliced
2 tbsp. finely chopped, firmly packed oregano or sage	½ lb. Italian pork sausage
	1½ cups chicken broth, divided
	6 extra-large eggs, beaten, divided

Grate enough bread in a food processor for 5 cups of large, firmly pressed crumbs. Transfer the bread crumbs to a mixing bowl, stir in the grated cheese, and season lightly with salt and black pepper. Add the parsley and oregano or sage.

Coat the bottom of a frying pan with olive oil, set it over medium-low heat, and sauté the onion and celery until soft. Add the garlic and mushrooms, season lightly with salt, and continue sautéing until the mushrooms are fully cooked. Transfer the sautéed items to the mixing bowl with the bread crumbs.

Remove the sausage from the casing and brown it in the frying pan over medium-low heat until fully cooked, breaking it up with the back of a wooden spoon. Transfer the sausage to the mixing bowl, toss everything together, and stir in 1 cup of chicken broth to moisten the mixture. Stir in 5 of the beaten eggs. The stuffing should be thick and moist but not soupy. If necessary, beat the last egg and stir it in or add the remaining chicken broth.

Fill the cavity of the turkey with the stuffing, leaving some room for it to expand.

Rub some olive oil over the turkey and season it with salt, black pepper, and whatever dried herbs you prefer. Roast the turkey as appropriate for its weight. If there is stuffing leftover, place it in a greased casserole dish, add just less than ¼ inch of broth on top, and tent it with aluminum foil. Bake the stuffing at 375 degrees until the broth has been absorbed by the stuffing and it has risen and become firm. Serve hot. Serve 8 to 10 adults.

Coniglio Rustico (Rabbit Braised in White Wine Sauce with Artichokes, Green Olives, and Capers)

BASILICATA

Italians love rabbit! In fact, Italy is one of the largest commercial producers of rabbit in Europe and ranks highest in rabbit consumption. It therefore is no surprise that the domestication of rabbits on the Italian peninsula dates back to the third century BC, when the Roman legions brought them back from North Africa and Spain. Today, in the small hilltop towns of Basilicata and Calabria, you are sure to see freshly butchered rabbits hanging in butcher shop windows. In fact, many modern Italians also raise their own rabbits as a food source, keeping them in small wooden hutches in the backyard until it's time for a delicious Sunday stew.

In the United States, rabbit has long been overlooked. Until recently, it was difficult to find in supermarkets and rarely seen on restaurant menus. How unfortunate! But finally, innovative American chefs and adventurous home cooks have come to realize what the Italians have known for centuries: rabbit is a truly versatile meat with delicious mild flavor that is similar to chicken. Here is a tasty recipe made with the best ingredients from the coastal regions of Basilicata and Calabria: fresh artichokes, plump green olives, and white wine from the hills near Ciro. If rabbit is not available at your local supermarket or butcher shop, use boneless chicken thighs or split Cornish game hens instead.

2 young rabbits (2½ to 3 lbs. each)
1 large Spanish or Vidalia onion, chopped
3 ribs celery, chopped
4 cloves garlic, sliced in half
1 small bunch whole Italian flat leaf parsley
2 bay leaves
2 cups light chicken broth
Salt and black pepper to taste
Flour, for dredging
Olive oil, for sautéing

1½ cups white wine
1 tbsp. finely chopped, firmly packed oregano
1 tbsp. finely chopped, firmly packed thyme
2 large lemons, divided
1½ dozen baby artichokes (about 2½ inches long)
½ cup capers in brine
1½ cups whole, pitted green Castelvetrano or Calabresi olives
2 tbsp. butter

First, dress the rabbit. Remove the legs at the joint. Remove the breast from the remaining carcass and chop the breast in half, cutting through the spine. Place the legs and breast pieces in a bowl and set them in the refrigerator. Place the remainder of the carcass (neck, back, rib cage, and flap meat) in a soup pot. Add the onion,

celery, garlic, parsley, bay leaves, and chicken broth to the pot. Add enough water to cover everything completely by 1 inch, season with salt and black pepper, set the pot over medium-low heat, and simmer for 2 hours. Strain the stock through a fine mesh sieve, and press the carcass and aromatics against the sieve with a wooden spoon to extract all of the juices. Then set the stock to the side.

Season the rabbit with salt and dredge it in flour. Coat the bottom of a 5½ quart frying pan with olive oil, set it over medium-low heat, and brown the rabbit on each side until lightly golden. Remove the rabbit from the frying pan and set it to the side. Drain off most of the oil from the frying pan and add the white wine. Return the rabbit to the frying pan, add the oregano and thyme, and pour over enough stock to cover the rabbit. Braise for 1 hour, turning the pieces every 15 minutes. Add more stock as necessary.

While the rabbit is braising, prepare the baby artichokes. Squeeze the juice of 1½ lemons into a large bowl of cold water, enough to cover the artichoke hearts completely. Remove the outer leaves of the artichokes until you reach the soft, pale inner cone. Remove the top ⅓ of the artichokes and peel the stems. Cut the artichokes in half and drop them into the acidulated water to prevent browning. When you are ready to use the artichokes, drain them and pat them dry.

After the rabbit has braised for 1 hour, transfer it to a serving platter and cover it with aluminum foil. Add the artichokes, capers, olives, butter, and juice of ½ lemon to the frying pan. Continue braising over low heat for another 10 minutes or until the artichokes are tender but still firm. Adjust the seasoning if necessary. Spoon the artichokes and sauce over the rabbit. Serve hot. Serves 6 adults.

A typical scene in any small town along Campania's costiera

IX

Liquori e Cose Dolce (Liqueurs and Desserts)

Strange Wheat in Santa Margherita di Belice

A Rambling in Sicily

One summer, while visiting my friends Rita and Salvo in Bagheria, Sicily, I spent a day rambling around the town of Santa Margherita di Belice. This is where my grandfather's family came from. I was excited to check it out! It was a warm day, and the hills were shades of sun-baked yellow. After driving for two hours, I finally came upon a sign pointing towards my destination: a sprawling mass of tightly packed houses perched on the flat top of a wide hill. I pulled over to the side of the road and took photographs. Beside me was a wheat field that had recently been harvested. I walked to the edge of the field and pulled a few of the remaining strands of wheat. It was the perfect souvenir! In Sicily, a small bouquet of wheat is kept in the home for good luck. What could bring more luck to my home than a bouquet of wheat from the town of my family's origin?

I then proceeded into the town and went for a stroll. It was now midday and the shops were closed. I came upon an old man selling garlic from a pull-cart. I asked him, "Does the Abruzzo family still live in this town?"

He looked at me quite puzzled and said, "Of course!"

I then asked, "How many Abruzzos are there?"

The old man explained, "Half of the people in this town are Abruzzos, and the other half are related to them." He then asked who I was looking for.

"No one in particular," I said.

The old man became suspicious. He raised his brow and the look on his face became stern. He demanded to know why I was questioning him. "If you are not looking for anyone, then why are you asking me about the Abruzzo family?"

I smiled and proudly exclaimed, "Because I am an Abruzzo from America whose family came from this town!"

Now exasperated, the old man replied, "Bravo Abruzzo! Now, do you want to buy some garlic?"

I left Santa Margherita later that afternoon with a handful of wheat and some garlic for my friends. I had a wonderful time exploring the home of my ancestors. When I returned to Bagheria, I told Rita and Salvo all about my exciting day. I showed them the bouquet of wheat that I picked from the field. Salvo took it in his hand and looked at it closely. He seemed puzzled.

"This is strange wheat," he said as he handed it to Rita.

She put her glasses on and examined the grains. Then she, too, exclaimed, "Yes, this is strange wheat! The grains are not plump."

Rita handed the bouquet back to me. "It appears that you have weeds from Santa Margherita," she said.

"Oh yes, those are just weeds," Salvo added.

Rita then apologized. "We are sorry to disappoint you, but if you bring these weeds back to your home, they will not bring you good luck."

Needless to say, I tossed out the bouquet of weeds and we all had a good laugh. When my stay in Bagheria came to an end, Rita and Salvo's daughter, Paola, presented me with a gift. As I opened the box, she said, "Hang this in your house for good luck!" It was a terracotta wall plate and on it was painted a bouquet of golden wheat. Rita explained, "We did not want you to leave Sicily without some wheat." I thanked them, and when I returned home I hung the plate on the wall in my kitchen. It is a pleasant reminder of my dear friends in Sicily and the strange wheat I picked that day in Santa Margherita.

A day at the beach in Cefalu, Sicily

Fancy marzipan is a Sicilian delicacy

The tiny harbor of Scopello, Sicily nestled between the rocks and the sea

The chic resort of Taormina is full of Sicilian charm

A quiet road through the Val di Salso, Sicily

Grapes in Viterbo, Lazio

Sweet almond brittle is a favorite snack in Southern Italy

Arancello e Limoncello (Sweet and Fragrant Citrus Liqueur)

CAMPANIA

I once stayed for two weeks at the home of my friends Salvatore and Anna in Palermo. They were delighted to have me as a guest and truly rolled out the carpet to make my stay special. When I arrived at their apartment, my friend Salvatore proudly announced that he installed a new American-style kitchen because I was coming. Anna gave me a big hug and proclaimed, "We also bought a longer bed for you to sleep in because you are so tall!" That was just the beginning of their fuss to make sure that I was comfortable and well-fed during my stay. Each morning, Salvatore's son, Lorenzo, would take a glass jar from the cupboard. He would shake the jar vigorously and then put it back. When I asked him what it was, he proudly exclaimed, "This is lemon liqueur that I am making to celebrate your stay! It will be ready before you leave." Inside the jar were lemon peels soaking in alcohol. "It is a specialty from the Amalfi Coast, where they grow the best lemons in Italy," Lorenzo explained. When the liqueur was ready, he strained out the peels and the liqueur was vibrant yellow. One evening, we all sat on the balcony and had a drink. It was the perfect nightcap. Before I left, I prodded him for the recipe, and he graciously obliged. When I make it, I sometimes use plump California oranges instead of lemons. But don't tell Lorenzo! Use whatever citrus fruit you like best. Either way, it is sure to be delicious.

14-16 California navel oranges or lemons

3 cups sugar

3 cups water

7 cups vodka

Use a potato peeler to remove the peel from the oranges or lemons without taking any of the pith. Place the sugar and water in a saucepan and boil gently over low heat until the volume has reduced by almost half.

Add the citrus zest, simmer for another 2 minutes, and then remove the saucepan from the heat. When the mixture has cooled to lukewarm, transfer it to a large glass container, stir in the vodka, seal the container tightly, and give it a good shake. Store the container in a cool, dark place for 10 days and shake the container once each day.

Strain the liqueur through a fine mesh strainer or cheesecloth and transfer it to bottles. Store at room temperature or in the freezer. Serve chilled.

Ciliegie Ubriaco (Drunken Cherries)

LAZIO

In Italian, ubriaco *means "drunken," which is the perfect name for these cherries, which have been allowed to rest in fine brandy, vodka, or rum for many weeks. Drunken cherries are a favorite after-dinner treat in the town of Celleno, where Italy's best cherries are grown. They are always sweet and succulent! The people of Celleno use them to make brandies, sweet liqueurs, syrups, jams, and much more. In fact, the local cherry liqueur called Maraschino Celleno is just as good, if not better, than the world famous Luxardo brand from Veneto. Made with a secret blend of sweet and sour cherries, Celleno's version of maraschino liqueur is flavorful, bold, and sure to knock you off your feet! If you prefer a sweeter, less potent liqueur, then try my drunken cherries recipe. Just be sure to use a high-quality brandy, vodka, or rum. Seal the drunken cherries in a glass jar and allow it to sit for at least one month to marry the flavors. The longer it sits, the more flavorful and delicious it will become! To serve my* ciliegie ubriaco, *I like to place two cherries in a shot glass and then top it off with the liqueur. Better yet, place a cherry on top of a scoop of vanilla ice cream and drizzle over a shot of the liqueur! Served chilled, it is the perfect nightcap on a warm summer evening in the countryside of Lazio.*

2½ lbs. Bing cherries (with stems), divided
1½ cups sugar

½ cup water
3½ cups brandy or vodka

Wash the cherries. Remove the stems and pits from 6 ounces of cherries and place them in a blender. Leave the remaining cherries whole with the stems intact and place them into 2 sterilized 1 quart mason jars.

Place the sugar in a saucepan with the water, bring it to a low boil, and simmer until it reaches the consistency of syrup. Add the syrup to the blender and puree until smooth. Strain the syrup through a fine mesh sieve, place it in a mixing bowl, and allow it to cool until lukewarm. Then stir in the alcohol.

Pour the liqueur over the cherries in the mason jars and seal the lids of the jars tightly. Allow the cherries to sit in the refrigerator for at least 1 month before serving. Serve two cherries in a shot glass with some liqueur as an accompaniment to biscotti or sweet ricotta cheese pies. The cherries will keep in the refrigerator nicely for up to 1 year.

Fragole Sotto Marsala (Strawberries in Sweet Marsala Wine)

SICILY

The countryside near Marsala is famous for two things: wine and strawberries. This simple recipe is the perfect marriage of both! It is a true taste of western Sicily, where rows of grape vines march up the low hills and strawberry fields stretch across the valleys in the springtime. Italians love to macerate fruit with wine or liqueur. It is always a delicious combination. My friends Rita and Salvo macerate sweet strawberries with Marsala wine. Their daughter, Paola, makes it for me whenever I am at her house for dinner. It is a light and refreshing dessert after a big meal. I like to serve macerated fruit for dessert when I throw a dinner party. It can be prepared ahead of time, and best of all it does not involve baking! My guests are always pleased when I present them with an elegant wine glass filled halfway with macerated strawberries and topped with a scoop of gelato or fresh whipped cream. Be sure to make this recipe in springtime, when the strawberries are best!

2 lbs. strawberries	½ cup sugar
Peel of 1 California navel orange	2 cups sweet Marsala wine
1½ cups water	

Thinly slice the strawberries and place them in a bowl and set aside. Use a potato peeler to remove the peel from the orange without taking any of the pith. Place the water, orange peel, and sugar in a saucepan and simmer over medium heat for 12 to 15 minutes or until the volume has reduced by almost half and the consistency has thickened to a light syrup. Remove the saucepan from the heat and let it sit for 1 minute. Then stir in the wine. When the wine mixture has cooled, pour it over the strawberries. Place the strawberries in the refrigerator and allow them to macerate for at least 6 hours before serving. Serve chilled. Serves 6 adults.

Torruna di Mandorle (Honey Almond Brittle)

CALABRIA

Almonds grow abundantly in Southern Italy. In some parts of Calabria, almond groves dot the landscape for countless miles. Almonds are a nice snack when toasted but are even better when plucked fresh from the tree and eaten raw! They are sweet, juicy, and delicious. Anyone who has seen an almond tree knows that the actual nut is encased in a leathery, green pod, which makes them challenging to extract. One afternoon, my friend Salvo gave me a bag of fresh almonds. "Enjoy these as a snack while you and your friends are travelling," he said. Unfortunately, Salvo did not give us a nutcracker, and as we drove up the coast of Southern Italy towards Naples, extracting the almonds from the pods proved to be a difficult task. We had no choice but to improvise. My friend Jeff, who was sitting in the front passenger seat, opened the glove compartment, wedged a pod in the crack, and then gave the glove compartment door a quick, hard slam. It proved to be an efficient—albeit somewhat messy—method! Soon we were munching on fresh almonds as we drove the autostrada through Calabria.

Almonds play a dominant role in Southern Italian cuisine and are used in both sweet and savory dishes. You can find them in everything from Sicilian fish stews to crunchy Roman biscotti. Almond brittle is a popular snack in Calabria, where it is often sold by vendors at street festivals. My family has made it for as long as I can remember. It is a tradition passed on by my grandmother, who always prepared a batch for special occasions and holidays. For Christmas, she shaped the brittle into a ring so that it looked like a wreath, and she decorated it with bits of candied citron and colorful nonpareils. Sometimes she made the brittle with hazelnuts instead of almonds. It was always a special treat! Here is her recipe, which is very typical of what you will find in Calabria and Sicily. It is quick and easy to make, so be sure to prepare some for your next festive occasion.

1½ lbs. whole blanched almonds	⅔ cup honey
4 cups sugar	Colored nonpareils, for decorating
½ tsp. salt	

Preheat the oven to 375 degrees. Toast the nuts for 7 to 10 minutes or until golden. Spray two non-stick baking trays with cooking spray and set them to the side.

Place the sugar, salt, and honey in a large saucepan over medium heat and stir constantly with a slotted spoon, scraping the mixture up from the bottom of the saucepan. After 10 minutes, the sugar mixture will turn to syrup. Continue stirring until the syrup turns a medium amber color. Then remove the saucepan from the

burner and quickly stir in the almonds while the syrup is piping hot. Use the slotted spoon to scoop up some of the mixture. Allow the excess syrup to run off, and then drop small clusters on the baking sheets. Sprinkle immediately with nonpareils. If you prefer, arrange the almonds into a ring or log. Allow the *torruna* to cool completely before serving. Makes 2 dozen small clusters.

Cucuzzata (Sicilian Squash Marmalade)

SICILY

By the end of August, there is sure to be a dozen or more cucuzza squash hanging from the arbor in my vegetable garden. Many will grow to be five feet long and will weigh more than fifteen pounds! But what does one do with so many squash? At my farm in Virginia, we make marmalade. I follow a traditional Sicilian recipe developed by the nuns at a convent near Palermo many centuries ago. The squash is ground into a pulp and boiled with sugar and other ingredients for hours, until it has thickened into a pale green marmalade called cucuzzata. *It is a most unusual but tasty treat from the mountains of the Palermo region. Sweet and delicious, it has a unique flavor that is reminiscent of honeydew melon. The Palermitani use* cucuzzata *as a filling for cookies, pastries, and fancy tarts. I eat it on a slice of bread, just as you would do with any other type of marmalade or jam. It is also a unique and delicious topping for vanilla gelato. For a savory treat, smear it on fresh, grilled Italian bread and top it with a slice of prosciutto.*

4 long cucuzza squash	7 tsp. lemon juice
7 cups sugar	1 tsp. salt

Peel the squash and slice them in half. Scoop out and discard all of the seeds and the spongy white flesh. Chop the squash into small pieces and then puree in a food processor until smooth. Process 14 cups of squash puree and then transfer the puree to a soup pot. (A tall pot is preferable as the marmalade with burp and splatter as it boils.)

Add the sugar and lemon juice. Simmer over medium-low heat, stirring frequently. When the marmalade thickens (after about one hour), lower the heat and stir or whisk every 2 minutes, scraping the bottom of the pot to prevent burning. Test the thickness by allowing a teaspoon of marmalade to cool to room temperature. When the marmalade is thick and rich, it is done. This will take anywhere from 1½ to 2 hours depending upon the moisture content of your squash.

Transfer the marmalade to sterilized mason jars. Seal them tightly and then process in boiling water for 13 minutes. Makes 6 one pint jars.

Gellu di Melone (Sicilian Watermelon Mold)

SICILY

Mount Etna rises above the picturesque fishing village of Aci Trezza. This is a rocky stretch of coast where ancient lava flows once reached the sea, creating a mysterious landscape that is a place of legend. According to Homer's Odyssey, the one-eyed cyclops lived here. As the story goes, the cyclops cornered Odysseus in a cave on Etna's slope. Fearing he would be killed, Odysseus blinded the cyclops with a hot iron and fled to his ship. The cyclops then hurled giant rocks at Odysseus, which landed in the sea. Odysseus escaped, and the rocks became islands that today stand guard over Aci Trezza's small harbor. These islands are now fittingly known as the Isole dei Cyclopi.

If you explore the Etna region, be sure to spend a day in Aci Trezza. Its quaint harbor is certainly a place of legend! It is also a great place to sample the distinctive cuisine of eastern Sicily. Etna's fertile green slopes produce a bounty of fruits and vegetables, including sweet watermelons that are always a summertime treat at the restaurants along Aci Trezza's Lungomare dei Cyclopi. With a bounty of Southern Italy's best fruits at hand, the hinterland of Etna has also become legendary for its unique desserts. Here is my favorite! It is a tantalizing and intriguing pudding made with fresh watermelon puree and pomegranate juice and flavored with cinnamon and vanilla. Set in a fancy gelatin mold and topped with shaved dark chocolate, it is truly a dessert that legends are made of!

1 medium watermelon	⅔ cup cornstarch
⅓ cup pomegranate syrup	¾ cup sugar
1½ tsp. vanilla extract	Shaved dark chocolate, for topping
¾ tsp. cinnamon	(optional)
¼ tsp. salt	

Cut the sweetest portions of the watermelon into chunks. Using a blender, make 5 cups of watermelon puree. Add the pomegranate syrup, vanilla, cinnamon, and salt to the blender and pulse a few times. Place one cup of the watermelon mixture in a small bowl, whisk in the cornstarch until smooth, and then set it to the side. Place the rest of the watermelon mixture in a large saucepan, add the sugar, set it over medium heat, and bring it up to a low boil, whisking constantly. When the sugar has dissolved, add the cornstarch mixture.

Lower the heat slightly to medium-low and continue simmering and whisking constantly for 10 minutes or until the puree is translucent and thick like pudding. Spray the inside of a gelatin mold lightly with cooking spray and pour the puree into the mold. If you prefer, use small ramekins instead. Let the puree cool to room temperature and then place it in the refrigerator for at least 6 hours to set.

Unmold the pudding by dipping the mold in warm water for a minute and then inverting it on to a serving plate. Serve chilled, with fresh fruit or topped with a few curls of shaved dark chocolate. Serves 4 to 6 adults.

Zeppole (Festival Doughnuts)

BASILICATA

In Italy, every city and town has a patron saint, and once each year, a festival is held in the saint's honor. Most festivals begin with a somber religious procession in which a statue of the saint is carried through the streets. Afterwards, the entire town gathers for a celebration. Zeppole and other deep-fried treats are sure to be served at any festival in Italy, and certainly on the feast day of a patron saint. They are also popular at Italian festivals in the United States. During the summer, you can even buy them at boardwalk stands in Coney Island and the Jersey Shore. Crisp and golden on the outside and soft and spongy in the middle, when topped with a blanket of powdered sugar, they are simply irresistible!

Here is my family's recipe for the crispiest Italian doughnuts ever. Zeppole is the Neapolitan name that most Italian Americans are familiar with, but in Sicilian dialect, they are called sfinge. *Although recipes for the dough may vary from region to region, one thing remains a constant—they must be fried at the right temperature or else they won't be crisp. We make them once a year: on New Year's Day, right after the stroke of midnight. It is my family's tradition for everyone to drop some dough into the hot oil and make a* zeppole *for good luck in the coming year. And, of course, we all have to eat one too! No matter what the celebration,* zeppole *are a festive and tasty treat. If you prefer, dip them in warm honey flavored with cinnamon and orange peel. Buona festa!*

2 lbs. all-purpose, pre-sifted flour	½ lb. confectioners' sugar, for dusting
1 tsp. salt	(optional)
¾ oz. fast-acting dry yeast	2 cups honey (optional)
3½ cups warm water	½ tsp. cinnamon (optional)
2 extra-large eggs	Zest of 1 California navel orange
4 tbsp. sugar	(optional)
1 gallon corn oil, for deep frying	

In a large mixing bowl, thoroughly combine the flour and salt. In a separate bowl, combine the yeast with the water and let it sit for 10 minutes. Beat together the eggs and sugar in another bowl, and then whisk the egg mixture into the yeast. Make a well in the middle of the flour and then add the liquid ingredients. Beat the liquid ingredients with a fork, slowly pulling in flour from the sides of the well. Continue until everything is combined to form a moist, sticky dough. Cover the bowl loosely with plastic wrap and allow the dough to rest for 1 hour or until it has doubled. Push the dough down with a wooden spoon, cover it again with plastic wrap, and let it rest for another hour or until it has doubled.

Heat the oil in a large pot. Push down the dough and then drop tablespoons of dough into the hot oil. Fry the *zeppole* until golden brown, turning them occasionally so that they fry evenly on all sides. Remove the *zeppole* with a slotted spoon and place them on a tray lined with paper towels to absorb the excess oil. Sprinkle the *zeppole* with confectioners' sugar or drizzle them with warm honey. If you prefer honey, place it in a small saucepan, stir in the cinnamon, add the orange zest, and let it simmer gently over low heat for 2 minutes and then sit for 3 minutes before drizzling. Serve hot. Makes 3 dozen *zeppole.*

Cicerchiata (Honey-Covered Fried Pastry Nuggets)

ABRUZZO/MOLISE

Fried pastry nuggets covered with honey are a popular holiday treat throughout Southern Italy. Each region calls them by a different name and has its own special way of preparing them. In Campania, they are called struffoli, *and the nuggets are tossed with lemon-scented honey. The Sicilian version is called* pignolata *because they are cut to resemble pine nuts; whereas in Abruzzo, the nuggets are rolled into tiny balls and called* cicerchiata, *which means "chickpea" in the local dialect. When sprinkled with colorful nonpareils,* cicerchiata *are a festive snack at the annual* carnevale *in Vasto, a charming seaside town that lies on Abruzzo's southern coast. If you head to Vasto in February for* carnevale, *you are sure to see mounds of sweet* cicerchiata *on display in pastry shop windows and on tables set up by street vendors who call out for you to have a try!*

Here is my family's recipe for the absolute best honey-covered fried nuggets! We cut the dough into small diamonds, but if you prefer round nuggets that resemble chickpeas, roll the dough into thin ropes and cut them into small rounds. We flavor the honey with cinnamon and toss in a handful of slivered almonds and candied citron. If you prefer, add chopped walnuts or candied orange peel instead. No matter how you make them, cicerchiata *are always a scrumptious and irresistible treat! I spoon them into cupcake wrappers for individual servings that are easy to grab and hold while eating. If you buy them at* carnevale *in Vasto, they will be handed to you in a small plastic bowl. But be forewarned, this is one sticky dessert that will have you licking your fingers!*

1 cup milk	1 gallon corn oil, for deep frying
1 cup sugar	12 ounces blanched slivered almonds
½ tsp. salt	64 oz. honey
6¼ cups all-purpose, pre-sifted flour	1 tsp. cinnamon
3 heaping tsp. baking powder	3 dozen cupcake wrappers
1 cup vegetable shortening	Colored nonpareils, for decoration
2 extra-large eggs	

Warm the milk in a saucepan on the stovetop, remove it from the heat, stir in the sugar and salt, and let it cool completely. Meanwhile, sift together the flour and baking powder in a large mixing bowl. Then cut the shortening into the flour and work it with your hands until the texture is like oatmeal. Form a well in the middle of the dry ingredients.

Beat the eggs and combine them with the milk mixture. Pour the liquid ingredients into the well. Beat the liquid ingredients with a fork, slowly pulling in flour from the sides of the well. Continue until everything has been combined to form a sticky dough. Turn the dough onto a lightly floured work surface and knead it until smooth and shiny. Cut the dough into 4 pieces, wrap them with plastic wrap, and let them rest for 1 hour in the refrigerator.

Roll out the dough on a lightly floured work surface to ¼ inch thickness. Cut off a ½ inch wide strip and cut it into small diamonds. Continue until all of the dough has been cut. Heat the oil in a large pot and fry the diamonds one handful at a time until golden. Remove them from the oil with a skimmer and place them on a tray lined with paper towels to absorb the excess oil.

Preheat the oven to 375 degrees and toast the slivered almonds for 7 to 10 minutes or until golden. Pour the honey in a wide saucepan and stir in the cinnamon. Bring the honey to a boil and then remove the saucepan from the burner. Place a handful of the *cicerchiata* and a sprinkle of toasted almonds in a small mesh strainer and dip it in the warm honey. Drain the excess honey, transfer the *cicerchiata* to cupcake wrappers, and sprinkle immediately with nonpareils. Reheat the honey when it cools down and becomes too thick to drain through the mesh strainer. Serve at room temperature. Makes 3 dozen.

Crostata di Albicocca e Mandorle (Almond and Apricot Tart)

CALABRIA

When you arrive at Salvatore and Anna's beach villa in Calabria, you are greeted by a small but glorious tree. It stands beside the walkway in the garden. When I visited one year in July, its branches were full of bright orange apricots. It is the crown jewel of the garden, and I dared not pluck a fruit without asking first! Salvatore and Anna's daughter, Gemma, said, "Go right ahead! If they are not picked soon, we will be cleaning spoiled fruit from the walkway." I gathered as many apricots as I could and ate a few while I was picking them. Wonderfully sweet and slightly tart, they were perfect for baking in a crostata. *Now, if I could only persuade Gemma to skip an afternoon at the beach in order to bake! Here is a recipe inspired by the sweet, ripe apricots I picked from the tree in Salvatore and Anna's front garden. It is a creation of my very own. Although this may not be a traditional Calabrian recipe,* crostata *are popular in all regions of Italy. Why shouldn't sweet, ripe apricots from Calabria be baked in one too? Make this tart in a fluted tart pan and arrange the sliced apricots in a fancy pattern. The creamy almond filling, crunchy sliced almonds, and tender crust make this an elegant dessert. It is something you might just find at a fancy pastry shop in Reggio or Cosenza.*

For the crust:	For the filling:
2½ cups all-purpose, pre-sifted flour	4 tbsp. butter
1 cup semolina flour	⅔ cup sugar
¾ cup sugar	1 tsp. vanilla extract
1 heaping tsp. baking powder	½ tsp. salt
½ tsp. salt	2 extra-large eggs
8 tbsp. vegetable shortening	8 oz. almond paste
4 tbsp. butter	⅓ cup semolina flour
3 extra-large eggs	14 apricots
	¾ cup apricot preserves
	⅔ cup sliced almonds

First, prepare the crust: In a large mixing bowl, combine the flour, semolina, sugar, baking powder, and salt. Cut the shortening and butter into the dry ingredients and work it with your hands until you achieve the texture of oatmeal. Form a well in the middle of the dry ingredients. Beat the eggs and pour them into the well. With a fork, beat the liquid ingredient, slowly pulling in flour from the sides of the well. Continue until everything has been combined to form a soft, sticky dough. Turn the dough onto a lightly floured work surface and knead it until smooth and shiny. Wrap the dough with plastic wrap and allow it to rest in the refrigerator for 1 hour.

Lightly grease an 11 inch diameter, 1 or 1½ inch deep fluted tart pan with a removable bottom. Roll out the dough to ¼ inch thickness on sheets of lightly floured plastic wrap. This will make it easier to move the dough from your work surface to the tart pan. As the dough is soft, it will otherwise be difficult to transfer to the tart pan without tearing. Press the dough firmly and evenly into the bottom and sides of the tart pan and trim any excess dough from the edges.

Next, prepare the filling: Using an electric mixer, cream together the butter, sugar, vanilla, and salt and then beat in the eggs. Beat in the almond paste a little at a time. When the mixture is smooth and creamy, beat in the semolina flour. Spread the almond filling evenly in the tart. Slice the apricots in half and arrange them on top, cut side up, in a circular pattern.

Preheat the oven to 350 degrees and bake the tart for 1 hour. Make a glaze by warming the apricot preserves in a small saucepan. Brush the top of the tart with the glaze after it has baked for an hour, making sure it gets into all the nooks and crannies. Then sprinkle the sliced almonds over top. Continue baking for another 10 to 15 minutes or until firm and golden brown. Check the firmness by inserting a toothpick in the center of the tart. The almond filling should be moist, but not runny. Allow the tart to cool before removing it from the tart pan. Serve at room temperature. Serves 6 to 8 adults.

Pizza Ricotta (Country-Style Sweet Ricotta Pie)

BASILICATA

Sweet ricotta pies are an Easter tradition in the regions south of Rome. They are the perfect way to celebrate the ending of Lent, which is the six week period before Easter when Catholics fast and abstain from eating meat and sweets. During the last week of Lent, there are sure to be many somber processions and ceremonies in small towns and big cities alike, as Catholics head to church to commemorate Good Friday. But when Easter finally arrives, the festivities begin! This is a time of celebration and indulgence after weeks of fasting. And there is nothing better than waking up on Easter morning to the smell of sweet ricotta pies just pulled from the oven. Oh, how wonderful Easter Sunday is in Italy!

The recipes for sweet ricotta pie vary from region to region. In the Neapolitan version, which is called pastiera, *grains of wheat are mixed in with the ricotta to add density and texture. Other versions include candied citron or chocolate chips. Here is my mother's recipe, which has been handed down in her family for generations. It is typical of what you will find in Basilicata, Apulia, and Southern Campania. As a child I enjoyed waking up to the smell of her pies on Easter morning! Unlike the dense* pastiera *of Naples, my mother's ricotta pie is light, creamy, and delicious. Her secret is to whip the ricotta filling until fluffy—it will melt in your mouth. If you like, sprinkle some semi-sweet chocolate morsels or some diced candied citron over top before baking.*

For the crust:	For the filling:
3 cups all-purpose, pre-sifted flour	2½ lbs. ricotta cheese
¾ cup sugar	2½ cups confectioners' sugar
1 heaping tsp. baking powder	1½ tsp. vanilla extract
½ tsp. salt	4 extra-large eggs
12 tbsp. butter	2½ tbsp. cornstarch
3 extra-large eggs	

This recipe makes 2 open-faced pies. First prepare the pie crust: In a mixing bowl, thoroughly combine the flour, sugar, baking powder, and salt. Next, cut in the butter and work it with your hands until you achieve the texture of oatmeal. Form a well in the middle of the dry ingredients and add the eggs. Beat the eggs with a fork and then slowly pull in flour from the sides of the well. Continue until everything has been combined to form a sticky dough. Turn the dough onto a lightly floured work surface and knead it until smooth and shiny. Cut the dough into 2 equal pieces. Wrap each piece with plastic wrap and allow the dough to rest in the refrigerator for 1 hour.

Next, prepare the filling: Bring the ricotta to room temperature in a large mixing bowl and then add the confectioners' sugar and vanilla. Beat everything together with an electric mixer for 2 to 3 minutes or until the ricotta is smooth and silky. In a separate bowl, beat together the eggs and cornstarch until smooth. Add the egg mixture to the ricotta and beat for 2 minutes or until light and fluffy.

Lightly grease two 10 inch diameter, 2 inch deep pie dishes. Roll each piece of dough to just less than ¼ inch thickness. Roll the dough on sheets of lightly floured plastic wrap. This will make it easier to move the dough from your work surface to the pie dishes. As the dough is soft, it will otherwise be difficult to transfer to the pie dishes without tearing. Set a sheet of dough into each pie dish. Press the dough gently into each dish and crimp the top edges with your fingers. Pour equal amounts of the filling into each pie shell.

Preheat the oven to 350 degrees. Bake the pies for 1 hour or until the crust is golden brown. The ricotta filling will be slightly loose in the middle but will firm up as it cools. Serve at room temperature. Serves 10 to 12 adults.

Torta di Castagne (Chestnut Sponge Cake with Walnuts)

LAZIO

When I finished this cookbook, my wife had one criticism. She said, "There is no recipe with chestnuts!" I shrugged my shoulders and remained silent. She then asked, "How can that be? Italians love chestnuts!" I defended myself with a simple explanation. "There are no chestnut recipes because I do not like chestnuts!" Then I explained that it would be disingenuous for me to include a recipe using something that I would neither eat nor cook with. Therefore, I said, "A chestnut recipe is out of the question!" My wife refused to accept this answer. "I cannot imagine an Italian cookbook without a chestnut recipe! Italians use chestnuts in all sorts of dishes! They even have festivals to celebrate the chestnut! You need at least one recipe!" By week's end, I was at the supermarket buying chestnuts—and lots of them.

After doing a little research and some experimenting, I came up with a simple recipe that to my surprise is damn good! It is a light chestnut sponge cake typical of the region near the enchanting town of Soriano in the Cimini Hills north of Rome. In Soriano, chestnuts are serious business. After all, Lazio's best chestnuts are grown here. The people of Soriano love their chestnuts and have incorporated them into many dishes, including wonderful sweet desserts. Head to Soriano's annual Sagre della Castagna, chestnut festival, in early October to try them. With a delicate chestnut flavor, this sponge cake can only be described as ethereal. Topped with a dollop of fresh whipped cream, it is a true taste of the Cimini Hills. What a perfect Southern Italian treat! And so, this is how a chestnut recipe made its way into my repertoire of Italian desserts! If you are not a fan of chestnuts, this recipe is sure to make you one.

1 jar (14 oz.) whole chestnuts	1¾ cups sugar
1½ cups all-purpose, pre-sifted flour	1¾ tsp. vanilla extract
4 tsp. baking powder	3 extra-large eggs
¼ tsp. salt	1½ cups milk, divided
1¼ cups butter	¾ cup walnuts, chopped

Using a food processor, grind enough chestnuts for 2 cups of fine meal. Sift together the flour, baking powder, and salt in a mixing bowl, and then stir in the chestnut meal. In a mixing bowl, cream the butter, sugar, and vanilla until light and fluffy, and then beat in the eggs.

Beat in one third of the dry ingredients. Once they are incorporated, beat in ½ cup of milk. Continue beating in the remaining dry ingredients and milk in the same fashion until everything has been incorporated and the batter is light, fluffy, and smooth.

Preheat the oven to 375 degrees. Pour the batter into a lightly greased 10½ inch springform pan and sprinkle the walnuts evenly over top. Bake for 50 to 60 minutes or until golden on top and a toothpick inserted in the cake comes out dry. Serve at room temperature with a dollop of fresh whipped cream. Serves 6 adults.

Ciambelle di Olio di Olive e Pignoli (Lemon Flavored Olive Oil Cake Topped with Pine Nuts)

ABRUZZO/MOLISE

In Italy, there are two types of bakeries—a pasticceria, *where they sell cakes, pastries, and cookies, and a* paneficio, *where they sell bread and savory biscuits. Whenever I stay with my friends Salvatore and Anna in Palermo, I go to the local* pasticceria *each morning for a pastry and espresso, and then I head over to the* paneficio *where their children Gemma and Lorenzo work. I chat with my friends for a while, distract them from their tasks, and then leave with loaves of fresh bread for the afternoon meal that Anna will prepare. It's a wonderful daily routine while staying with friends! I just adore living* la vita Italiana!

Ciambelle signifies any sort of ring-shaped dessert, regardless of whether it's a cookie, doughnut, or cake. In Abruzzo, Molise, and Apulia, sweet ring-shaped biscuits brushed with sugar glaze are also called *ciambelline or* taralli. *Ring mold cakes are popular along the Adriatic coast of Italy from Emilia Romagna and Le Marche in the north down to Abruzzo and Molise. No doubt, you will find them at any* pasticceria *in Teramo. Here is a wonderful recipe for a light* ciambelle *made flavorful and moist with olive oil. Fresh lemon zest and a good sprinkle of pine nuts on top make this cake delicious and bright, like the Adriatic sun. Enjoy it in the morning with your espresso or serve it as a light dessert after a special meal.*

2 cups all-purpose, pre-sifted flour	Zest of 1 lemon
2 heaping tsp. baking powder	1½ tsp. lemon juice
½ tsp. salt	¾ cup olive oil
3 extra-large eggs	½ cup milk
1¾ cups sugar	1 cup pine nuts
1 tsp. vanilla extract	

Preheat the oven to 375 degrees. Sift together the flour, baking powder, and salt. In a mixing bowl, cream the eggs and sugar until light and fluffy and then beat in the vanilla, lemon zest, and lemon juice. Next, add one third of the flour mixture and beat until smooth. Continue by beating in the olive oil, then half of the remaining flour, then the milk, and then the rest of the flour. When the batter is smooth and fluffy, pour it into a lightly greased ring mold or 10 inch springform pan and sprinkle the pine nuts evenly over top. Bake for 35 to 40 minutes or until golden on top and a toothpick inserted in the center comes out dry. Serve at room temperature. Serves 6 adults.

Torta di Ricotta con Ciliege (Rustic Ricotta Cake with Cherries)

LAZIO

If you drive from Rome to the hills of Celleno in early March, the cherry trees are sure to be covered with pale pink and white blossoms. As you approach Celleno travelling on the autostrada provinciale, a road sign proudly announces "Terra di Ciliegie." This means that you have arrived in the "land of cherries." Be sure to explore Celleno's enchanting centro storico *or old town, which sits atop a rocky hill with beautiful views of the nearby cherry groves. Complete with a medieval castle and crumbling stone buildings, it is an impressive place full of character! In June, the cherries will be ready to harvest, so be sure to head back to Celleno for the annual cherry festival, Festa della Ciliegie. There is a parade with decorative floats, a cherry pit spitting contest, and plenty of music, food, and drink. The festival goes on for two weeks and ends with the unveiling of the crostatona, an enormous cherry tart that is over fifty feet long! All festival goers are invited to have a taste!*

Here is a recipe for ricotta cake loaded with sweet cherries from Celleno. It is typical of Northern Lazio's rustic cuisine and something you just might find at one of the food stalls at the Festa della Ciliegie. The fresh cherries add a burst of sweetness with every bite. Baked in a large, round tin, this is country-style cooking at its best—simple and uncomplicated! There is no fancy frosting or decorative details. Just be sure to sprinkle over plenty of sugar that will caramelize and make the top of the cake golden brown and crackly. If fresh cherries are out of season, use drunken cherries instead (see page 250)! The added kick from the alcohol is reminiscent of an old-fashioned Italian rum cake.

2½ cups all-purpose, pre-sifted flour	1 tsp. salt
4 rounded tsp. baking powder	2½ tsp. vanilla
2½ cups ricotta cheese	Zest of 1 lemon
2 sticks butter, softened	1 tsp. lemon juice
4 extra-large eggs	2 cups pitted, halved Bing cherries,
2¾ cups sugar	divided

Sift together the flour and baking powder. Pulse the ricotta in a food processor until smooth and creamy. In a standing mixer, beat together the butter, eggs, sugar, salt, vanilla, lemon juice, and lemon zest on medium speed until light and fluffy. Add the ricotta and continue mixing until thoroughly combined. Incorporate the flour ½ cup at a time until you achieve a smooth batter.

Preheat the oven to 350 degrees. Grease a 10 inch diameter round springform pan with butter. Pour half of the batter into the pan and sprinkle over half of the cherries. Pour over the remaining batter, smooth it out, and sprinkle the remaining cherries over top. Bake for 30 minutes, then spray the top lightly with cooking spray and sprinkle with sugar. Continue baking for another 20 minutes or until golden and crackly on top and a toothpick inserted into the cake comes out clean. Serves 6 to 8 adults

Pizzelle (Anise Wafer Cookies)

ABRUZZO/MOLISE

Pizzelle *are sweet wafer cookies that are popular in the Abruzzo region. When I was a child, I enjoyed them at my friend's home. His mother was of Abruzzese descent and always made them fresh. They were a treat that my family was not familiar with, so it was certainly worth getting the recipe!* Pizzelle *are typically flavored with vanilla, lemon, or anise and dusted with powdered sugar. I like anise best! In the rural hill towns of Abruzzo, they are still made using a traditional* pizzelle *iron. A scoop of dough is placed on the iron, which is then closed and set upon the embers of a fire. Today, most Italians have an electric iron, which makes the task easier and more enjoyable. This is how I make mine, and they are always perfectly crispy and delicious. We always eat them while they are still warm! You can purchase an electric* pizzelle *iron at your local Italian market or simply order one online. Just be sure that the iron will impart a fancy, intricate design to the wafers. Serve them with a scoop of gelato at your next dinner party. They are the perfect light dessert after an elegant meal.*

1 cup butter	1½ tsp. anise extract
3½ cups all-purpose, pre-sifted flour	½ tsp. salt
3 rounded tsp. baking powder	¾ cup confectioners' sugar, for
6 extra-large eggs	dusting
1⅔ cups sugar	

Melt the butter and allow it to cool. Whisk together the flour and baking powder. In a separate bowl, beat the eggs and sugar until light and fluffy, and then beat in the melted butter, anise extract, and salt. Beat in the flour one cup at a time. The dough should be smooth and sticky.

Spray your *pizzelle* iron lightly with cooking spray, drop a rounded tablespoon of dough onto the iron, and close it. Cook the *pizzelle* for about 1½ minutes or until golden. Allow the *pizzelles* to cool and then sprinkle them with confectioners' sugar.

Biscotti di Regina (Crunchy Sesame Seed Cookies)

SICILY

Passagiata *is another Italian tradition that I adore! On summer nights, Italians take to the streets for a stroll, or* passagiata *as it is called in Italian. They walk off an evening meal, meet up with friends, or head to a* gelateria, *which is Italy's version of an ice cream shop. Whenever I visit my friends Rita and Salvo, we always head to a nearby seaside town to stroll down the lungomare, which is a waterfront boulevard or promenade. In large resort towns, the lungomare is sure to be bustling with activity and pedestrians. This is always the best place for a* passagiata *because there you will find plenty of cafes and ice cream shops. You will also find street vendors displaying piles of roasted nuts, candies, and cookies. They are tempting treats, and I can never resist buying a bag! Crisp sesame cookies called biscotti di Regina are my favorite snack to munch on while strolling on the* lungomare *with my dear friends. These are a simple, rustic butter cookie from the Sicilian interior. Rolled in sesame seeds and baked until crisp, these treats are irresistible. They are the perfect snack for when you want something that is not so sweet.*

3 extra-large eggs	½ tsp. salt
1 tsp. vanilla extract	12 tbsp. butter
2 tbsp. Grand Marnier liqueur	¾ lb. sesame seeds
3¼ cups all-purpose, pre-sifted flour	2 extra-large egg whites
1¼ cup sugar	1 tbsp. water
1 heaping tsp. baking powder	

Beat 3 eggs with the vanilla and Grand Marnier and set the bowl to the side. In a mixing bowl, thoroughly combine the flour, sugar, baking powder, and salt. Next, cut the butter into the flour, working it with your hands until the texture is like oatmeal. Form a well in the middle of the dry ingredients and pour the beaten eggs in the well. Beat the liquid ingredients with a fork, slowly pulling in flour from the sides of the well. Continue until everything has been combined to form a sticky dough. Turn the dough onto a lightly floured work surface and knead it until smooth and shiny. Cut the dough into 4 equal pieces, wrap them with plastic wrap, and let them rest in the refrigerator for 1 hour.

Preheat the oven to 375 degrees. Place the sesame seeds in a shallow bowl. Beat the 2 egg whites with the water in another bowl. Roll the dough into ½ inch diameter cords, and cut them into 1 inch pieces. Dip each pieces of dough in egg wash, roll it in sesame seeds, and place it on a lightly greased baking sheet. Bake the cookies for 25 minutes or until golden. Makes 5 dozen cookies.

Biscotti di Pistacchi (Pistachio Cluster Cookies)

SICILY

The best pistachios in Europe are grown near the small town of Bronte. Perched on Mount Etna's western slope, this ancient town looks out upon vast groves of pistachio trees that sway in the mountain breezes. In this region, pistachios are used primarily in desserts, but they also make their way into all sorts of pasta, meat, and vegetable dishes. There is even a version of pesto sauce that is made with pistachios instead of pine nuts. Head to Bronte's pistachio festival, Sagra del Pistacchi, that's held each October to sample these dishes and many more. It is sure to be a delicious event with plenty of music, dancing, and food stalls! Be sure to try Bronte's signature pistachio sponge cake that is baked in enormous sheets and shared with everyone.

If you ask me, the best place for Bronte's fine pistachios to wind up is at a fancy pasticceria *in Taormina, where they will be chopped and sprinkled over cannoli, ground into meal for pistachio cakes, and baked into tasty pistachio cluster cookies. The cookies are my absolute favorite. Whenever I'm in Taormina, I head to the nearest* pasticceria *to pick some up. They are crunchy, sweet and chock full of pistachios. After I returned from a trip to Sicily, I set myself upon the task of recreating this wonderful cookie. After a few tries, I nailed it down! Here is the recipe. If you don't have whole, raw pistachios, try using pine nuts or slivered almonds instead.*

2¼ cups all-purpose, pre-sifted flour	¼ cup corn oil
1¾ cups sugar	1 tsp. vanilla extract
3 rounded tsp. baking powder	1¾ lbs. pistachios, pine nuts, or
¼ tsp. salt	slivered almonds
¾ cup milk	1 cup confectioners' sugar

Preheat the oven to 350 degrees. In a mixing bowl, thoroughly combine the flour, sugar, baking powder, and salt. Then add the milk, corn oil, and vanilla extract and beat well to form a loose, sticky dough. Place the nuts in a separate bowl. Drop a rounded teaspoon of dough into the bowl of nuts and press the nuts into the dough. Transfer the nut cluster to a lightly greased baking sheet. Space the nut clusters at least 2½ inches apart on the baking sheet, and bake for 15 to 20 minutes or until golden on the bottom. Allow the cookies to cool completely and then dust them with confectioner's sugar. Makes 5 dozen cookies.

Anginetti (Sugar Glazed Vanilla Cookies)

CAMPANIA

At the beginning of the twentieth century, my grandmother's family and many others from southern Campania settled in Newark, New Jersey. They brought with them many simple and tasty recipes from the rural towns and villages of the Salerno and Avellino provinces. Today, the children and grandchildren of these immigrants continue to make many of the traditional foods from the region, such as anginetti, *which can now be found at Italian bakeries in New Jersey and New York. This recipe for an Italian American classic has been handed down in my family for at least four generations—and rest assured, it is far better than any version you might find at a bakery!*

Anginetti are soft cookies, similar to cake, that simply melt in your mouth. They are flavored with vanilla, dipped in a sweet sugar glaze, and then decorated with colorful nonpareils. They are traditionally served at weddings and on holidays and festive occasions. You are sure to find many different versions of anginetti *in southern Campania. Depending upon the town, they may be flavored with vanilla, lemon, anise, or almond extract and decorated with candied cherries or citron. In some places the cookies are shaped into an* s, *while in others the dough is twisted into a knot or braid. Regardless of the preparation, they are sure to be sweet and scrumptious. They are quick and easy to make, so give them a try!*

For the cookies:	For the sugar glaze:
6¼ cups all-purpose, pre-sifted flour	3 extra-large egg whites
6 heaping tsp. baking powder	½ tsp. vanilla extract
2 sticks butter, softened	½ tsp. orange juice
1¼ cup sugar	½ tsp. lemon juice
2 tsp. vanilla extract	1 lb. confectioners' sugar
2 tsp. orange juice	Colored nonpareils, for decoration
2 tsp. lemon juice	
½ tsp. salt	
6 extra-large eggs	
2 extra-large egg yolks	

Whisk together the flour and baking powder. In a mixing bowl, cream together the softened butter, sugar, vanilla, orange juice, lemon juice, and salt until light and fluffy. Add the whole eggs and egg yolks to the creamed ingredients and continue beating until smooth and fluffy. Fold in the flour mixture 1 cup at a time until the dough pulls together.

Preheat the oven to 375 degrees. Turn the dough out on a lightly floured work surface and knead it until smooth. Roll the dough into ½ inch diameter cords, and then cut them into 5 inch pieces. Shape each piece into an *s* and place them on a lightly greased baking sheet. Bake for 15 minutes or until the bottom of the cookies are golden.

Allow the cookies to cool. Meanwhile, prepare the sugar glaze: Beat together the egg whites, vanilla, orange juice, lemon juice, and confectioners' sugar in a mixing bowl until smooth and fluffy. Dip the tops of the cookies in the glaze, sprinkle immediately with nonpareils, and place them on wax paper to dry for an hour. Makes 6 dozen cookies.

Cuccidati (Turnover Cookies Filled with Figs, Nuts, and Raisins)

SICILY

No visit to Sicily would be complete without stepping foot inside a traditional Sicilian pasticceria, *or pastry shop. They are places of joy and fantasy, where you will see cakes, pastries, and confections that are true works of art. Fancy cakes called* cassata *are decorated with colorful candied fruits and white icing that is piped into intricate designs.* Marzipano, *sweet almond paste, is molded into the shapes of different fruits and vegetables, and each piece is then hand-painted with such detail that it looks like the real thing. Even the cannolis are decorated to perfection with candied orange peel and pistachios! With such a variety of fanciful masterpieces, you won't leave empty handed. However, there is just one problem—they are so beautiful you won't want to eat them!*

Cuccidati *are festive Christmas cookies. You are sure to find them at any Sicilian* pasticceria *during the holidays. To celebrate the Feast of the Seven Fishes, my grandmother shaped her* cuccidati *into fish and decorated them with eyes, scales, and fins. No doubt, she spent many hours skillfully crafting each cookie, just as her mother did in Sicily. On Christmas Eve, a platter of the fancy fish cookies would be proudly displayed on the dessert table for everyone to see. I continue the tradition with my own spin. Having no patience and little free time, crafting a few dozen fish cookies is inconceivable. Instead, I make one gigantic fish, which we then slice to serve. My grandmother would be proud—although she might say that I am lazy. In keeping with her tradition, I decorate my* cuccidati *with intricate details. They are so beautiful, it is truly a shame to eat them!*

For the dough:
1 cup milk
1 cup sugar
½ tsp. salt
6¼ cups all-purpose, pre-sifted flour
3 heaping tsp. baking powder
1 cup vegetable shortening
2 extra-large eggs

For the filling:
1½ cups chopped walnuts
1½ cups chopped almonds
1½ cups chopped hazelnuts
3 cups chopped, firmly packed dried figs
¾ cup chopped, firmly packed golden raisins
¾ cup chopped, firmly packed dark raisins
½ cup chopped, firmly packed candied orange peel or citron
1½ cups honey
1 rounded tsp. cinnamon
2 tbsp. Arancello or Grand Marnier liqueur

Warm the milk in a saucepan on the stovetop, remove it from the heat, stir in the sugar and salt, and let it cool completely. Meanwhile, sift together the flour and baking powder in a large mixing bowl. Cut the shortening into the flour and work it with your hands until the texture is like oatmeal. Form a well in the middle of the dry ingredients. Beat the eggs and combine them with the milk mixture. Pour the liquid ingredients into the well. Beat the liquid ingredients with a fork, slowly pulling in flour from the sides of the well. Continue until everything has been combined to form a sticky dough. Turn the dough onto a lightly floured work surface and knead it until smooth and shiny. Cut the dough into 4 pieces, wrap them with plastic wrap, and let them rest for 1 hour in the refrigerator.

Meanwhile, prepare the filling: Preheat the oven to 375 degrees and toast the walnuts, almonds, and hazelnuts for 7 to 10 minutes or until golden. Combine the nuts with the figs, golden raisins, dark raisins, and candied orange peel in a mixing bowl. Place the honey in a saucepan, bring it up to a simmer over low heat, remove the pan from the heat, and then stir in the cinnamon and liqueur. Pour the warm honey over the nut mixture and stir well so that everything is coated.

Roll out the dough to ¼ inch thickness. To make turnovers, cut the dough into 5 inch diameter circles. Place a generous portion of the filling on top of each circle and then fold the dough over and seal the edges. To make 2 large fish-shaped cookies, divide the dough into 2 equal pieces and roll them to ¼ inch thickness. Arrange half of the filling on each in a crescent shape, and then fold the dough over and seal the edges. Decorate the cookies by snipping the dough with the tip of a scissor to make scales and poking a raisin into the dough for an eye. Cut out fins and a tail from the scraps of dough. Beat an egg white with a splash of water to adhere the fins and tail, and then brush the whole cookie lightly with the egg wash.

Preheat the oven to 350 degrees. Place the cookies on an ungreased baking sheet and bake for 25 minutes or until golden brown. Makes 2 dozen small cookies.

Tozzetti (Crunchy Orange Hazelnut Biscotti Dipped in Dark Chocolate)

LAZIO

My friend Salvatore works for the Sicilian regional government. When I arrived for a visit one summer, he happily announced, "Since you are staying with us, I will not go to work this week." A gracious host, Salvatore planned day trips to keep us busy. Each day before setting out, we drove to Salvatore's office. He would run in for a minute, and then we would go to the pasticceria across the street and have espresso and biscotti. After a few days, I asked Salvatore, "Why must you go to the office every morning if you have taken off of work?" He replied, "Because I must sign in." I questioned him further, "Why must you sign in?" Salvatore cracked a smile and exclaimed, "Because I still want to get paid!" I then asked, "But what if your boss sees you here?" Salvatore laughed and explained, "He would think nothing of it. We take many breaks each day for espresso and biscotti!"

This recipe is for a twice-baked cookie from Lazio. They are a common sight in bakeries and cafes in all regions of Italy. My friend Salvatore loves them and so do I! The baking method is quite simple. First, the dough is shaped into a log and baked until golden. Then, it is sliced into cookies, which are baked again for a few minutes until crisp. They are perfect for dunking in a cappuccino at one of Rome's chic coffee bars. The traditional recipe from Lazio calls for hazelnuts, but any other type of nut will do just fine. It is a simple recipe that you can make all your own. I make my tozzetti extra special by adding a splash of orange liqueur and tossing in a handful of sweet candied orange peel for a burst of bright flavor. For added decadence, I dip them in Italian dark chocolate from Perugia. What could be a better treat?

3 cups coarsely chopped hazelnuts, divided

10 tbsp. butter, melted

1¾ cups sugar

3 extra-large eggs

2 tbsp. Grand Marnier or Arancello liqueur

2 tsp. vanilla extract

4 cups all-purpose, pre-sifted flour, divided

1 heaping tbsp. baking powder

½ tsp. salt

1 extra-large egg white

12 oz. dark chocolate

Preheat the oven to 375 degrees. Toast the hazelnuts for 7 to 10 minutes or until golden. In a large mixing bowl, whisk together the melted butter, sugar, eggs, liqueur, and vanilla extract. In a separate bowl, sift together 3¾ cups of flour, the baking powder, and the salt.

Combine the flour mixture with the liquid ingredients and then stir in half (1½ cups) of the chopped hazelnuts. Turn the dough onto a lightly floured work surface and knead until smooth. If the dough is too sticky, work in the remaining ¼ cup of flour. Divide the dough in half and shape each portion into a 10 inch long, 4 inch wide log. Transfer both logs to lightly greased baking sheets. Whisk 1 egg white in a small bowl with a splash of water and brush the logs with the egg wash.

Preheat the oven to 350 degrees. Bake the logs for 30 minutes or until golden. Remove them from the oven and let them cool for 5 minutes. Use a serrated knife to cut the logs on the diagonal into ¾ inch wide slices. Arrange the slices cut side down on the baking sheets and return them to the oven. Bake for 3 minutes and then turn the biscotti over and bake for another 3 minutes. Allow the biscotti to cool completely.

Fill a saucepan halfway with water and bring to a low boil. Place the chocolate in a bowl that fits snugly on top of the saucepan. Remove the saucepan from the heat, place the bowl on top of the saucepan, and stir the chocolate until it is melted and smooth. Dip the top of each biscotti in the chocolate, sprinkle with the remaining hazelnuts, and set them on a tray until the chocolate hardens. Makes 28 to 36 biscotti.

'Nfasciateddi (Honey-Covered Almond Twists)

SICILY

My Sicilian grandmother made delicious honey-covered cookies filled with sweet almond paste. The cookies are called 'nfasciateddi in Sicilian dialect. When I was young, the name was difficult for me to pronounce so I called them "honey S" cookies. According to my grandmother, in Sicilian dialect 'nfasciateddi means "something wrapped in a diaper," which certainly describes how the cookie dough is wrapped around the filling. My grandmother was the only person that I ever knew to make these cookies. I never saw them at Italian American bakeries and none of my Italian American friends made them. Once, when I travelled to Palermo, I brought these cookies to my friends—they too had never seen or heard of them!

A few years after my grandmother passed away, I travelled to Agira, Sicily, to see the town where her family was from. Perched atop a steep mountain, the views over the Salso Valley and Mount Etna were breathtaking. I explored the narrow, winding streets and walked all the way to the top, where there was an old castle. Afterwards, I headed to a pasticceria, or pastry shop. Many of the sweets on display were familiar to me, and one made me smile. It was my grandmother's "honey S" cookie! I pointed to the cookies and asked the old woman behind the counter what they were called. "'Nfasciateddi!" she proudly exclaimed. The sound of that word rolling off her tongue was music to my ears. It brought back fond memories of my grandmother baking up a storm in the small kitchen of her apartment. I could not resist buying some. They were sweet and delicious, just like the ones my nonna made. What a pleasant ending to my day! Be sure to give these cookies a try. They are not only unique but also truly delicious.

For the filling:
24 oz. whole, blanched almonds
3 rounded tbsp. all-purpose, pre-sifted flour
1 tsp. cinnamon
1¼ cups honey

For the cookie dough:
1 cup milk
1 cup sugar

½ tsp. salt
6¼ cups all-purpose, pre-sifted flour
3 heaping tsp. baking powder
1 cup vegetable shortening
2 extra-large eggs

For the honey coating:
12 oz. whole blanched almonds
2½ lbs. honey
½ tsp. cinnamon

First prepare the filling: Toast the almonds in a preheated 375 degree oven for 10 minutes or until golden brown. Allow the almonds to cool and then grind them into a fine meal using a food processor. Place the almond meal in a mixing bowl and stir in the flour and cinnamon. Add the honey and thoroughly combine everything to form a sticky dough. Turn the dough onto a lightly floured work surface and knead until smooth. Shape the filling into a brick, wrap it in plastic wrap, and set it in the refrigerator for at least 6 hours or overnight.

Prepare the dough: Warm the milk in a saucepan on the stovetop, remove it from the heat, stir in the sugar and salt, and let it cool completely. Meanwhile, sift together the flour and baking powder in a large mixing bowl. Cut the shortening into the flour and work it with your hands until the texture is like oatmeal. Form a well in the middle of the dry ingredients. Beat the eggs and combine them with the milk mixture. Pour the liquid ingredients into the well. Beat the liquid ingredients with a fork, slowly pulling in flour from the sides of the well. Continue until everything has been combined to form a sticky dough. Turn the dough onto a lightly floured work surface and knead it until smooth and shiny. Cut the dough into 4 pieces, wrap them with plastic wrap, and let them rest for 1 hour in the refrigerator.

Preheat the oven to 350 degrees. Roll out the dough on a lightly floured work surface to just under ¼ inch thickness. Cut the dough into strips 1 inch wide and 5 inches long. Cut a piece of the almond filling from the brick and roll it into a cord about 3 inches long and ½ inch in diameter. Place it on a strip of dough and then roll or twist the dough around the filling. Shape the cookie into an *S* and place it on a baking sheet. Continue preparing the cookies in this way, placing them 2 inches apart from one another on the baking sheet. Bake for 25 minutes or until golden brown and then let the cookies cool.

Meanwhile, toast the almonds for the honey coating in a preheated 375 degree oven for 10 to 12 minutes or until golden brown. Allow the almonds to cool and then grind them into a fine meal using a food processor. Sprinkle some almond meal on two baking sheets. Pour the 2½ pounds of honey in a wide saucepan and stir in the ½ teaspoon of cinnamon. Bring the honey up to a boil and then remove the saucepan from the heat. Use tongs to dip each cookie in the warm honey. Allow the excess honey to drip off and then set the cookies on the baking sheets and sprinkle with the remaining almond meal. To serve, arrange the cookies in a tall mound on your serving platter. Makes 3 dozen cookies.

Casatelli d'Agira (Turnover Cookies Filled with Chocolate and Chickpea Paste)

SICILY

Chickpeas and chocolate add intrigue to this traditional cookie from the town of Agira, Sicily. The combination is unexpected, exotic, and delectable! The origin of Agira's signature cookie is equally fascinating. The ancient town is perched atop a mountain with commanding views over the Sicilian interior. In days gone by, it was a strategic outpost for ancient Greeks, Romans, Arabs, Normans, and Spaniards who all, at one time or another, ruled the island. Each civilization brought their own cooking traditions and ingredients to Sicily, leaving their mark on what would eventually become Sicilian cuisine. No doubt, the inventive use of ground chickpeas in this cookie is a legacy from the Arabs, and the use of chocolate came from the Spaniards, who brought it back from the new world. How fascinating and tasty! Be sure to give casatelli *a try. The creamy chickpea and chocolate filling is sweet, nutty, and delicious. The hints of orange and cinnamon add even more interest. This is one cookie that is truly beyond compare.*

For the filling:	For the cookie dough:
16 oz. whole, blanched almonds	6 cups all-purpose, pre-sifted flour
2 cups water	½ tsp. salt
2 cups sugar	3 heaping tsp. baking powder
¾ cup cocoa powder	1¼ cups vegetable shortening
Zest of 1 California navel orange	2 extra-large eggs
2 tbsp. Grand Marnier or Arancello liqueur	1½ cups sugar
½ tsp. cinnamon	Confectioners' sugar, for dusting
¼ tsp. salt	
1 cup chickpea flour	

First, prepare the filling: Toast the almonds in a preheated 375 degree oven for 7 to 10 minutes or until golden. Allow the almonds to cool and then grind enough almonds in a food processor for 2 cups of fine meal. Place the water in a saucepan. Set the saucepan over low heat and add the sugar. When the sugar has dissolved, whisk in the ground almonds, cocoa, orange zest, liqueur, cinnamon, and salt. Simmer over low heat for 2 minutes, and then slowly add the chickpea flour, whisking constantly. Continue simmering on low, whisking all the while, for another 3 to 5 minutes or until the mixture has thickened to the consistency of a thick batter. Transfer the filling to a bowl and let it sit in the refrigerator for 8 hours or overnight.

Prepare the cookie dough: Sift together the flour, salt, and baking powder. Cut the shortening into the flour and work it with your hands until the texture is like oatmeal. Form a well in the middle of the dry ingredients. Beat together the eggs and sugar and pour the mixture into the well. Beat the liquid ingredients with a fork, slowly pulling in flour from the sides of the well until everything is combined. Then add approximately 1 cup of cold water, a little at a time, until the dough pulls together. Turn the dough onto a lightly floured work surface and knead it until smooth. Cut the dough into 4 pieces, shape them into balls, cover them with plastic wrap, and let them rest in the refrigerator for 1 hour.

Preheat the oven to 350 degrees. Roll the dough to just less than ¼ inch thickness and press out circles of any size with a cup. Place some filling in the middle, fold over the dough, and seal the edges by pressing down with the tines of a fork. Set the cookies on an ungreased cookie sheet and bake for 15 minutes or until golden. Allow the cookies to cool and then dust them with confectioner's sugar. Makes about 4 dozen cookies.

Biscotti al Ciocolato e Noce (Sugar-Glazed Chocolate Walnut Cookies)

CAMPANIA

Here is another cookie from Campania that is simply irresistible. I ate them as a child when I visited my grandmother's oldest sister, Anna, who was the best baker on the Campanese side of my family. Flavored with coffee and wonderful spices such as cinnamon, nutmeg, and allspice, these chocolate cookies have a depth of flavor that is rich and intriguing. We always called them "Aunt Annie's Chocolate Cookies" because she was the one who baked them. Unfortunately, I therefore do not know their proper name, and despite my research efforts I have been unable to pinpoint the town of their origin. However, the sugar glaze is a tell-tale sign that this recipe must have originated in the Avellino or Salerno provinces! You are likely to find them on any Campanese dessert table along with anginetti, struffoli, *and sweet ricotta pies. They are an unusual and tasty treat that will have your friends and family asking for the recipe. So why not make them your signature cookie?*

2½ cups regular coffee	2 cups chopped walnuts
3 sticks butter, melted	8 cups all-purpose, pre-sifted flour
3 extra-large eggs, beaten	6 heaping tsp. baking powder
½ rounded tsp. salt	
½ rounded tsp. cinnamon	*For the glaze:*
½ rounded tsp. allspice	3 extra-large egg whites
½ rounded tsp. nutmeg	½ tsp. vanilla extract
1 tsp. vanilla extract	½ tsp. orange juice
1½ cups sugar	½ tsp. lemon juice
1½ cups brown sugar	1 lb. confectioners' sugar
6 oz. cocoa powder	Colored nonpareils, for decoration

Brew the coffee, allow it to cool, and pour it in a large mixing bowl. Add the butter, beaten eggs, salt, spices, vanilla, sugar, brown sugar, and cocoa and whisk until smooth. Stir in the walnuts. In another mixing bowl, thoroughly combine the flour and baking powder. Stir the flour into the wet ingredients 1 cup at a time to form a soft dough. Turn the dough onto a lightly floured work surface and knead it until smooth. Form the dough into a ball, cover it with plastic wrap, and then let it rest for 30 minutes.

Preheat the oven to 375 degrees. Cut the dough into 6 pieces. Roll each piece into a ¾ inch diameter log, and then cut the logs into 1½ inch pieces. Place them on an ungreased cookie sheet and bake for 20 minutes or until golden on the bottom.

Allow the cookies to cool. Meanwhile, prepare the sugar glaze: In a mixing bowl, beat the egg whites, vanilla, orange juice, lemon juice, and confectioners' sugar until smooth and fluffy. Dip the tops of the cookies in the glaze, sprinkle immediately with nonpareils, and place the cookies on wax paper to dry for an hour. Makes 8 dozen cookies.

X

Ramblings in Virginia

I hope you enjoyed our ramblings through Southern Italy and Sicily. It certainly has been an incredible journey! Now, I invite you back to my farm in the beautiful countryside of Virginia. This is where I recreate all of the wonderful recipes from my travels. Let me tell you a little more about where my wife, Jen, and I live. Our home is located in the quaint village of Hume, Virginia (population 524). Here, cows probably outnumber people 2 to 1. We have a small post office, but no supermarket, convenience store, or gas station. However, we do have three wineries, and if you include all the wineries within a ten-mile radius of the village, there are almost two dozen.

Our house sits at the top of a hill and looks down upon our barn and eleven-acre hay field. We hope to put in a vineyard soon! There are woods at one end of our property where we gather wild cardoons and dandelions in the spring and raspberries in the summer. We also have a large black walnut tree that drops plenty of nuts each fall. They are easy to pick from the ground, but a real job to crack open! The vegetable garden and fig trees are strategically positioned between our house and detached garage, where marauding deer seldom venture. We do not worry about rabbits nibbling on our lettuce and herbs because the fox living in our field keeps the rabbit population down. We have refrained from planting more fruit trees because they attract bears. Besides, the "U-pick" orchards up the road have wonderful fruit at a reasonable price. The orchard shops are also a great place to pick up local honey, syrups, and homemade jams.

Although we do not keep animals, many of our neighbors raise cattle, pigs, sheep, and poultry and hunt deer in the fall. Therefore, fresh, organic meat is widely available. When we first moved in, a cattle farmer nearby welcomed us with a big smile and five pounds of ground beef. He handed it to me and exclaimed, "We just slaughtered a cow, welcome to Hume!" His grass-fed black angus beef is beyond compare. Our neighbor who keeps chickens provides us with fresh brown eggs that are infinitely better in taste and texture than the white eggs at the supermarket. For other high-quality foods, we head to the weekend farmer's markets in the larger nearby towns. There, we find all sorts of specialty produce and artisanal cheeses and bread. They even have a vendor who trucks in fresh seafood from the Chesapeake Bay. Sometimes fish even fall from the sky at my farm! One afternoon, I was on my tractor cutting hay when I saw a fish flopping around in the middle of the field. How crazy, I thought! The talon marks of a bald eagle were the tell-tale sign of how it got there. The nearby streams are a more reliable source for fresh rainbow trout. Out here, an hour or two of fly fishing in the morning means a delicious dinner that evening. What more could you want or need?

Let's Head into My Kitchen

When guests come to my house, they love to peek into my refrigerator and pantry closet. That is where every wonderful dish begins. Let me show you! Both are always well-stocked with plenty of Italian ingredients so that I can cook up a wonderful dish at any time. And for me this is important. Living in the countryside, I do not have the luxury of a corner supermarket or convenience store. Running out of an ingredient while cooking or not having it means a long ride into one of the larger nearby towns. Now that will certainly spoil the fun! Keeping a well-stocked pantry is quite easy. Most of the items I keep have a long shelf life, and refrigerator items will stay fresh for a week. I shop for meats, seafood, and other perishable items every four or five days, and I stock up on jarred, canned, and nonperishable pantry items every two or three months. If you're inspired to cook with an Italian flare, then there are essential ingredients that you should keep stocked in your pantry and refrigerator. If you open the doors to my pantry and fridge, here is what you will find:

SHELF AND PANTRY ITEMS

DRIED HERBS, SPICES, AND SEASONINGS: coarse sea salt, black pepper, white pepper, crushed red pepper flakes, paprika, saffron, cinnamon, nutmeg, whole and ground cloves, allspice, fennel seeds, anise seeds, oregano, basil, parsley, thyme, bay leaves, sage, rosemary, marjoram, tarragon, anise extract, and vanilla extract.

Oils, Vinegars, and Wines: Red and white wine, olive oil (for cooking), extra virgin olive oil (for salads), corn oil (for deep frying), red wine vinegar, white vinegar, and balsamic vinegar.

Starches and Legumes: Italian 00 flour (for making pasta), semolina flour, chickpea flour, polenta, country-style Italian bread (for cooking and grinding into coarse crumbs), finely ground dry bread crumbs (for dredging and frying), small pasta for soup (tubbetini, orzo, acini pepe, etc.), assorted short pasta (penne, ziti, rigatoni, etc.), assorted long pasta (spaghetti, tagliatelle, papardelle, etc.), couscous, long-grain rice, short-grain rice for risotto (arborio, canaroli, or vialone nano), canned or dried beans (cannelini, borlotti, kidney beans, chickpeas), dried lentils, and dried fava beans.

Other Items: Broth (chicken, light beef, and vegetable), San Marzano tomatoes (whole peeled and crushed), tomato paste, olives (green, black, and Kalamata), salt-preserved capers (for cooking), capers in brine (for salads), sundried tomatoes in olive oil, jarred artichoke hearts in olive oil, jarred Italian tuna in olive oil, jarred Italian anchovies in olive oil, anchovy paste, dried porcini mushrooms, dried chestnuts, walnuts, almonds, pine nuts, sesame seeds, almond paste, assorted dried fruits (raisins, candied orange peel, citron, figs, apricots), and honey.

REFRIGERATOR ITEMS

CHEESES AND MEATS: Soft cheeses for casseroles and desserts (ricotta or mascarpone), melting cheeses (mozzarella, fontina, asiago, telaggio, or caciocavallo), hard cheese for grating (Parmigiano-Reggiano, Pecorino Romano, aged asiago, or grana padana), Italian bacon (pancetta or guanciale), cured ham (prosciutto, speck, or capocollo), cured pork sausage (Genoa salami or soppressata), and fresh pork sausage.

<u>Aromatic Vegetables, Fresh Herbs, and Other Items</u>: Garlic, Spanish or Vidalia onions, green onions, celery, carrots, lemons, oranges, oregano, basil, Italian flat leaf parsley, thyme, bay leaves, sage, rosemary, marjoram, mint, and tarragon.

OTHER ODDS AND ENDS

Butcher string (to tie stuffed roasts and roulades), bamboo skewers (3 and 6 inches in length, to fasten stuffed meats and seafood), and cheesecloth (to strain or remove moisture from soft cheeses and other items).

Let's Head Out to My Vegetable Garden

Now that you have seen the pantry, let me show you my vegetable and herb garden! My guests always love to walk through the garden and admire the vegetables. I give them a shopping bag and tell them to pick whatever they want to take home. Some guests are bashful and grab only a tomato or a few peppers. Others fill the bag up with lots of everything.

When I was a child, I helped my father plant a vegetable garden every spring. I enjoyed lending a hand, and he taught me everything that I know. My grandfather and uncles also planted vegetable gardens. By mid-summer, everyone was competing to grow the largest tomato, the longest zucchini, or the most peppers. It was always such fun. Today, my brother and I continue the family tradition of planting a vegetable garden, as does my brother-in-law. They both live in suburban New Jersey, but we all grow wonderful vegetables. And yes, there is some rivalry! Although my brother's garden does not produce an abundance of large tomatoes and zucchini like mine, I must admit he always has a few monstrous pumpkins for the kids. As for my brother-in-law, he and my sister now live in the house that was once my childhood home. He plants his garden in the same plot that my father and I used twenty years ago. For some reason, his tomatoes just don't grow as plump as ours did. I have the photographs from my childhood to prove it!

If you love to cook Italian food, consider planting an Italian vegetable garden in your backyard. The fresh vegetables and herbs will make all of your dishes extra special. You don't need a green thumb or a big yard. In my garden, I have three 6 by 6 foot plots and three 6 by 12 foot plots. I use one small plot for herbs, one for beans, and one for peppers and eggplants. I use one large plot for tomatoes, one for zucchini, and one for greens, root vegetables, and anything else I decide to grow. During the summer, not a single day goes by without a fresh tomato salad, pasta topped with fresh herbs, grilled vegetables drizzled with olive oil, or roasted meats flavored with sprigs of rosemary and sage. My garden produces more vegetables and herbs than we could possibly eat during the summer, so we jar and freeze the rest. There is always plenty to last through winter. Here are the herbs and vegetables you should consider for your Italian vegetable garden. Even if you choose not to grow your own, be sure to incorporate these into your repertoire of Italian dishes.

Herbs: Basilico (Genovese basil), origano (Italian or Greek oregano), prezzemolo (Italian flat leaf parsley), rosmarino (rosemary), salvia (sage), timo (thyme), maggiorana (marjoram), mente (mint), and dragoncello (tarragon).

Tomatoes: Pomodori (large tomatoes for salad), pomodorini (cherry tomatoes), and pomodori Romani (plum tomatoes for sauce).

Peppers: peperone (sweet bell peppers,) friatelli (sweet cubanelle peppers), peperoncino (hot peppers for dried spice), pepperoncini lunghi (hot long peppers for frying), peperoni tondi (sweet or hot cherry peppers)

Other Vegetables: Zucchine Genovese (zucchini), melanzane (eggplants), cetriolo (cucumbers), fagiolini (string beans), cipolle (sweet onions), cipolloto (green onions), and aglio (garlic).

Unique Italian Vegetables and Varieties: Borlotti (cranberry beans), fave (fava/ broad beans), fagiolini Romani (Italian flat beans), cocuzza (Sicilian long squash), zucca (Italian pumpkin), carciofi (artichokes), carduna (cardoons), finocchio (bulb fennel), finocchio selvatico (Sicilian long fennel), scarola (escarole), bietola (Swiss chard), cavolo nero (Tuscan kale), radicchio di Treviso (long radicchio), rucola (arugula/rocket), and borrana (borage).

The view from my garden

Zucchini and rosemary

Getting ready to harvest Swiss chard

Zucchini blossoms

Cucuzza squash hanging from a trellis

Harvesting zucchini

Italian flat beans

Harvesting Italian flat beans

Young white onions

Getting ready to jar vegetables

A bounty of sweet yellow onions

Now, I Must Say Goodbye

With a well-stocked pantry and fresh vegetables from your Italian vegetable garden, you will be ready to cook all of the amazing recipes we encountered while rambling through Italy. It is now time for you to head into your own kitchen. Roll up your sleeves, sharpen your knives, and turn on the stove. I hope I have ignited a passion in you; it's time for you to cook! Use the best ingredients possible and please be creative! If you like an ingredient, use it. If you don't like an ingredient, substitute something else. And by all means, incorporate ingredients unique to your geographic area whenever a recipe calls for something that is not available to you. Think of my recipes as building blocks. I have shown you the cooking techniques; now make my recipes all your own!

That being said, I must now say goodbye. I enjoyed our journey rambling through the heart of Italy. Thank you for coming along. I hope you enjoyed meeting my family, friends, and the other colorful people I introduced you to, as well as your visit to my farm. I look forward to sharing more incredible journeys with you in the future. *Ci vediamo presto!*

Getting ready to make sauce

Index